The Art of
MICHAEL FELL

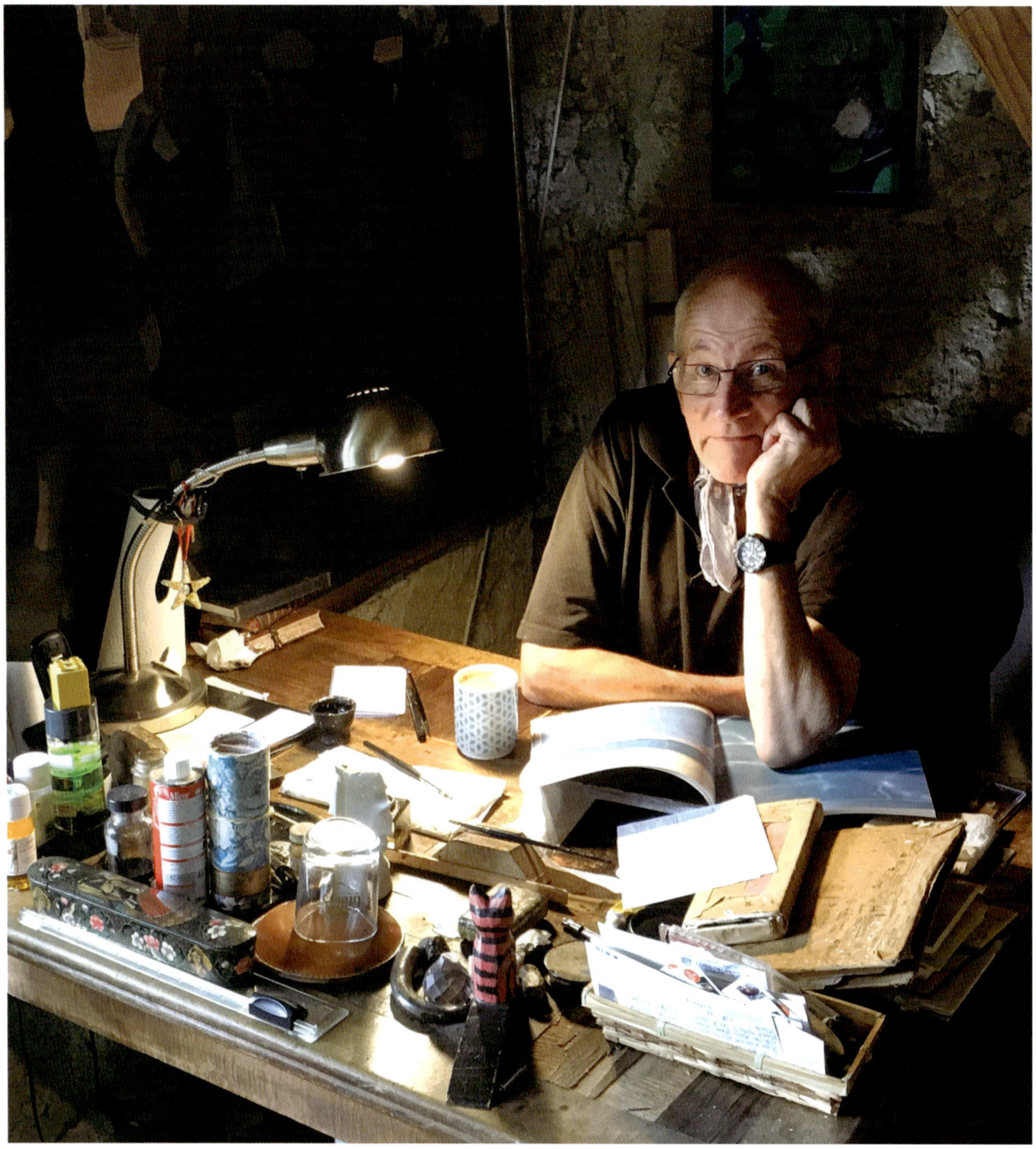

The Art of
MICHAEL FELL

Edited by Andrew Wilton

Unicorn Press

First published in Great Britain in 2024
by Unicorn Press
60 Bracondale
Norwich
NR1 2BE

tradfordhugh@gmail.com
www.unicornpublishing.org

A CIP record of this book can be obtained from the British Library
ISBN 978-1-739164-05-8

Designed by Karen Wilks
Printed in Malta by Gutenberg Press Ltd

Front cover: *Drive at Routgès*, *c.* 2000, oil on canvas, 104 x 91 cm
Back cover: *St John Southworth in Westminster Cathedral*, 1980s, oil on canvas, 122 x 91 cm
Frontispiece: Michael Fell at his desk in his studio at Barrère on 12 September 2017

Contents

Introduction

Andrew Wilton

I first came to know Michael Fell when I was looking for instruction in printmaking at the City & Guilds Art School in Kennington, south London. I had been recommended to it by a Cambridge friend, who was studying carving and gilding there: the school was well known for its courses in the applied arts. During the time I was at the school several students were applying paint with distemper-rollers to create large colour-field paintings in the contemporary American style; one student was working on a large canvas depicting the Battle of Waterloo, with figures studied from nude models, and so learning about anatomy, lighting and composition.

Our teacher in the print department was Henry Wilkinson, who had trained as an engraver on gun-metal and specialised in plates depicting hunting scenes with dogs. Technical competence was the yardstick by which success was judged. I treasured a remark he once made: ‘My wife can’t cook, but, by Jove, she mixes concrete like an angel.’ Michael Fell, a very different character, possessed the same businesslike practicality and adhered to the same exacting standards, but applied his assiduously acquired technical mastery in several media to a huge range of ideas.

While I was at Kennington he was living in a studio flat with his Australian wife Maureen. He sent some pictures to an exhibition mounted by a gallery in Halesworth, close to his family home in Suffolk, and happened to show me one of the canvases he was about to dispatch. It struck me as original in ways that were quite unlike any modern painting I had seen, and although this was a fleeting view I remembered it over many decades until I encountered a black-and-white photograph of it recently. Its current whereabouts are untraced and so it is sadly unavailable for reproduction in this book, except in that form; but I now learnt its title: *The Nun’s Family* [1]. Unusual as it was, it had emerged directly out of Fell’s current life, which involved earning money as a driver for a school run by nuns. Characteristically, that job reflected the values that ruled his life, a circumstance that no doubt explains why he chose to paint it.

The subject consists of a small group of children being transported in the care of a nun in the van Fell was driving. In presenting this unusual subject he incorporated scenes in the road glimpsed through the windows of the van, so creating a composite subject that represented different aspects of the suburban incident he was depicting. The individual children are vividly differentiated, the earnest dedication of the nun herself is

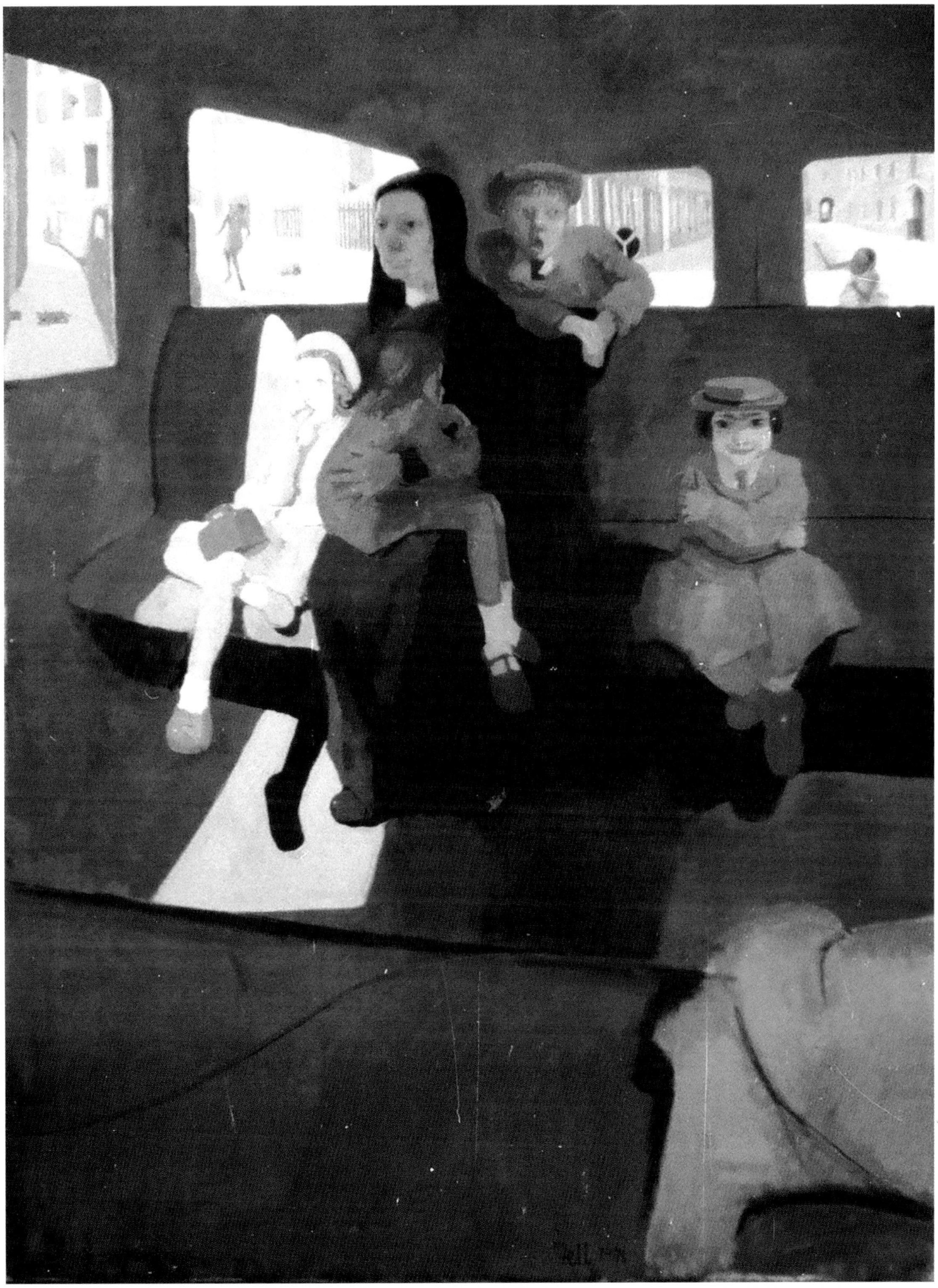

1. *The Nun's Family*, 1971, oil on canvas, dimensions unknown
Image obtained from the artist's papers

clear from her posture and expression. The compressed immediacy and informality of the composition, as well as the clear indication of an ongoing narrative and the vivid realisation of the participants with their individual personalities, have the effect of a still from a film. Insofar as the piece could be related to other English painting of the time, it perhaps derived from the symbolically weighted realism of Stanley Spencer (with its aspect of gentle satire), who looked back consciously to the Pre-Raphaelites. But what struck me about the picture was its freshness and independence of thought. It was by no means 'Victorian' in either approach or technique, rather instead firmly engaged with the contemporary world.

The setting of *The Nun's Family* [1] is of a piece with most of Fell's early work, which took for its subject matter the life of London's streets: commuters, pedestrians, men and women in bars and cafés, old people and children, often the disadvantaged or disabled – a very urban *dramatis personae*, studied close up. The setting rarely involved green spaces, but when it did, they became a focus for the perceptive study of nature confined for urban purposes. Kennington Park, close to the City & Guilds, is the context of some scenes of social interaction, though on occasion the enjoyment of an expanse of green lawn becomes the subject itself, a subjective evocation of the magical feeling of sitting in an urban space surrounded by nothing but grass.

Another early picture, *A Lovely Summer's Day, if you can see it* [2], is an admiring tribute to the planting and lake in Regent's Park as well as a witty, if wry, comment on our relation to the experience of nature. The details of water and foliage, blossom, birds and footbridge, all crisply and matter-of-factly observed, include a dog that, we gradually realise, is waiting at the end of the bridge for a figure in the far distance: a woman feeling her way over the bridge with the aid of stick: she is blind. The composition enacts the distance she must cover in a steep perspective. The point of the sardonic title is made almost casually, certainly not sentimentally, but once made, governs our view of the whole scene. We see that the artist has registered his appreciation of nature as a privilege not to be taken for granted.

More than this, the picture is a manifesto of Fell's intentions in painting. How do we 'see' the lovely day? Is that vision a visceral response to something of fundamental importance to us? Fell makes us understand that such beauty is precious, and that his action in painting the scene is a

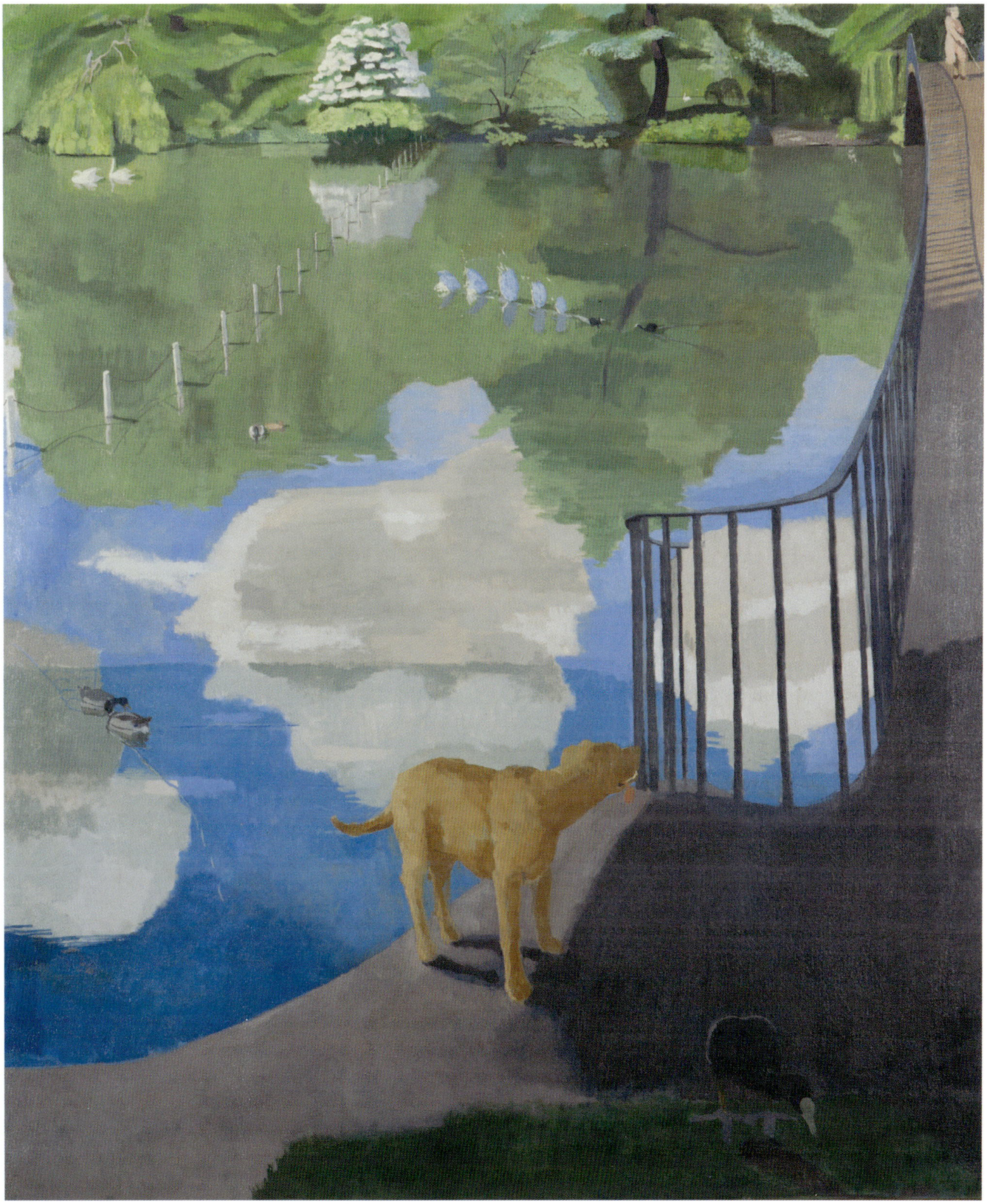

2. *A Lovely Summer's Day, if you can see it*, 1970s, oil on canvas, 110 x 90 cm

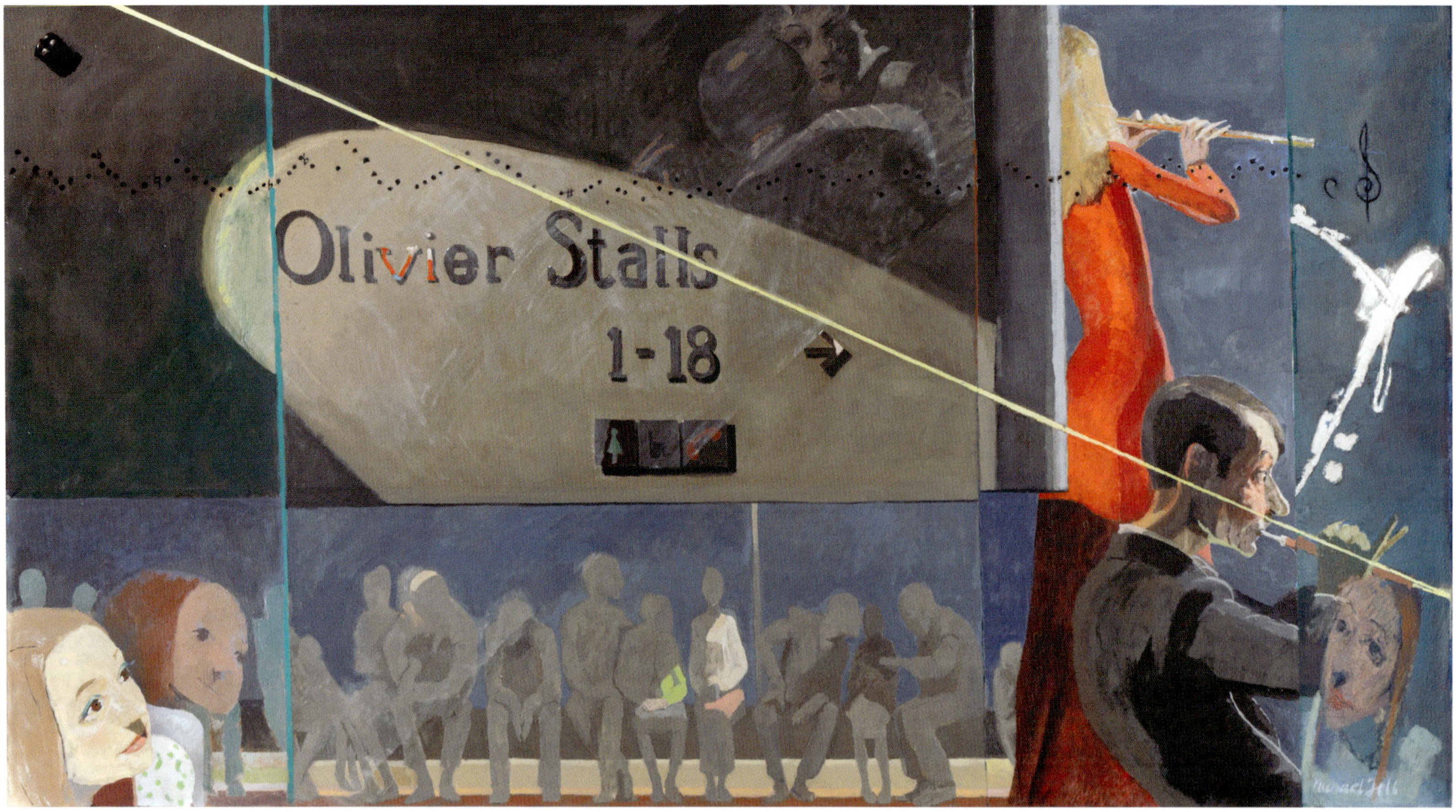

3. *Olivier Stalls*, mid-1980s, oil on canvas, 80 x 150 cm

declaration of faith. He had been brought up a devout Catholic, and in the context of his religious outlook on life as a whole that observation is important and is bound to colour our response not only to the paintings but to the innumerable prints into which he poured much of his inventive energy.

He applies the same analytical method to a quite different aspect of urban life: listening to music, and the way we process sound. *Olivier Stalls* [3], painted in the mid-1980s, while it assembles many details of the experience of a visitor to a theatre or concert foyer, becomes in the process a veritable essay on sound and how it can be represented in paint. The composition grows from a listening head in the lower left corner, which is mirrored twice by reflections at both sides of the canvas: the different attitudes of a listener in the course of hearing a piece. Fell studies the expressions of the human face in the act of listening to, or indeed the very act of producing, with greater or less effort, different musical sounds – sounds, from an oboe and a flute, that are represented as notes without a stave, on the canvas but in reverse as though the very notes were hanging in the air, to be apprehended from all sides, as indeed music is (here Fell borrows a technique regularly used in illustrated strip cartoons); or as a ruler-straight line of bright yellow cutting across the space; or as a burst of white light (the reflection of an incandescent tube in a pane of glass): all superimposed to evoke the undisciplined noise of a public space. Added to all this is a 1930s film that is being projected somewhere: the Babel that surrounds us is emphatically modern. Great sheets of plate glass, a ubiquitous component of modern life, become the structural underpinning of the very composition of the picture. It's as though the painter was building up his aesthetic out of the components of his observed surroundings.

Music was important to Fell, as was literature. The depth and breadth of his reading were not apparent in his notably unpretentious conversation, but when he came to set up a regular seminar in painting and art history in response to local demand at Barrère, the Gascon farmhouse he lived in for the last twenty years of his life, he could avail himself of a personal library covering the whole range of European art until the present. A print that illustrates this particularly well is a technically rather unexpected plate, *The Window*, a silvery lithograph that with miraculous precision presents the tracery of the beautiful 14th-century rose window that is all

4. *The Window*, 1980s, lithograph, 51 x 77 cm

that remains of the Bishop of Winchester's Palace in Southwark, by the Thames close to Southwark Cathedral [4].

The medieval tracery appears, ghost-like, against an old – but not medieval – brick wall, and is accompanied with verses both from the 14th-century English poem *Perle* and Wilfred Owen's famous First World War sonnet *Anthem for Doomed Youth*, the texts inscribed in the plate as though part of the torn advertising and accidental graffiti accumulated on the old masonry. The palimpsest reminds us of the beauty and loss woven into the physical fabric that constitutes our experience of the historical environment. *The Window* places its main subject in a context that is not only architectural but also historical and literary, with these passages of poetry slotted in like stones in the wall. Fell often presents us with images that are at least in part illustrations of poems: he seems to need both word and image to explain his thought.

A large etching, *The Gates of Hell* [5], seems in its apparently diverse throng of characters to have grown out of scenes sketched at random in a café. But it forces us to focus on a single poignant figure, a young woman in the foreground, who is evidently going through some deep personal agony which can't be explained to anyone in the crowd around her. This private drama is signalled by the almost imperceptible bitten lip of the young woman, and is enacted also in the glass of water and the sugar caster in front of her. The negligible accessories of life are integral to our experience of it, and sometimes the most profound of our feelings are prompted by the most trivial of incidents, which may be almost imperceptible in the hubbub of intrusive but unrelated activity.

Behind her on the wall appears a quotation that, we sense, sheds illumination on this scene:

> They knew the way and went to seek you along the narrow lane, but I wandered abroad into the night for I was ignorant.
> I was not schooled enough to be afraid of you in the dark, therefore I came upon your doorstep unaware.
> The wise rebuked me and bade me be gone, for I had not come by the lane.
> I turned away in doubt, but you held me fast, and their scolding became louder every day.

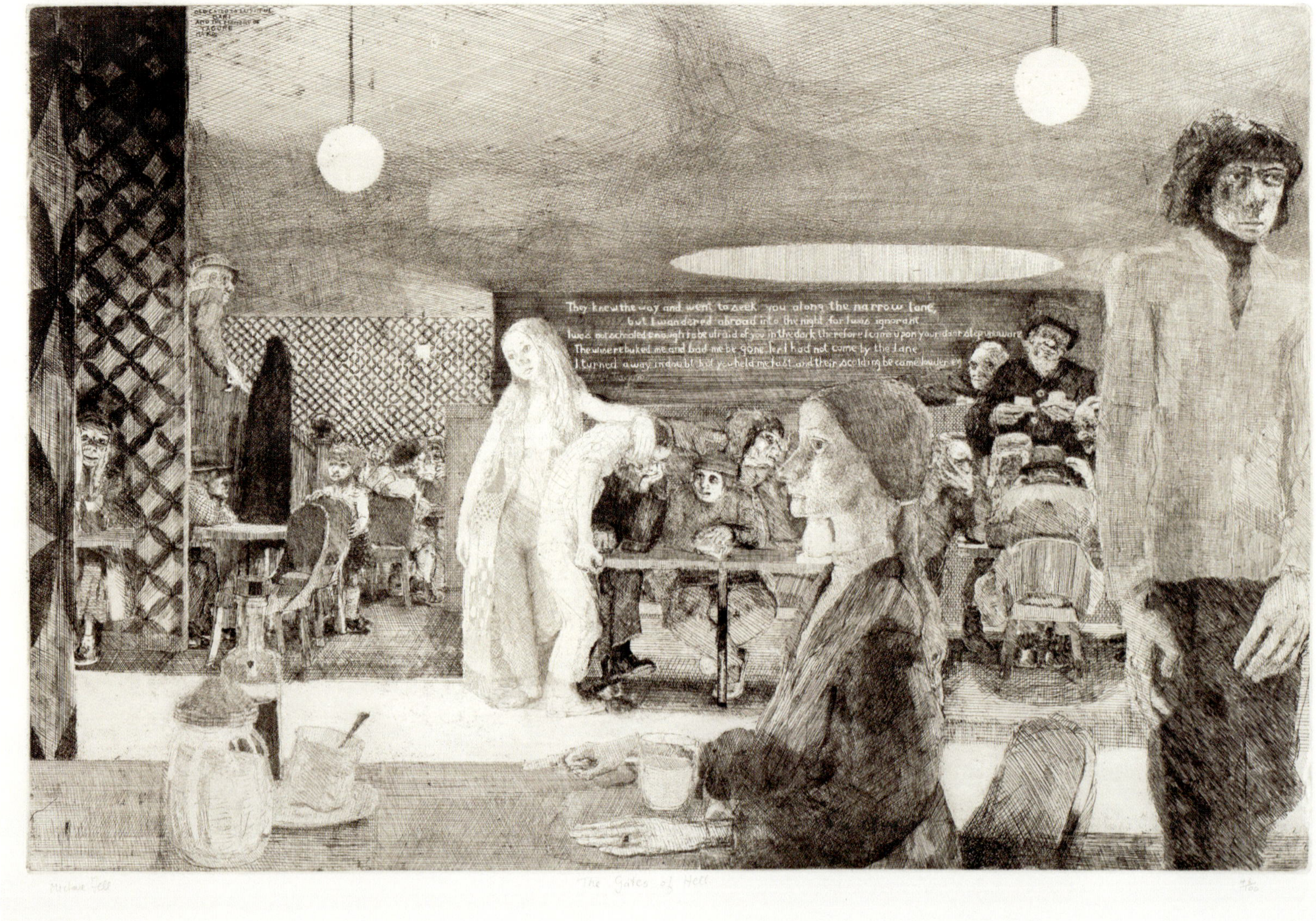

5. *The Gates of Hell*, 1974, etching and aquatint, 43 x 66 cm

This is a poem from *Fruit Gathering*, by the Bengali writer Rabindranath Tagore (1861–1941), whose blend of mysticism and compassion corresponds aptly to Fell's preoccupations in *The Gates of Hell* [5]. These, we learn, are clues to the silent drama of the young woman's anguish. The overriding sense is of isolation, of the insurmountable barriers between individuals and the inescapable ignorance that prevents each of us from reaching out to those who might most readily support us.

When Fell moved with his family to the Suffolk town of Bungay he characteristically chose subject matter that reflected, and sometimes closely illustrated, the character of the place. Their home was the elegant 18th-century Music House, where Chateaubriand had stayed when exiled during the French Revolution. Its handsome front door and staircase featured in several prints and paintings. The large canvas *Robert at the Music House* [16] brings together two contrasting aspects of Fell's productivity: one of his young sons is engaged in homework, next to the huge printing press that had become a central element in Fell's own creative life an artist.

Meanwhile he was still occupied at the City & Guilds, and staying in Norbury with friends, Robin and Pamela Ollington. Robin was a graphic designer, Pamela 'an elegant and forceful personality (with dramatic white hair)'. Their household became the subject of a witty 'scrapbook' – a painting that combines the personalities of the couple and their son Crispin in an affectionate evocation of Fell's daily life with them [98]. He himself is a diminutive figure at the top of the house (up a steep flight of stairs), working away at a desk. So tightly is the composition organised it seems that details like the iron trivet on the wall and the vase of three flowers must have meaningful relevance.

When he discovered the rural landscape of the Gers in southwest France, Fell's response was like a shout of glee at the replacement of impersonal crowds by a warm, creative group of friends and, most of all, by the brilliance of the Gascon light. He was stimulated to produce a large number of paintings, filled with the saturated, sometimes almost blinding colour of the landscape round his farmhouse at Barrère [52, 53, 56]. The careful husbandry of the Gers countryside is projected in his pictures in the meticulous ordering of forms and colours describing the patterns of the agricultural year, the growth and flourishing of crops and trees dictating the texture and rhythms of his brushwork.

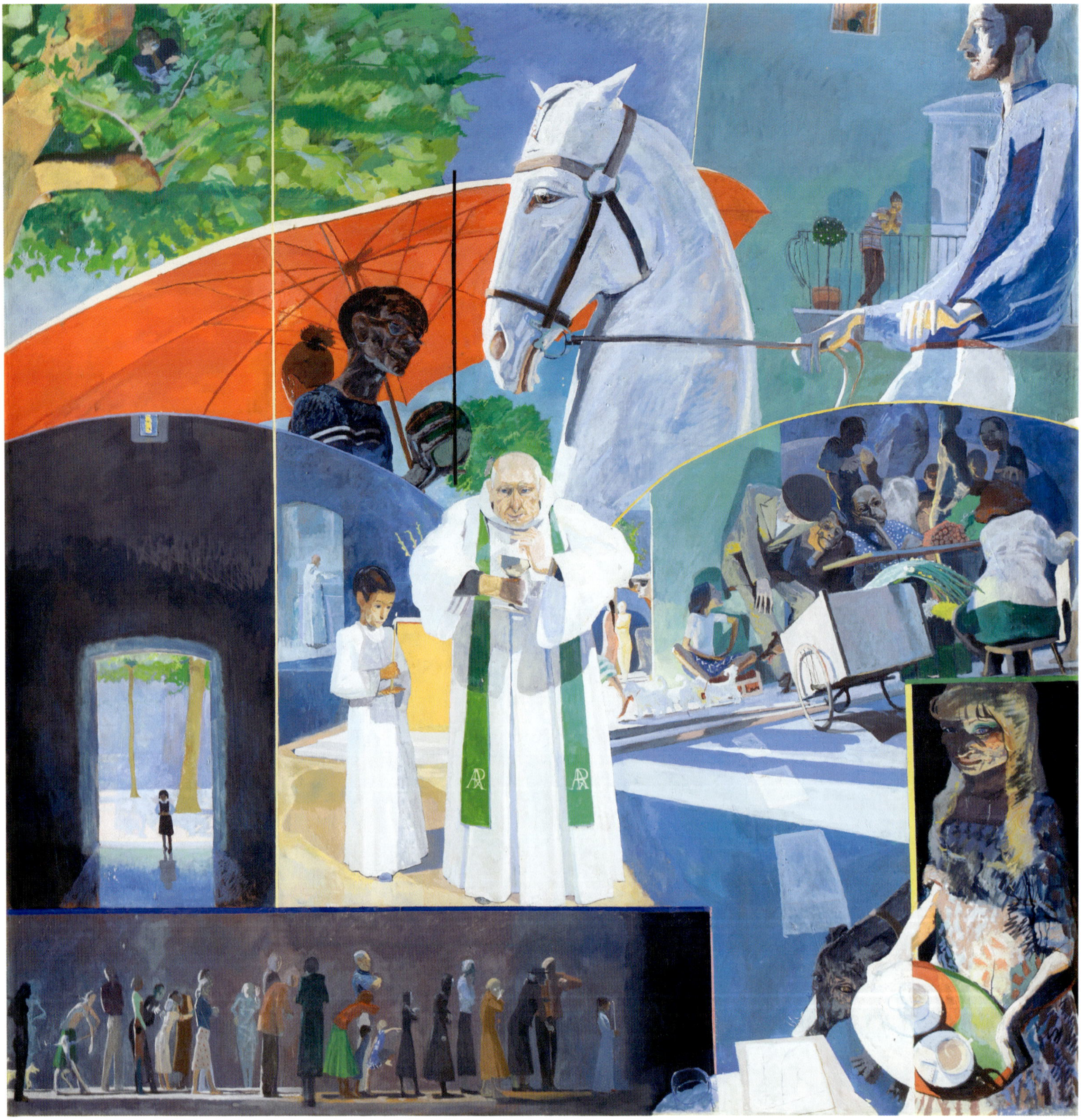

6. *Painting of the Priest (L'abbé Fabère)*, early 2000s, oil on canvas, 181.7 x 182.1 cm

On a quite different scale he also embarked on a sequence of paintings based on a penetrating analysis of the interrelationship of light and shadows on, in and under the water of the small fish pond beneath the south wall of the farmhouse [54, 60, 61]. These pictures focus on a few feet of dark, sometimes sunlit water. The sequence is brought to a climax in an exceptionally large treatment [54], upright this time, and stripped of the lily-leaves, reeds and goldfish that form the staffage of most of the others. Suffused with the brilliant light of the place it is in other respects austere, a starkly abstract study of the geometry of walls and surfaces, sunlit or reflected, two-, three- or even four-dimensional. A few stray wisps of algae denote the flat plane of the water which is perceived as a complex of other planes interlocking in the reflected space of the water.

The stark abstraction of this powerful image seems to belie the development of Fell's social life in the Gers, which blossomed in new ways. It inspired pictures (and many prints) with numerous figures: a summer fête in the village [49], a friend's family Christmas [102], the atmosphere of the church, St Pierre, in the local town of Vic Fezensac. The old acuteness of feeling for individuals among a crowd is here still, sometimes sharpened by witty characterisation. Fell's son Mark provides a helpful summary of one of the most complex of the paintings of this time, a large composition forming a characteristic 'scrapbook' of life in Vic Fezensac, which he dates to the early 2000s [6]:

> It draws heavily on his Sunday morning routine. Every Sunday morning (at least in spring and summer) he would go into Vic-Fezensac early, and have a coffee in one of the local cafés sitting outside. Whilst he was in the café, he would observe and sketch the local characters. Opposite the café, on the other side of the road, was a small Sunday morning market where one could buy the local melons, flowers and vegetables. After drawing he would go to mass at the Église Saint Pierre in Vic. As well as having a church, Vic Fezensac also has a bull-ring about five minutes walk from the café and not far from the Église Saint Pierre, at which they had *corridas* (a bull fight to the death) and *courses landaises* (a bloodless form of bull fighting in which the participants do acrobatics over the bull accompanied by traditional music).
>
> The central figure, the priest, is L'abbé Fabère, who was the local parish priest for many years; he would preside over Sunday morning Mass. He is shown administering communion.

> The bottom left shows a line of people queuing to receive communion, led by an altar girl holding a candle. The interior of Saint Pierre was always quite dark, and a girl is shown entering the church from the brightly lit square outside.
>
> The bottom right shows the waitress who worked at the café for many years, bringing coffee to people sitting outside. I remember she gave off a strong aura of sadness. To her left is a dog; there were always dogs with their owners at the café, hoping for some croissant crumbs. To the left of the dog is Dad's table with some drawing paper sitting next to a glass of water. Directly in front of him across the road is a part of the market, with produce in a cart and some locals chatting, one wearing a traditional beret. There are three rather smart white dogs being led past the locals, and one can see the elegant leg of a (Parisian) lady wearing a kitten heel, leading the dogs.
>
> On the top left a scene from a melon stall features, with an orange umbrella. Someone is inspecting a melon. On the top right, the horseman is wearing the white trousers often worn by participants in a bull fight.

I have often wondered how Fell saw himself fitting into the story of painting and printmaking in England. He came a couple of generations too late for the Etching Revival of the early 20th century, and didn't espouse the new techniques, like screen printing or acrylic paint, that became fashionable about the time I got to know him at Kennington, though he was as inventive and fertile as any of its practitioners. His love of unexpectedly orchestrated strong colour suggests a link with Expressionism, but the large *My Pond* [54], just described, illustrates how colour, however strong, is rigorously controlled by his sense of pictorial structure, embodied in consistently precise draughtsmanship and disciplined brushwork. Another constraint is the rigorous thinking that, as I hope I have shown, underlies all his visual ideas. He is an artist on his own, compelled into independence by a firmly held philosophy and by the confident subjectivity of his approach.

Life

Life

Katie Alice Fitz Gerald

Michael Fell was born on 31 January 1939, seven months before the outbreak of the Second World War, which would have a profound effect on his childhood as on everything else, including, of course, the arts. In the early years of the war Fell and his family – his parents, Anthony and June Fell, and his younger sister Patricia – were based in Epping, a suburb to the east of London. Following some uncomfortably close encounters with bombs, Michael and Patricia were sent to boarding school in rural England. Shortly after they had settled, the school itself was bombed, and the deputy head teacher was killed. The two children returned to London, but with the dangers of the blitz all too present young Michael was evacuated to Newcastle. This was one of the formative experiences of the war that stayed with him throughout his life. He was immediately displaced, and his parents lost track of his whereabouts. When they did finally make contact they found him undernourished and infested with lice. His own recollection was that his shoes had been taken from him shortly after his evacuation, and that he had subsisted on a diet made up almost solely of chips.

Following this traumatic period, Michael saw out the rest of the war under happier circumstances in rural Wales with his mother and sister. They eventually reunited with his father, and lived for a time near Guildford, where it was said that Michael began his compassionate interest in people, often inviting waifs and strays or young soldiers home for meals. It was also during this time that he acquired another sibling, a boy named Nicholas, who was born with severe congenital anomalies and sadly died very soon after his birth.

Shortly after the war the family moved to Wroxwell, a small village outside Chelmsford in Essex, and later lived in Chelmsford proper. Anthony Fell was beginning a political career which would eventually see him elected in 1951 as Member of Parliament for Great Yarmouth, a seat which had been held by his grandfather, Sir Arthur Fell, in the early 20th century. A forthright character touchingly and outspokenly proud of his modest son's talent, he started to encourage him to nurture his skills. He sought actively to enhance his family's education through the museums of London, making sure to highlight the great masters alongside his other enthusiasms – ceramics and antiquities. So began Michael Fell's lifelong commitment to both the fine and the decorative arts. After a turbulent early education through the war, attending several London schools including St Thomas More in Chelsea and the London Oratory School in Brompton Road, he was sent to St George's in Weybridge, where he completed his formal education and made a commitment to developing his practice as an artist.

> Just on 6 ft tall, large-boned, hungrily thin, with brown eyes and hair and large thickly veined expressive hands, Michael at seventeen, though awkward and unsettled, had nonetheless a determined chin that spoke of guts, and an easy smile which while seldom breaking into laughter was infectious enough to attract strangers. He was never transparent or easy to sum up, never egocentric enough to allow anyone to master and evaluate his opinions. He was easy to talk to on most subjects, but closed his mouth in a thin oyster line when the topic was himself and his future.[1]

So Michael Fell was described by his father, as he enrolled in a foundation course at St Martin's School of Art. The school was gaining notoriety through the sculpture department under the stewardship of Frank Martin, the young sculptors Antony Caro, Elizabeth Frink and Eduardo Paolozzi being on rotation to teach there. The foundation course, while giving Fell an introduction to the practice of art in a more general sense, didn't seem to provide the structure, philosophy or historical depth that he was after. Despite artists such as Peter Coker being part of the teaching faculty – Coker became and remained a lifelong advocate of Fell's work – Fell himself was seemingly untethered.

He had maintained a spate of jobs from waiting tables at night to cleaning department stores early in the morning, and he was invariably burnt out and unable to muster the energy or inclination to paint. However, the interest and compassion he had shown at such a young age towards other people continued to grow, and he would often frequent places where 'real people' could be found, observed and sketched. When he wasn't working in one of his numerous jobs he would take his sketchbook to Lyons cafés or Covent Garden market, noticing the array of characters, many of whom visibly wore traces of life's hardships. He would even discreetly sketch on the London tube, attracted by the nuances of character and expression that he'd find on his subjects in face or body. His compassion and empathy drew him to those with visible disabilities; they would become the heroes of Fell's drawings.

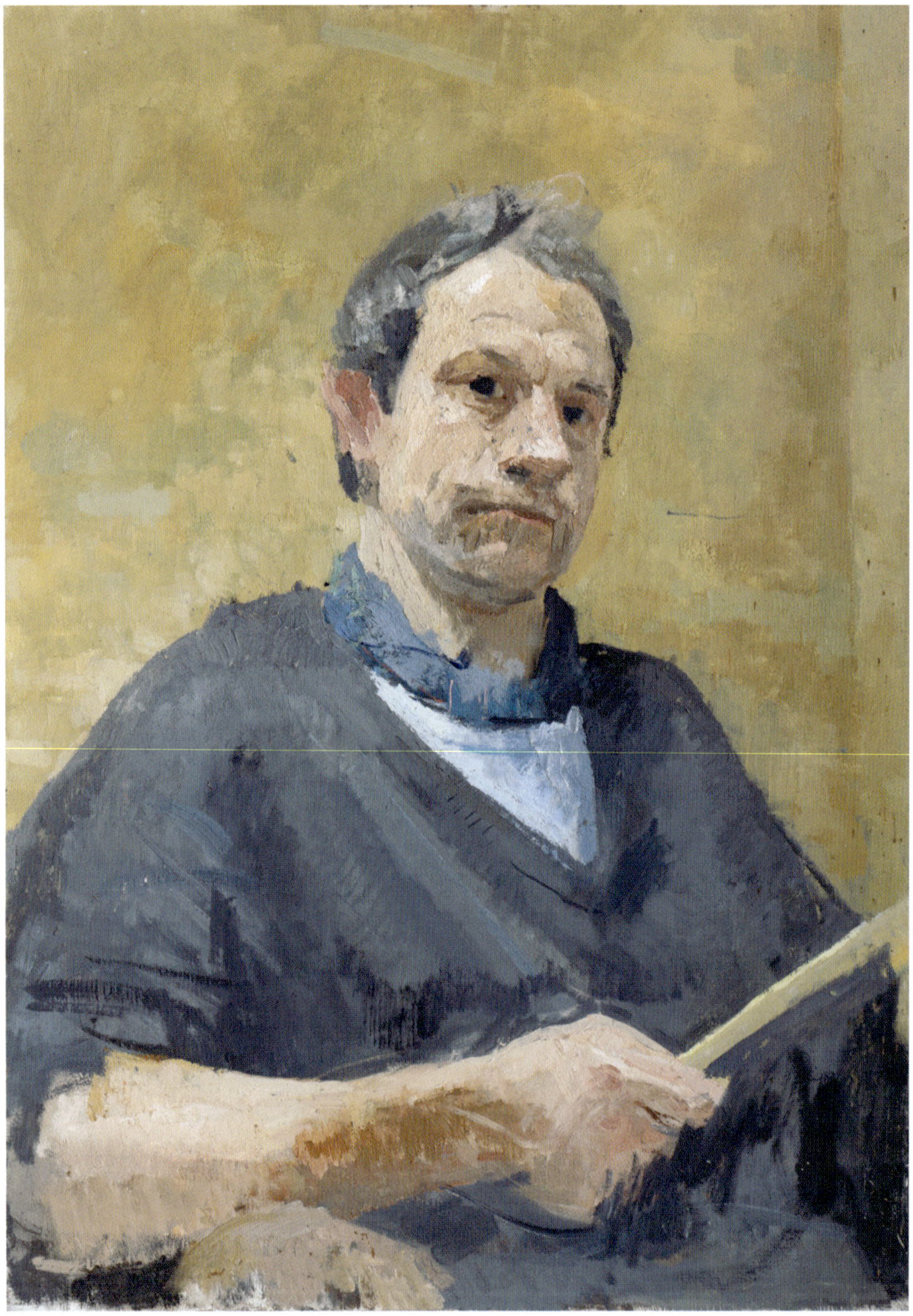

7. *Self Portrait,* 1970s, oil on board, 60 x 43 cm

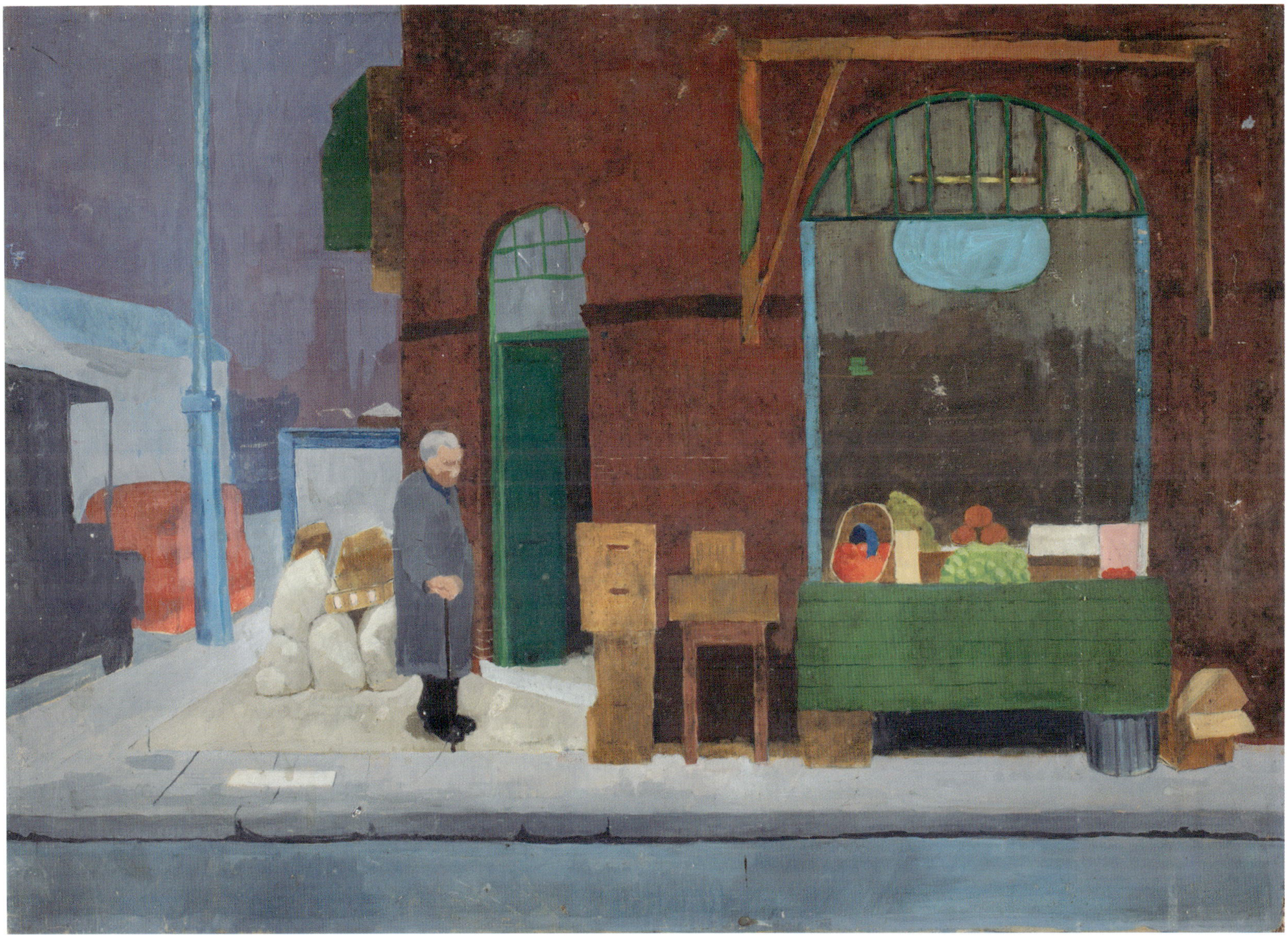

8. *London Scene*, 1960s, oil on board, 43 x 61 cm

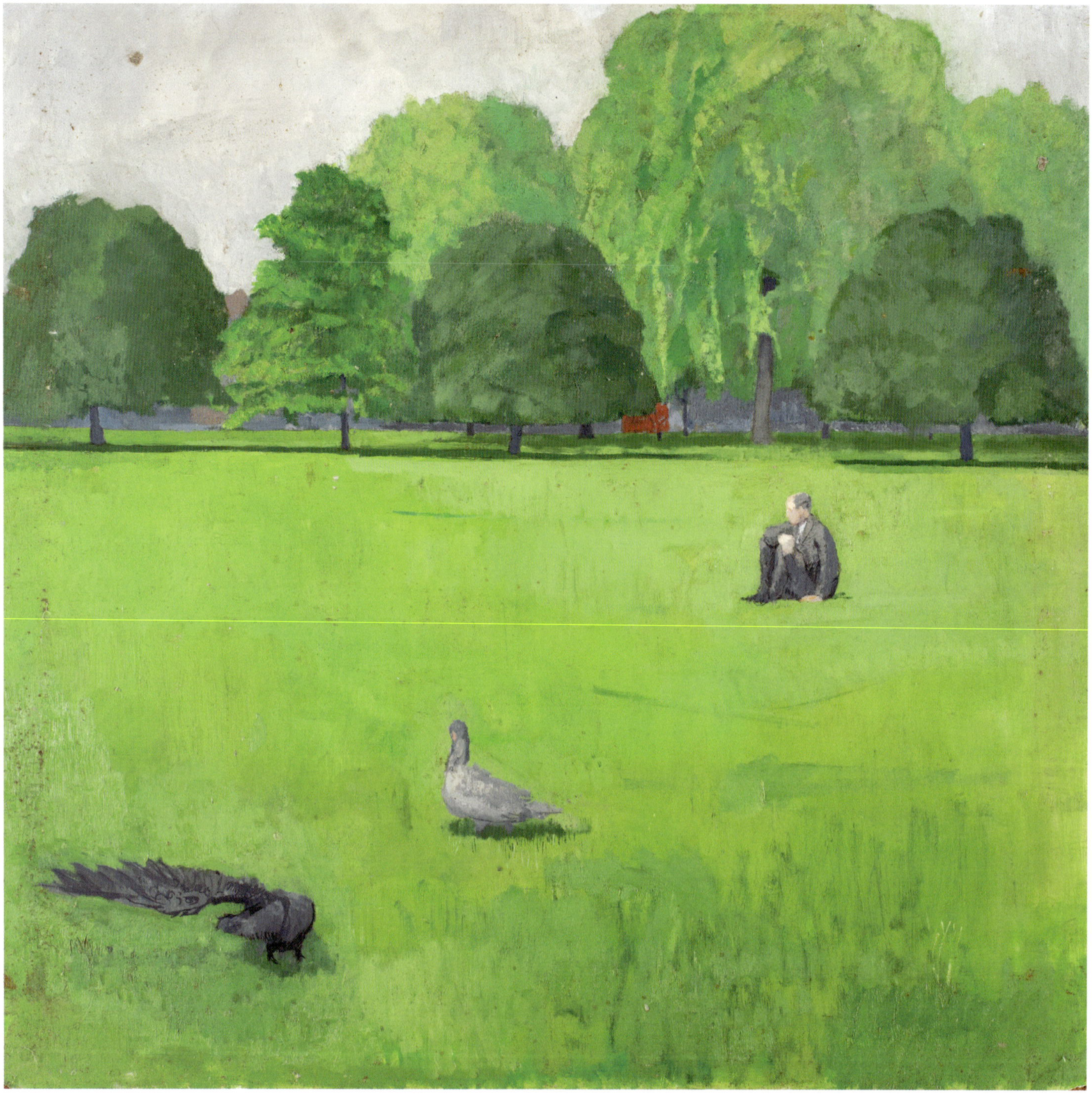

9. *On the Grass in the Park*, 1960s, oil on canvas, 61.9 x 64 cm

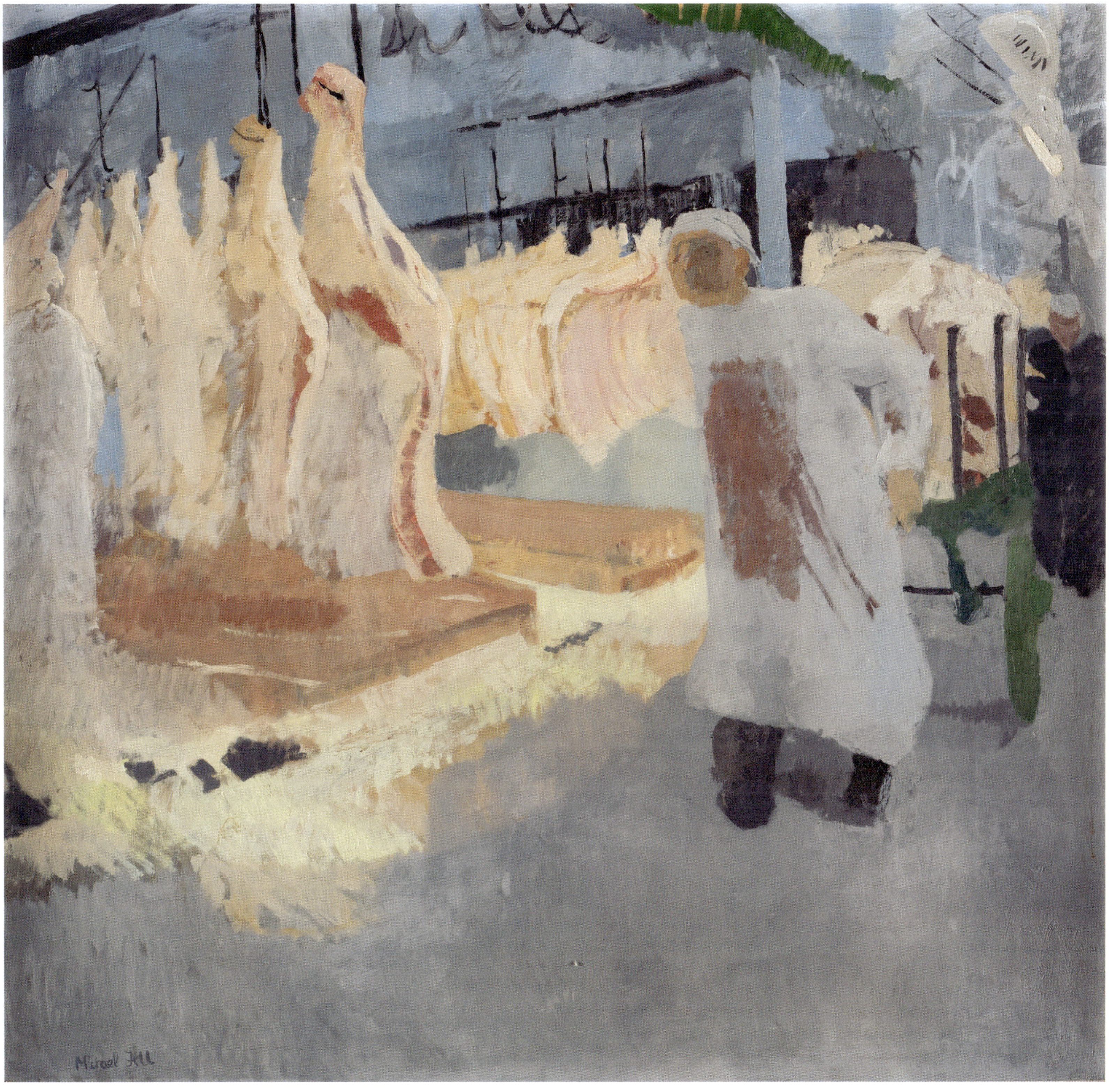

10. *Smithfield Butcher*, 1960s, oil on canvas, 91 x 85 cm

St Martin's proved not to be the context in which he would establish his artistic identity. He left the institution to embark on his own adventure overseas. His intention, following the holistic education instilled in him through his father's weekend tours of museums of London, was to extend his experience of the great masters of the Renaissance at first hand. His preliminary education through the collections of the National Gallery and the Victoria and Albert Museum opened him up to the traditions of painting, and he felt a deep pull to Italy, to bring himself closer to the true lives of Renaissance artists like Raphael, Michelangelo and Botticelli. This period of travel, particularly a long stint in Florence, opened his eyes and heart to new ideas and social experiences, giving him a stronger sense of himself as both man and artist.

His financial and artistic struggles continued after his return to London. The range of jobs he undertook eventually led to him canvassing for the Fulham Conservative Association, and his affability and aptitude for making friends found him successfully supporting his father's political career in Great Yarmouth. As an artist, however, he was still anxiously seeking a breakthrough. There were times when he felt so disheartened that he would not paint for months on end, wrestling with a sense of his own inadequacy compared with his heroes – what his father saw as a necessary but not noble struggle. This internal conflict would always haunt him as an artist. His father made clear his view that while it was imperative for Michael to commit himself to his talent, commercial success was not something to be sought after and could indeed corrupt the value of his creativity.

It was at the City & Guilds Art School in Kennington that Fell worked most intensively to develop that creativity across the disciplines of oil painting, drawing and printmaking. In 1965 he won a scholarship to study fine art there under the guidance of the Principal, Elizabeth Fitz Gerald, and painters in the faculty such as Bernard Dunstan and Henry Wilkinson who ran the print department. Fell had been introduced to the school by his close friend Bill Jordan, who was a sculpture student there. Jordan would go on to found the Jordan Gallery in Camden where Fell had several solo exhibitions alongside other rising artists of his generation, including David Hockney.

Shortly after beginning his studies, Fell moved into a house in Kensington with his friend Edmund Fairfax Lucy and a cohort from the City & Guilds. Their only rule, not to allow women to move in, was swiftly broken. Following the addition of Fairfax Lucy's sister to the house, Fell met a young Australian, Maureen Lean. It was 1966, and he entered his stride as an emerging artist, forming a group alongside other City & Guilds students such as P. John Burden, Pat Regnart and Tom Dowling, who titled themselves the 'York Street Artists'. They had chosen the name in reference to their occasional gallery which was on the lower floor of Anthony Fell's antique shop in Marylebone. Fell senior had become a more serious collector and dealer in antique porcelain, and set up this lesser-used space of his dealership as a gallery for Michael and his colleagues. It was also during these years that Michael, while still dedicated to painting, found himself drawn to the print studio at the City & Guilds.

The halcyon period that followed saw him gaining momentum in both his painting and printmaking practices, in parallel with his blossoming relationship with Maureen Lean [13]. This was cemented in their marriage at Farm Street Church, Mayfair, in 1967. A second scholarship followed, this time to study in Rome. It was awarded by City & Guilds as a prize to the student judged to be producing the best work in their final year. While it provided some travel costs and a small stipend, the couple decided to make it part of a larger adventure and honeymoon across Europe, sowing the seeds for a lifelong passion for the Continent. On their return they moved to a bedsit in Islington, which, while comfortable enough, lacked a studio. Elizabeth Fitz Gerald provided a solution. She had always been a strong advocate of Fell's work, and was keen for him to return to the City & Guilds for a postgraduate degree. She found lodgings in a postwar cluster of buildings on the Duchy of Cornwall Estate in Kennington, close to the art school. These had been specifically designed for and leased to artists by the Duchy. A single room with a mezzanine, the Cardigan Street flat [20] was vast compared to the Islington bedsit and accommodated both a studio and Maureen's framing and gilding business.

The early years living in Kennington saw Fell embark on a new variety of jobs to help pay the bills as well as save for more ambitious purchases, which included a splendid Swedish printing press. Printmaking drew him ever closer to both his subjects and his creative interests, including poetry. Several works combined literary references: *The Gates of Hell* [5], a large etching, includes a poem from the Indian poet and philosopher Rabindranath Tagore's *Fruit Gathering*.

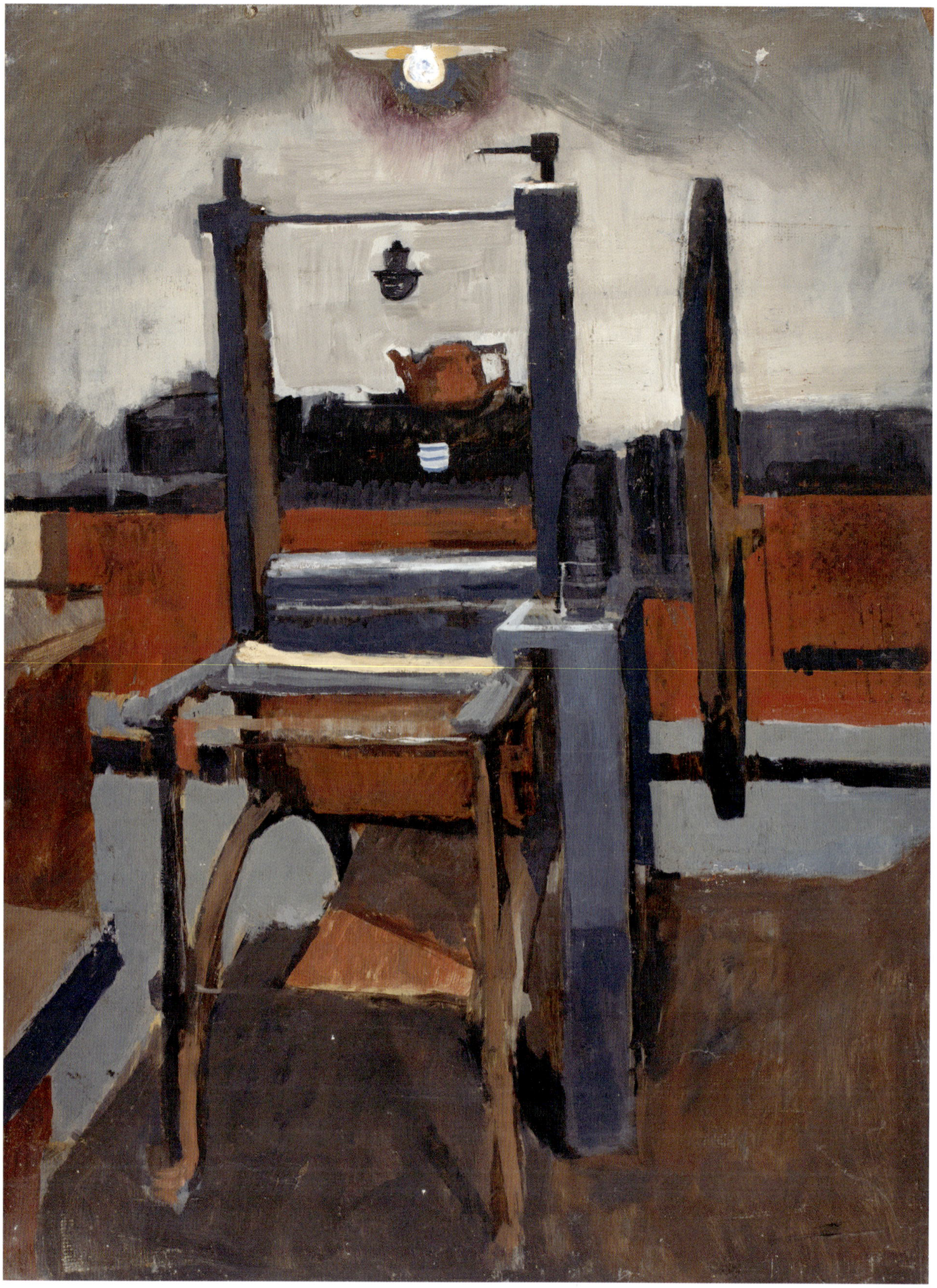

11. *Printing Press at City & Guilds*, 1960s, oil on board, 61 x 46 cm

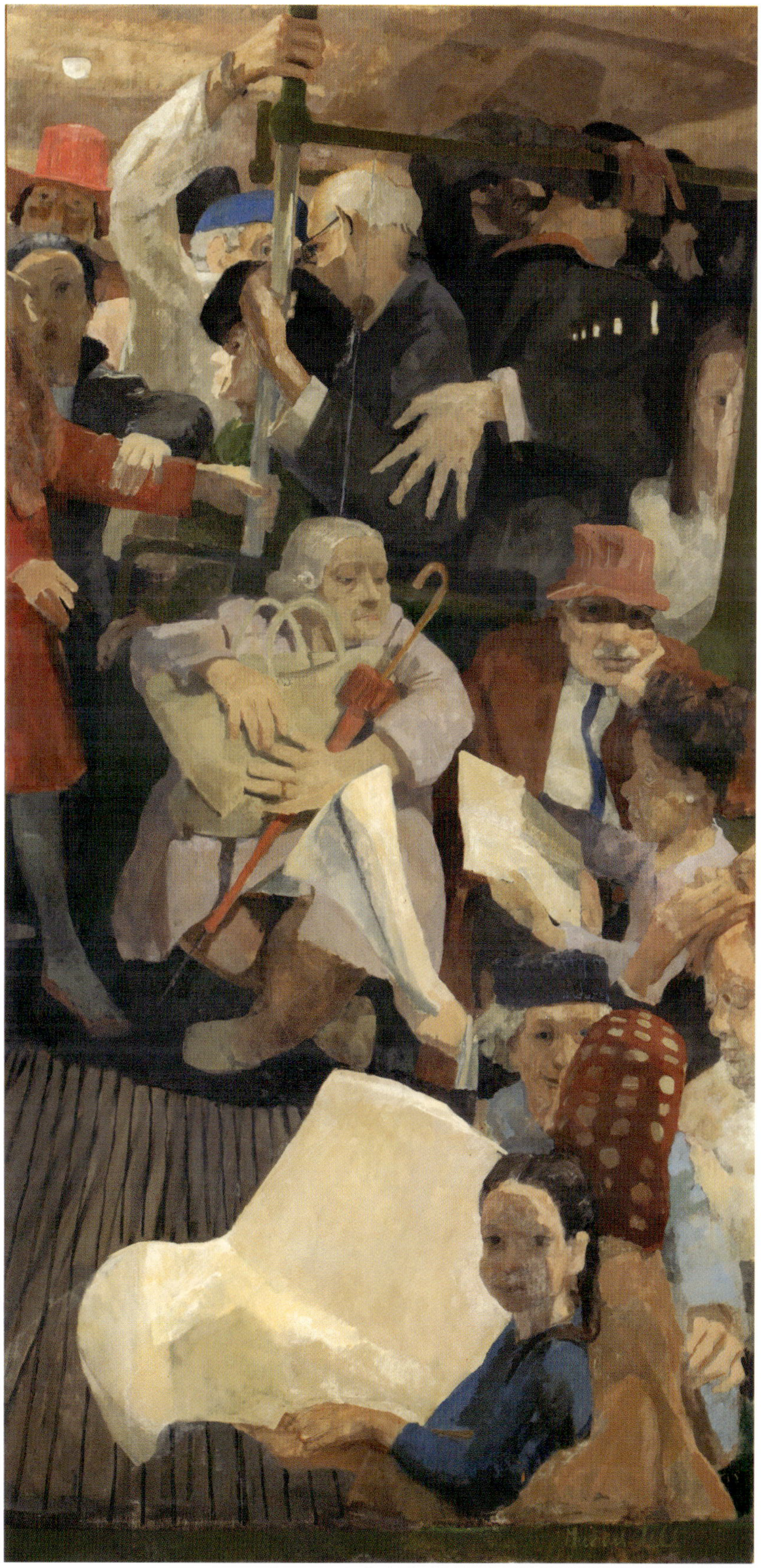

12. *Tube Train*, 1972, oil on canvas, 152 x 76 cm

Fell was introduced to Tagore's poetry by his dear friend Luthful Bari, who had come from India; they met in Fell's early years of waiting tables at the famous Talk of the Town night club. Poetry and music were hugely important to Fell; several of his works concern literary texts, such as *The Burning Babe* [18, 19] by the 16th-century English poet and Catholic martyr Robert Southwell. Some would include both musical and poetic references. Fell's paintings of this time, however, grew from the characters and situations he encountered in London. From the hordes of drawings and sketches that he was constantly making he created finished works such as *Tube Train* [12] and *The Nun's Family* [1]. He was also spending time on portraiture, working on the final composition through several iterations of drawing, requiring long and numerous sittings for the subjects. His early portraits include his parents and his wife, subjects that he could work on with his sitters at hand. Despite his practice growing into more ambitious lyrical works and landscapes he would return to portraiture, with both his children as well as close friends.

It was in the late 1960s that Michael and Maureen Fell met Sheila Arbuthnot, who had founded the Halesworth Gallery, a non-profit space in Suffolk, with her husband Jack in 1966. The gallery occupied a floor in a row of almshouses in the town of Halesworth and had been running exhibitions showing artists with a connection to East Anglia, including Elizabeth Frink. Sheila Arbuthnot initially asked Fell to participate in a group exhibition in 1969. She then invited him back for a solo exhibition in 1971. The prospect of producing work for a solo exhibition was both exhilarating and daunting. Fell approached his task with painstaking care and assiduity, working over the course of a year to produce oil paintings, prints and drawings.[2]

The early 1970s saw significant developments for Fell. Following his exhibitions at the Halesworth Gallery, he began exhibiting in earnest at the Jordan Gallery, run by his friend Bill Jordan. He showed drawings and etchings, and sales started to gain momentum. In 1972 a selection of Michael Fell's etchings was included in the British Museum's *Modern Prints and Drawings* exhibition, and four works, *Covent Garden – early morning* (1968) [33], *Covent Garden – late morning* (1968) [35], *Victoria Station* (1968) [37] and *St Anne's Vauxhall* (1969) [36], were acquired by the museum.

By 1973 the Fells were feeling the strains of living in London. Michael was working both as a van driver for a local school run by nuns [1] and for a cottage industry making 'glass paintings' from photographs printed on glass to replicate antiques. The couple were looking for some respite from the relentlessness of the city and were starting to consider a move elsewhere, outside London or further afield.

It was by chance that they learned about the Gers, a rural area of southwest France. Elizabeth Fitz Gerald, who had recently stepped aside as Principal of the City & Guilds to make way for the more established painter Roger de Grey, managed again to come to the Fells' rescue. She held a dinner party at which she introduced them to her nephew Maurice Fitz Gerald [17] and his wife, Jenny [104]. The young Fitz Geralds had been living in Paris until Maurice had been sent on secondment to the Gascon city of Auch, in the heart of the Gers. Very quickly they had become besotted with the region nestled in the foothills of the Pyrenees and purchased a small cottage, untouched by modern conveniences. The Fells, hearing this story and feeling their own desire to possess a plot in that French paradise, made an impromptu trip to the Gers and there found Barrère near the village of Rozès, a place Fell described as 'a ruin', surrounded by landscapes where skies were 'extraordinarily blue, the buildings sit white-hot, the vines shimmer and dance and the range of leaves and shapes is limitless'.[3] Thus began a new chapter for Michael who, with Maureen, would lovingly rebuild the 'ruin' over the next thirty years into a place which would become his permanent home and studio [26–28, 101].

In the mid-1970s the couple oscillated between their life in London and their project in France. During this time Michael Fell was asked by Roger de Grey to return to the City & Guilds to work alongside Daphne Casdagli and Joe Busuttil in the printmaking department. Fell would work 2–3 days at the school, leaving him time to continue painting, etching and participating in exhibitions at the Jordan Gallery.

In 1979 their son Mark was born [14]. The couple took the arrival of the new baby in their stride, continuing to live and work at the studio in Kennington, Maureen framing when she could and Michael teaching, painting and printmaking. It was not until Robert, their second son, was born in 1982 that they started to feel the constraints of their living arrangements, and finally two years later, in 1984, they decided to move

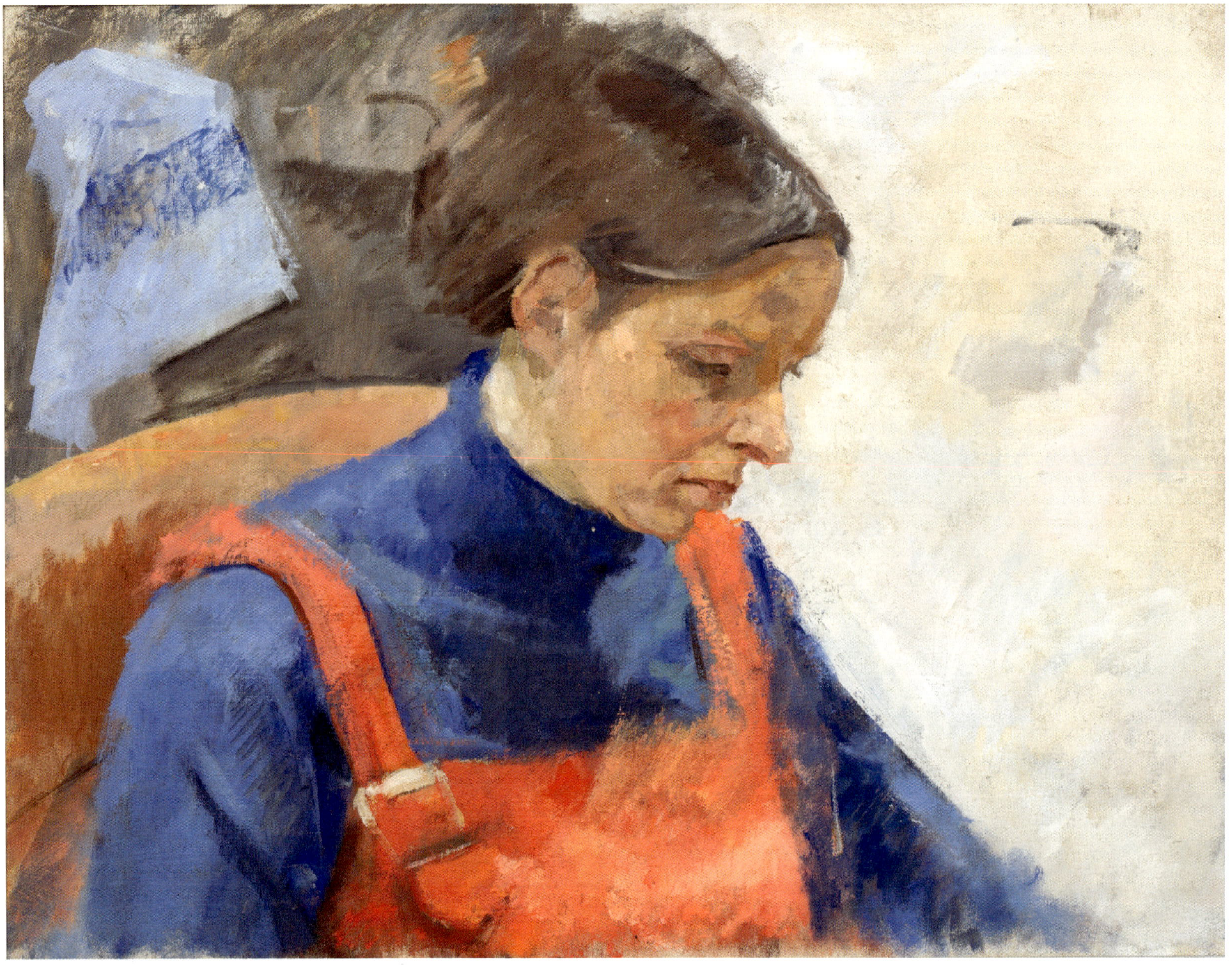

13. *Maureen*, 1970s, oil on canvas, 45 x 60 cm

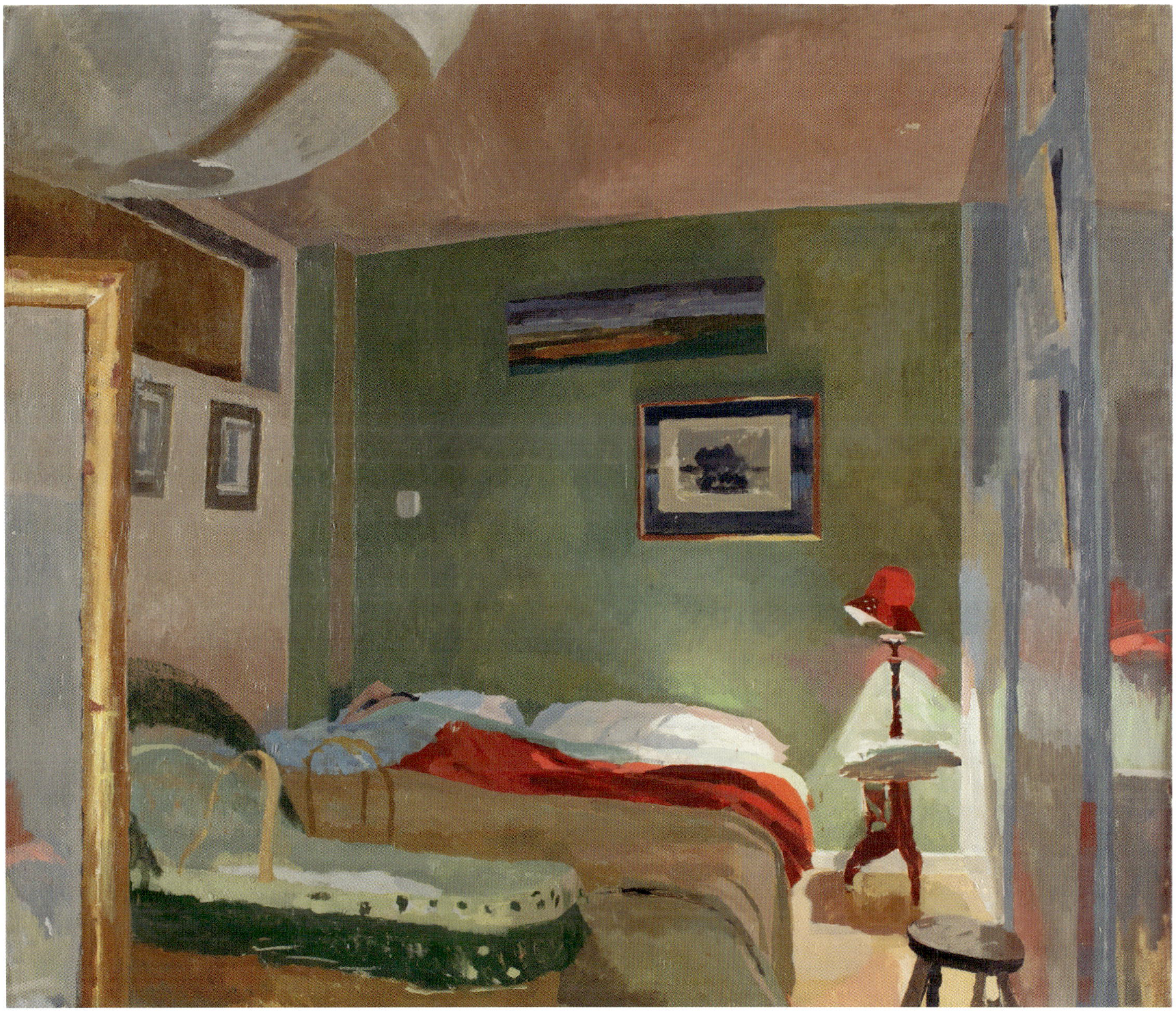

14. *Mark is born*, 1979, oil on canvas, 63.1 x 75.8 cm

away from the city to Bungay in Suffolk [21]. There they bought the Music House, a neglected but fine 18th-century property where the French aristocrat and writer Chateaubriand had once stayed, a fugitive from the Revolution. They undertook its restoration and had a blue plaque installed to commemorate its history.

Bungay provided an artistic community for the young family, situating them close to the British painter Sargy Mann, the historian and writer Frank Welsh, and the novelist Elizabeth Jane Howard. Fell would travel to London to continue teaching at the City & Guilds, but with access to more space and light he embarked on some of his most ambitious works, including the large canvases *Bungay* [15] and *Robert at the Music House* [16]. During the summer months the family would move to the Gers, camping in the garden as they rebuilt Barrère. In the early 1980s they realised that rebuilding the entire property was too demanding, and they offered to sell the barn next to the house to their close friend Frances Dakers. She was to become a lifeline for the family and even more so for Fell when he eventually moved there permanently.

When Fell was offered the role of Head of Foundation at the City & Guilds he used it as an opportunity to ensure that students could get a taste of all the facilities and education offered by the art school, including conservation, lettering, and both the illustrative and the decorative arts. By championing the range of art forms, the City & Guilds stood out from the other art schools in its egalitarian approach to art. Along with his leadership role at the City & Guilds Fell became Chair of the Society of Designer Craftsmen in 1984, remaining until 1987. He used his position to argue for a broader range of contemporary art – from emerging to established – to be included in museum and gallery collections, and curated the exhibition *Vision and Innovation* in 1987, the Society's centenary year.

While maintaining his role as teacher and faculty head Fell continued to produce work and to exhibit, at the Galleria Renata in Chicago, the Belanthi Gallery in New York, and the Royal Academy in London. He also founded the St Quitterie Press, named after the patron saint of Gascony. Together with twelve other artists, including Daphne Casdagli, Michael Estorick, Richard Bawden and Torie Begg, Fell created a portfolio of prints to illustrate the Prologue to the *Canterbury Tales* [43], showcasing an array of printing techniques, which was intended to fund bursaries at the City & Guilds.

In 1993 he showed work at the Chappel Galleries in Essex and with the painter John Lessore in Perpignan; a solo exhibition at the Chappel Galleries in 1999 was preceded by one at the Grosvenor Gallery in London in 1996. The Grosvenor Gallery had been established by Eric Estorick, father of Michael Estorick whom Fell had taught and collaborated with at the City & Guilds. Eric Estorick, an early collector and dealer in Italian modernism, set up an international programme showing artists such as Prunella Clough and John Hoskin as well as Francis Newton Souza and Sydney Kumalo. Fell's solo exhibition, *A Taste of Armagnac*, focused on a body of work that he had built up during his time in the Gers, together with select pieces from Bungay such as *Robert at the Music House* [16]. It was the only time Fell would write at any length about his work, stating quite frankly:

> I have always felt uneasy discussing my work. Once, when asked to talk a painting through I found myself totally tongue-tied but was saved by wise Peter Coker who said quietly 'I am sure Michael and the picture have talked it through', which we had. One is dealing with earthy things which are touched by heaven; it is the stuff of thought untrammelled. I fear that for me the process can be diluted or upset by too much discussion and explanation.[4]

The year 1996 also saw the family move again, this time to Ipswich, where Michael began working on his monumental picture *Crucifixus* [88]. His bigger pieces would occupy an ongoing part of his practice, often representing personal and philosophical quests which he would puzzle through for years. His son Robert remarked that *Crucifixus* followed the artist's moods and life events, getting darker and more sombre in palette in Fell's own dark years and becoming brighter when he found more happiness.

During the 1990s the City & Guilds went through some bigger changes in leadership and direction. Michael Kenny replaced Roger de Grey as the Principal and looked to align the school with others across the country, formalising BA degree programmes for Fine Art, Conservation, and Sculpture. With this the more holistic approach where teaching encompassed diverse art forms was set aside, and Fell found his ideas moving at odds with the school. In 1996 he left his position as Head of

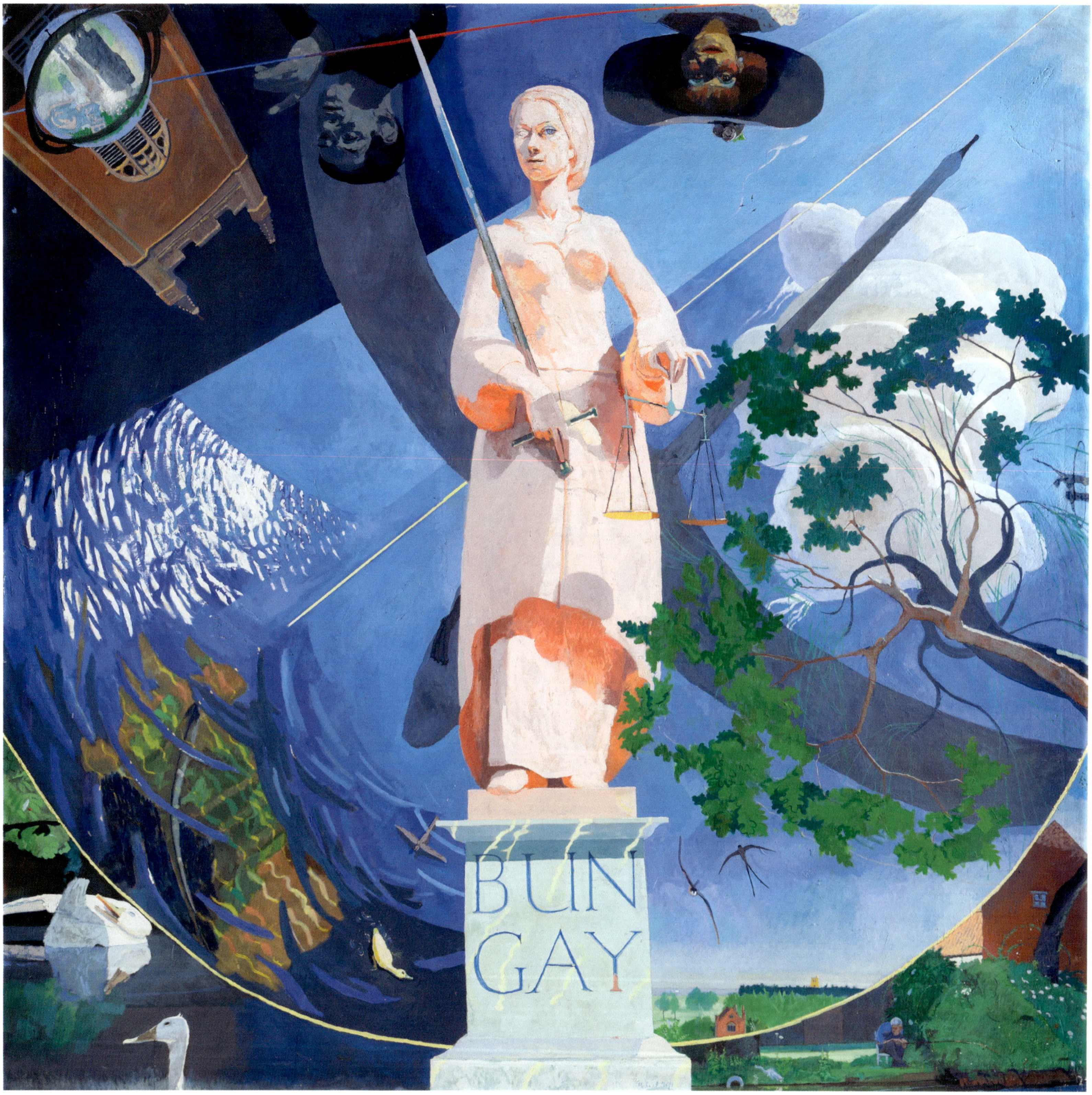

15. *Bungay*, 1990s, oil on canvas, 172 x 177.4 cm

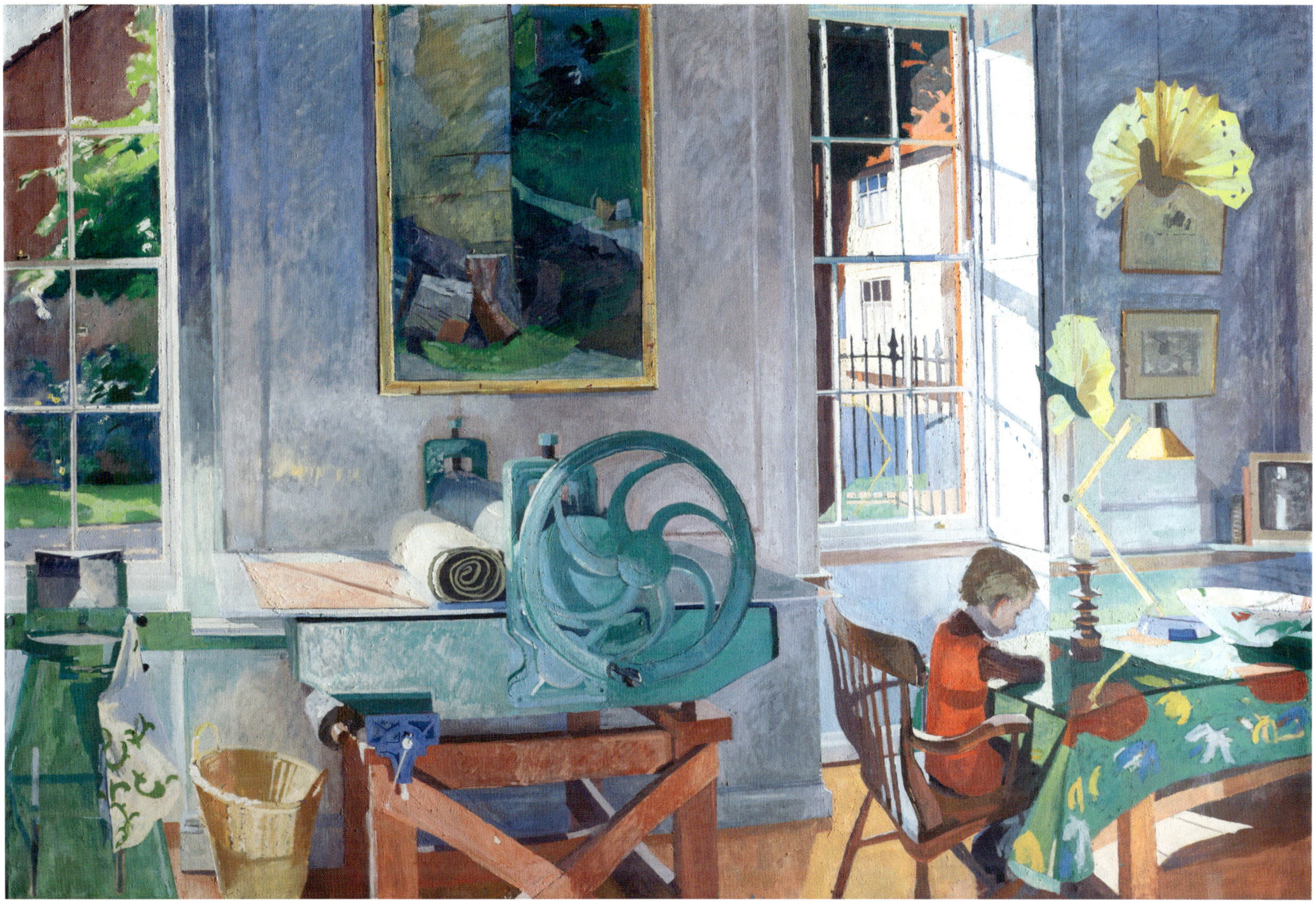

16. *Robert at the Music House*, 1993, oil on canvas, 121 x 182.2 cm

Foundation to focus more on his own practice. In 1998 he was elected an honorary fellow of the Royal Society of Painter-Printmakers. Things were shifting across all facets of his life, both personally and professionally: in 2000 he and Maureen separated. While not a happy time for either, this new freedom allowed Fell to move permanently to the Gers, where he set up his studio and home in Barrère.

The Gers was an extraordinary inspiration for Fell, in its landscape, spirituality, and importantly its people. He had set up an outdoor print studio, with two presses and other equipment, but the Gers was a place that inspired an emphasis on painting and prolific drawing. The early years were not easy, as the artist reconciled himself to his new life ahead. The frugality and remoteness were something of a comfort; he felt that destiny was synonymous with artistic excellence and integrity – which also met with his father's ideals of the 'great artist'. Anthony wrote of

> the frozen indecisiveness born of disbelief in one's ability that is part of the life of almost every creative artist. For it is a momentous solitary world and the sort of mind possessed by the artist most likely to produce worthwhile work is a mind that has in it a strong streak of humility, disbelief that he could possibly scale such heights.[5]

The breakdown of Fell's marriage cast a shadow over the early 2000s and led to a complicated relationship with his faith at this time. Several of his works provided a foil to work through his own discord. Gradually, through friendships and his dedicated practice, he started to resolve some of these internal conflicts and settled into a life of conscientious routine – painting daily, and church on Sundays, preceded by coffee at the Café de la Bourse, where he would sit and draw [6]. The pillars of his life became his loyalty to his Catholicism, his art practice and the group of close friends, both French and English, which grew as he became further embedded in his Gers life. The community that had built up in the region since the Fells first bought near the village of Rozès had grown into a lively ensemble of musicians, collectors and art enthusiasts. Fell would often include members of his close circle in his work, painting the Fitz Geralds [17, 104] who had become dedicated patrons, commissioning several paintings of the region; the Dufaus, who owned the fortified Château de Bazian; and the large Catholic Branthomme family, local sheep farmers, the subject

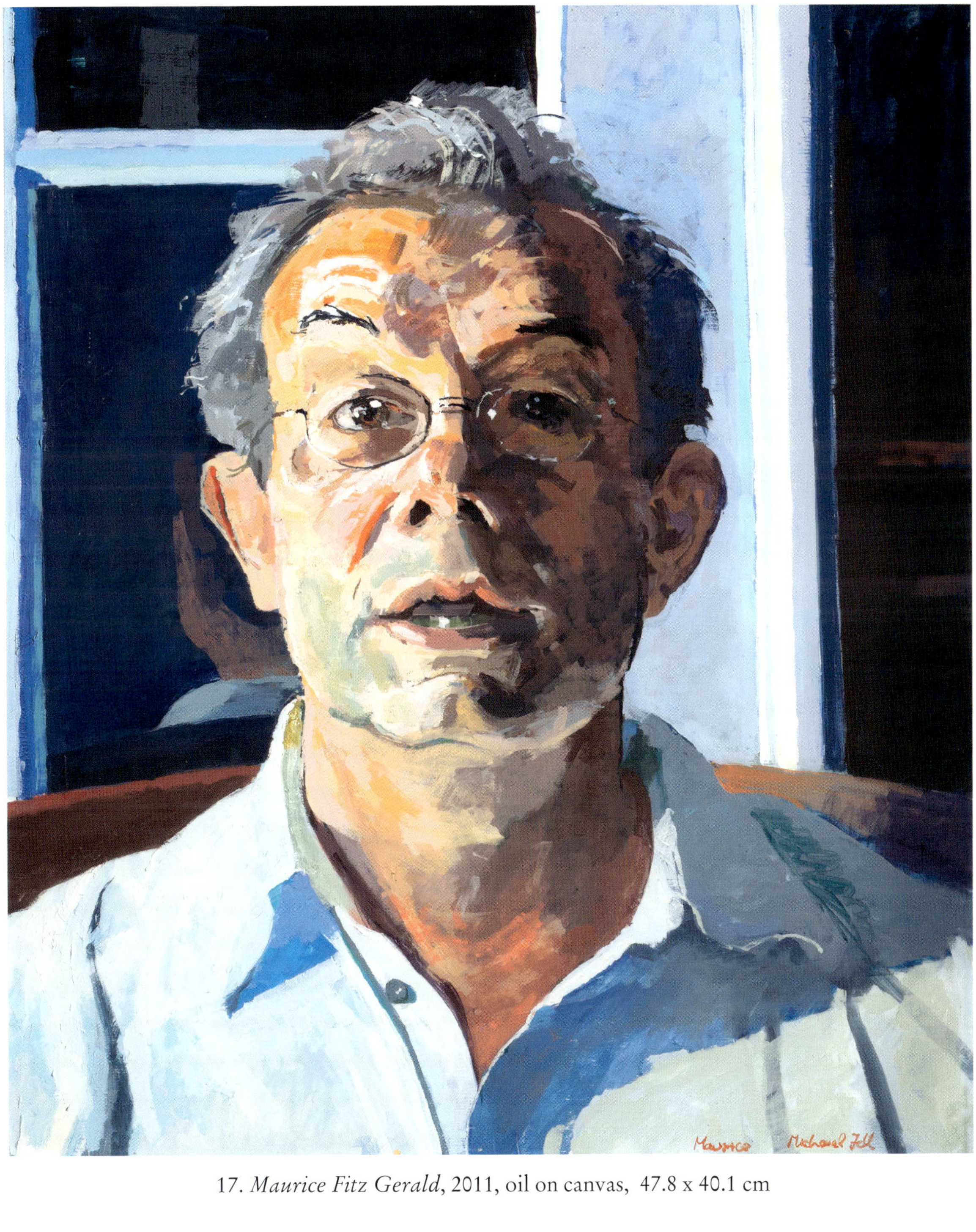

17. *Maurice Fitz Gerald*, 2011, oil on canvas, 47.8 x 40.1 cm

of two large paintings he was working on at the end of his life [102, 103].

At the request of several close friends Fell began teaching art and art history on Saturdays. His dedicated group of interested students included different nationalities; depending on who attended, he would often conduct the lessons in both English and French. He would start with basic still-life drawing, insisting that looking, seeing and understanding subjective perception were the most important acts of an artist. He would also include a lesson in art history, reading from one of the many art books in his own library. These lessons would jump around, sometimes focusing on specific artists such as Goya, Lucian Freud or Euan Uglow, at other times dealing with a larger period of classical or modern art. Through these art classes Fell met Isabelle Martinez, who became a lifelong friend and creative influence. He painted several portraits of her [24, 25], requiring her to sit for him routinely at Barrère. The collection of these works would speak of their intimate friendship, and the hours Fell spent painting her cemented their mutual understanding.

As Fell settled in and his collector base grew in the Gers he was encouraged to participate in more exhibitions both locally and back in London. One of the earliest was in 2002 in L'Isle de Noé, in a house owned by Arnaud and Anne Guinard. Fell had met the Guinards through mutual friends, Ted and Andrée Gorton, who owned a house in the village of Bazian. The Guinards had only recently purchased the property, and invited Fell to exhibit thirty of his paintings while the house still lay empty. The exhibition was informal, with the works nonchalantly placed through the rooms, propped against walls or placed on the sparse furniture scattered here and there; however it proved to be a pivotal moment for Fell, revealing enthusiasm and support for his work in the influential new Gers community. Soon after the exhibition he received requests from the de Margerie family to paint their home, one of the most important in the Gers, the Château de Mazères. He also received commissions from Michael Estorick, who had bought a Gers farmhouse called Routgès. Fell created a body of work including drawings and paintings around both properties. More exhibitions followed, notably in the Abbaye de Flaran, known for its ambitious programme, as well as in Condom, Valence, and his home village Rozès. In 2010 he presented a solo exhibition at the Bankside Gallery in London called *With Love from France*, which included some of his larger paintings alongside prints and drawings.

Fell experienced some health problems which led to less printmaking, but he continued to paint avidly until his death, maintaining his strict routine – rising early and following the light to work on either his landscapes outdoors or other pieces in his studio. On 12 March 2023 he was found collapsed at Barrère, dead at the age of eighty-four. Although he had reached a decent age, his death came as a shock to friends and family who had experienced his relentless work ethic and warm and mischievous sense of humour right up to the end. He had been up late the night before preparing for his Saturday art classes, making notes on artists he wanted to discuss. He never sought to be a great promoter of his work or his practice. He wanted people to have their own subjective experiences and interactions with his paintings, prints and drawings, and for his legacy to be the artwork rather than his own analysis or interpretation. He shared this view with Goya: 'There are no rules for painting ... Even the artist who has achieved more than most is hard put to explain how he reaches that deep understanding and appreciation of things, which is necessary for great art.'[6]

[1] Description by his father Anthony Fell, in his unpublished notes and memoir of Michael Fell written in 1971.

[2] The paintings exhibited included *Smithfield Butcher* [10], *Children's Playground*, *Summer Football* [89], *Autumn in Berwick Street*, *Mother and Daughter*, *The Nun's Family* [1], *Winter*, *Spring*, *Garden*, *Louise Villa*, *Still Life* and *Austrian Grasses.*

[3] From 'A Taste of Armagnac and the Comfort of Friends', written by Michael Fell to accompany his exhibition *A Taste of Armagnac* at the Grosvenor Gallery, March 1996.

[4] ibid.

[5] See note 1.

[6] A personal note by Francisco Goya, from *Goya: Drawings from His Private Albums* by Juliet Wilson Bareau (Ben Uri Gallery & Museum, London, 2001), p. 14.

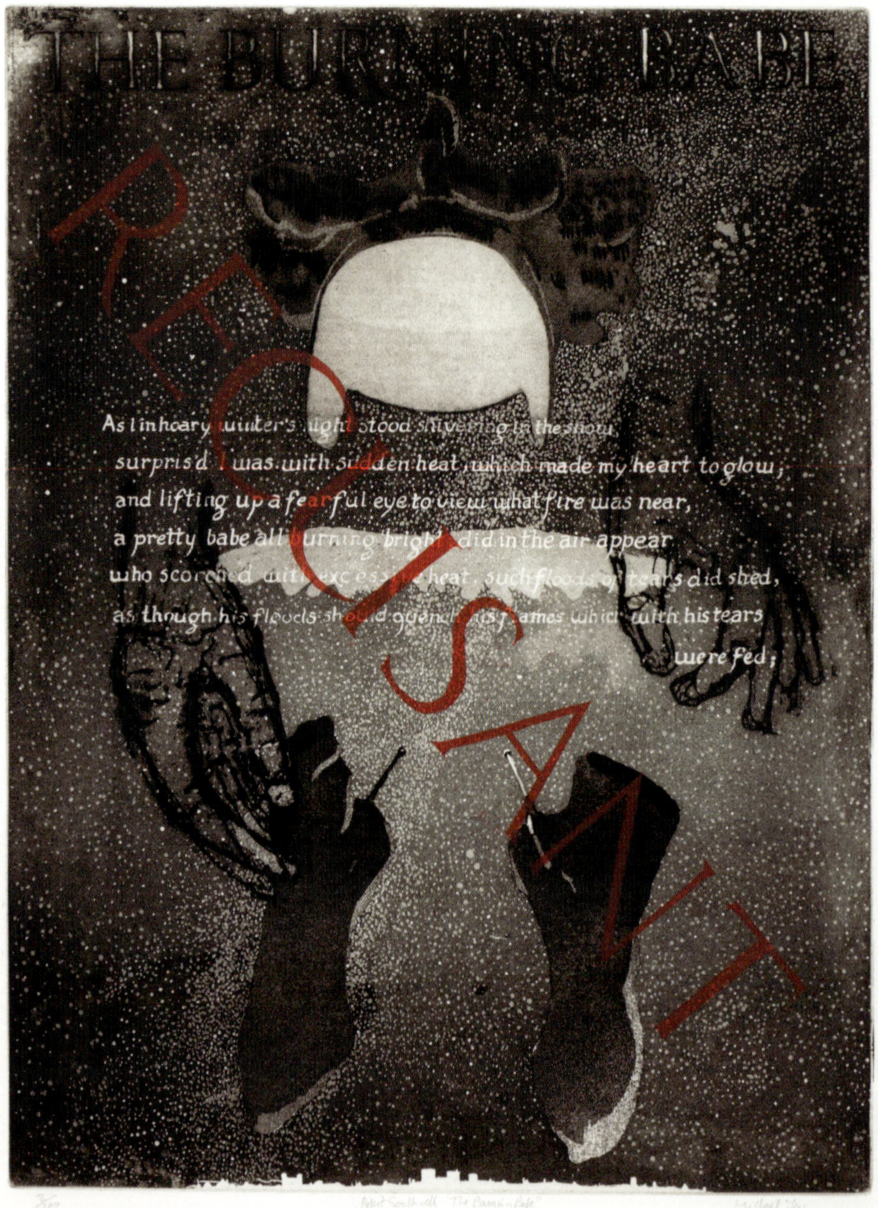

18. *The Burning Babe 1*, 1970s, aquatint, 59.5 x 45 cm

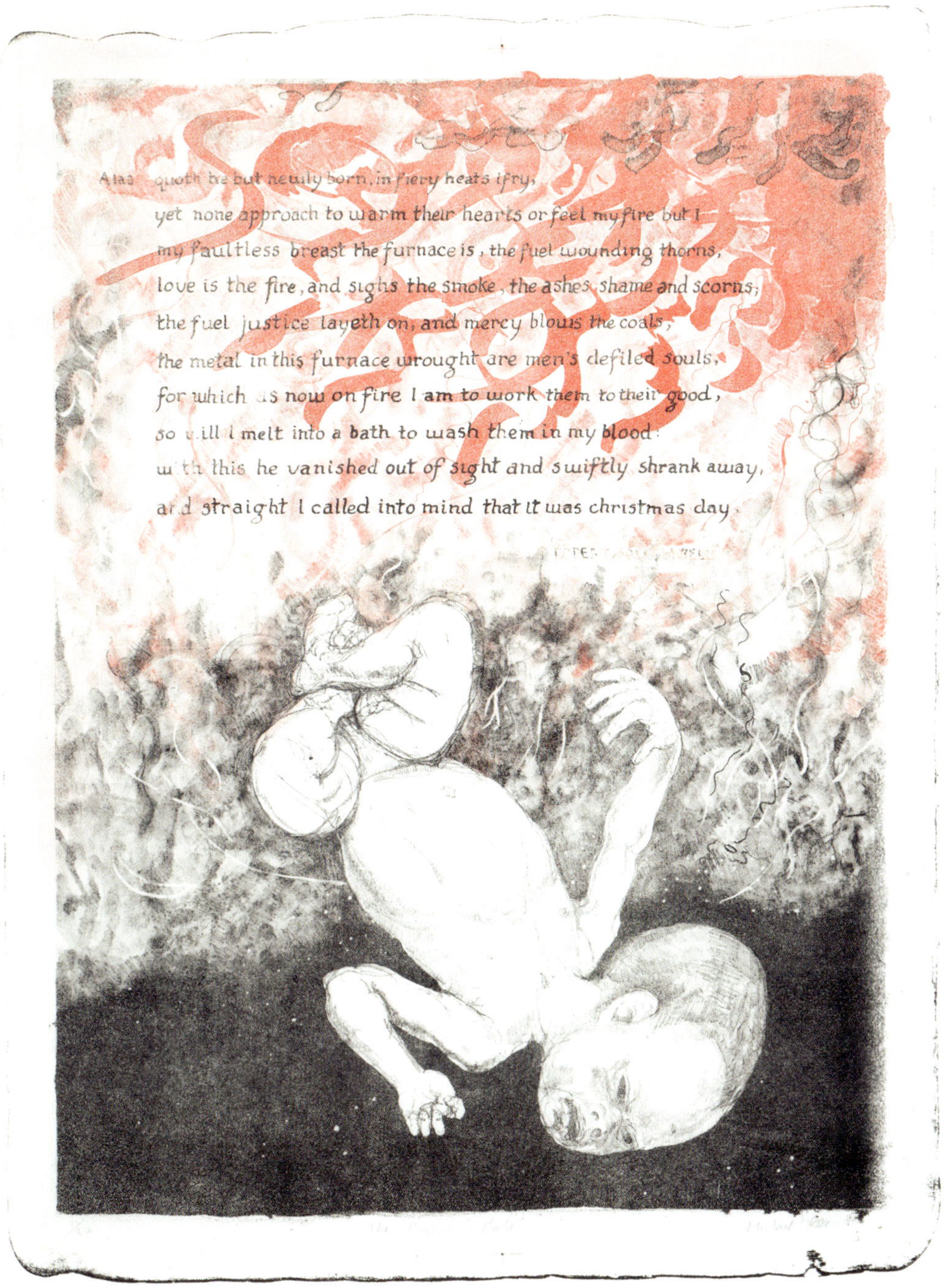

19. *The Burning Babe 2*, 1970s, aquatint, 66.5 x 50.8 cm

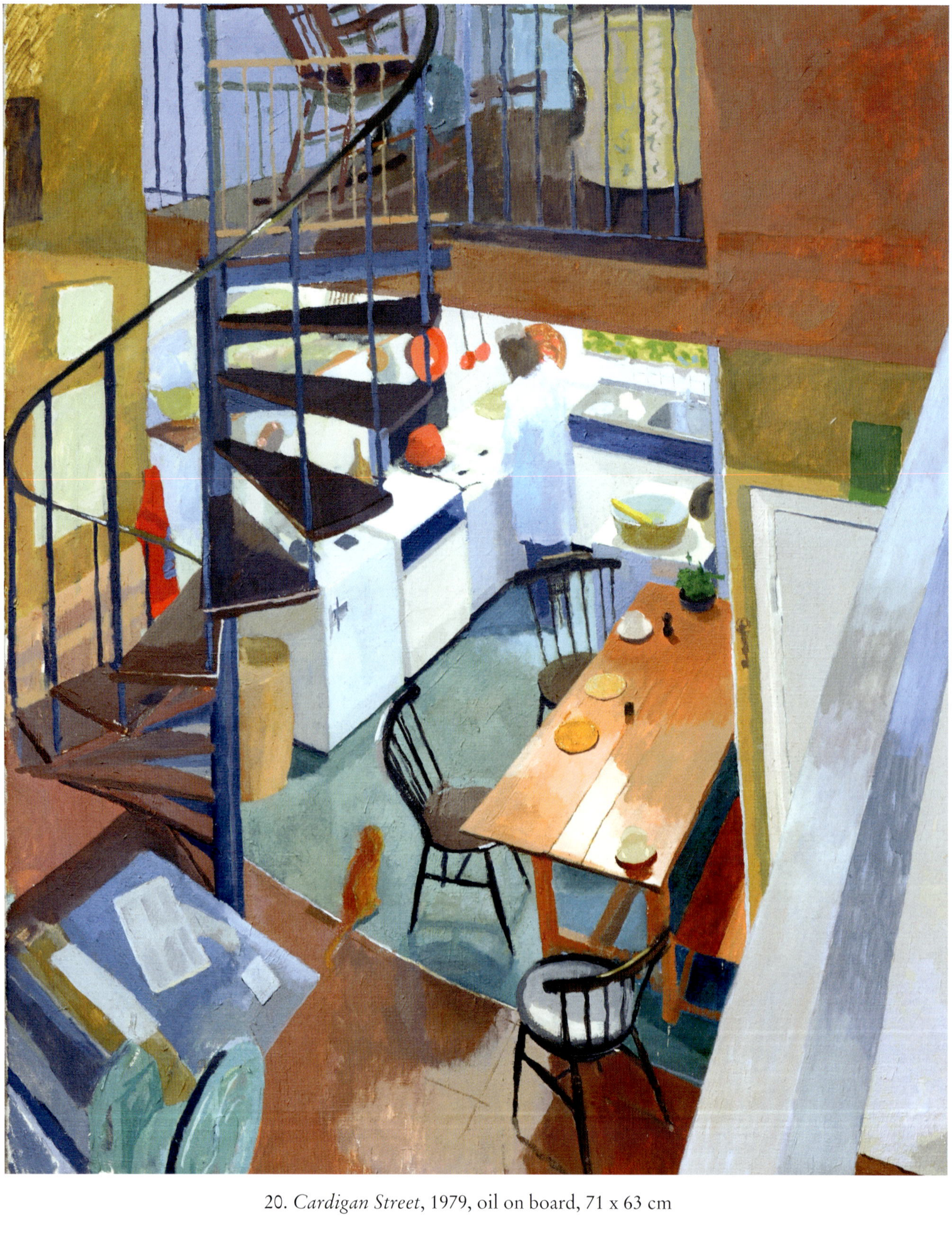

20. *Cardigan Street*, 1979, oil on board, 71 x 63 cm

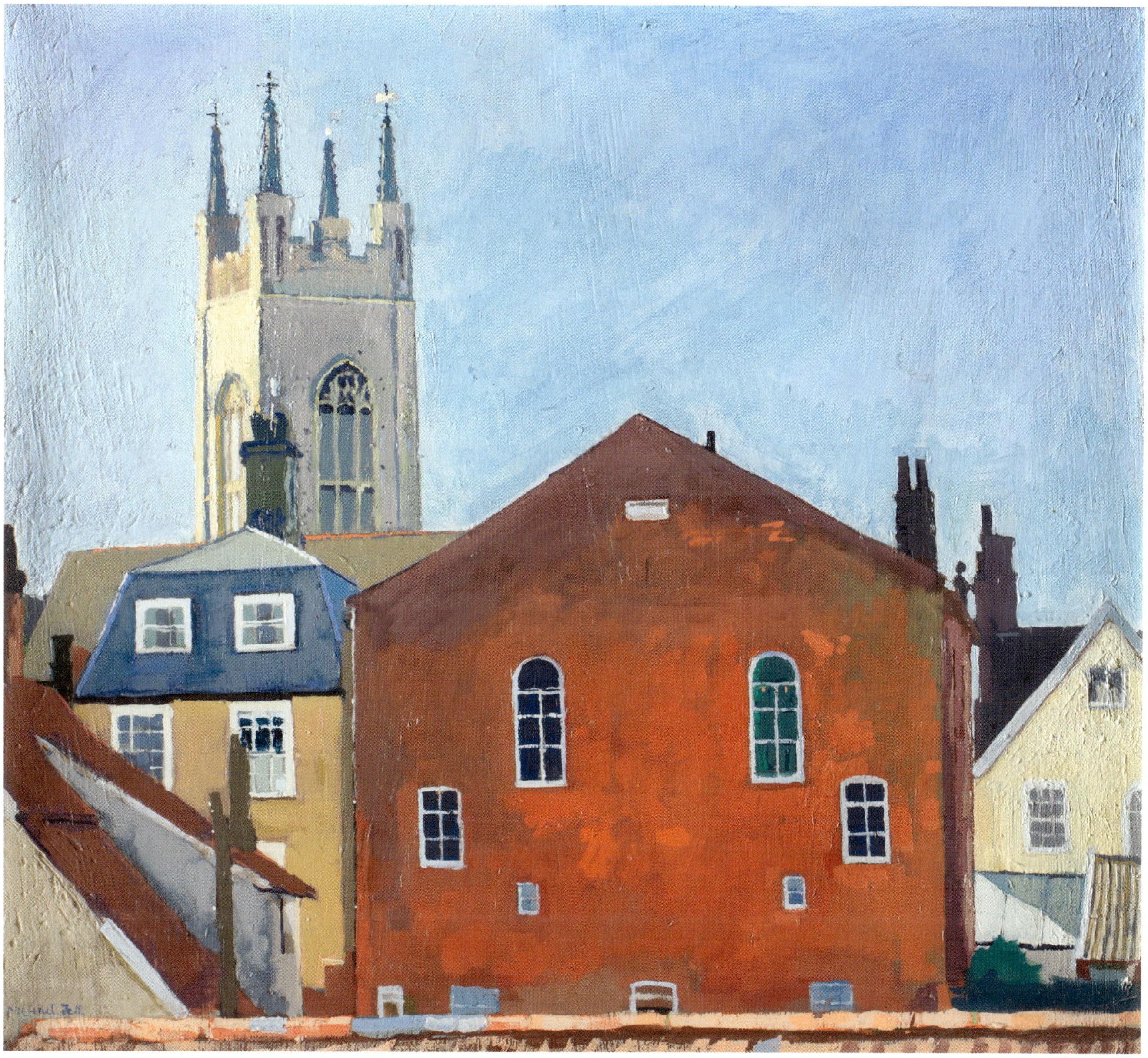

21. *St Mary's at Bungay*, 1980s, oil on canvas, 32.5 x 37 cm

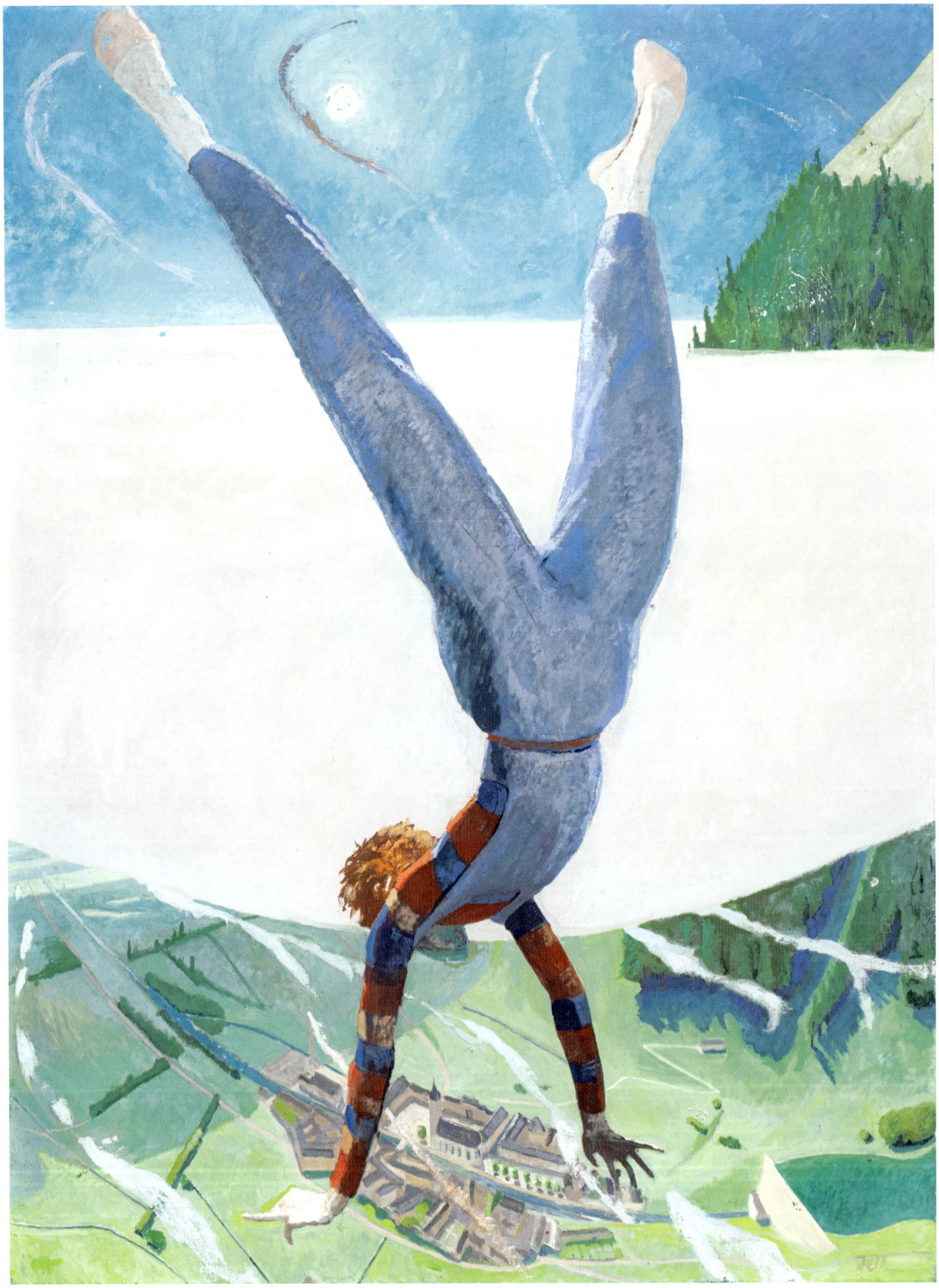

22. *Virginie*, 1990s, oil on canvas, 121 x 91 cm

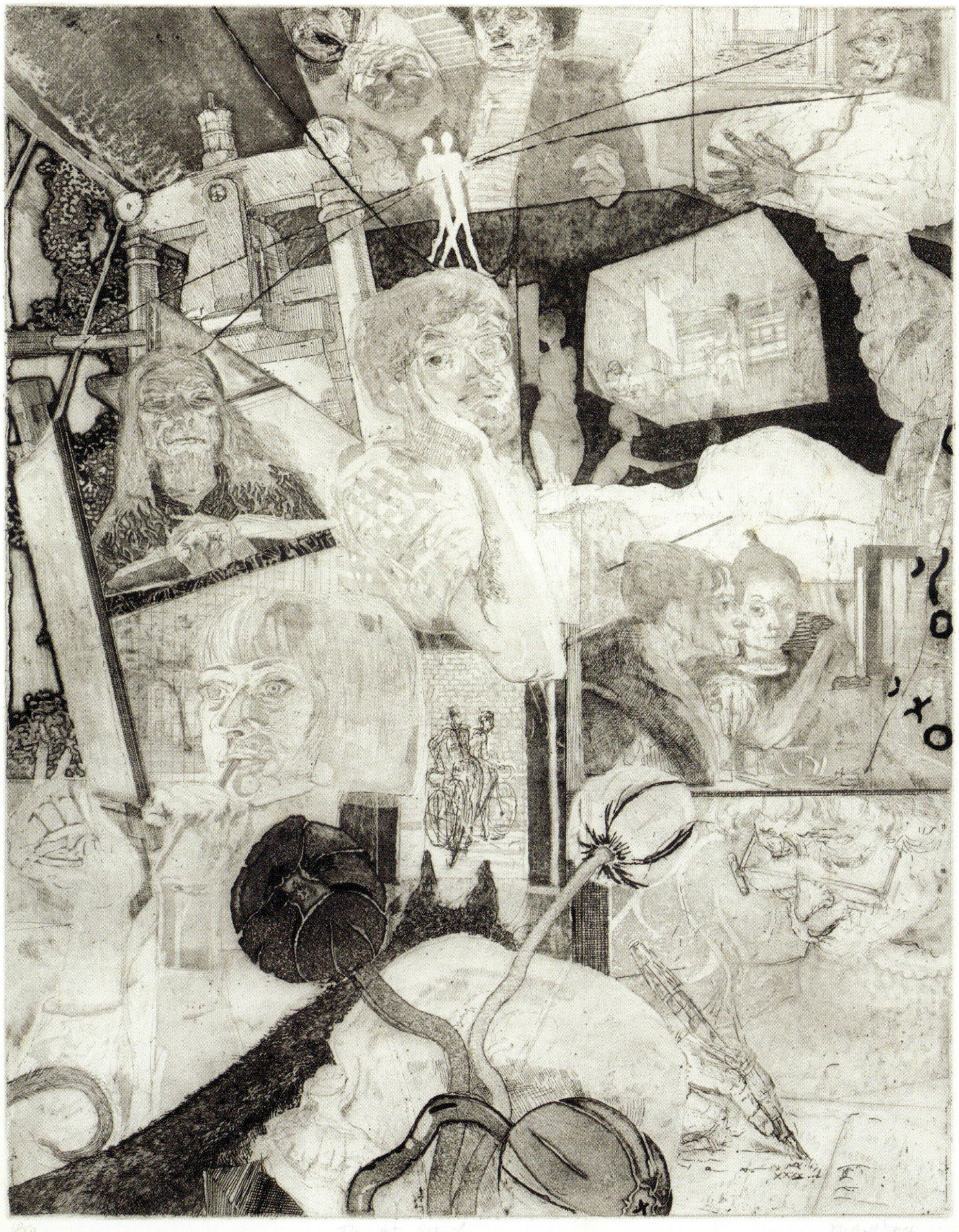

23. *The Art School*, early 1990s, etching and aquatint, 59.5 x 48 cm

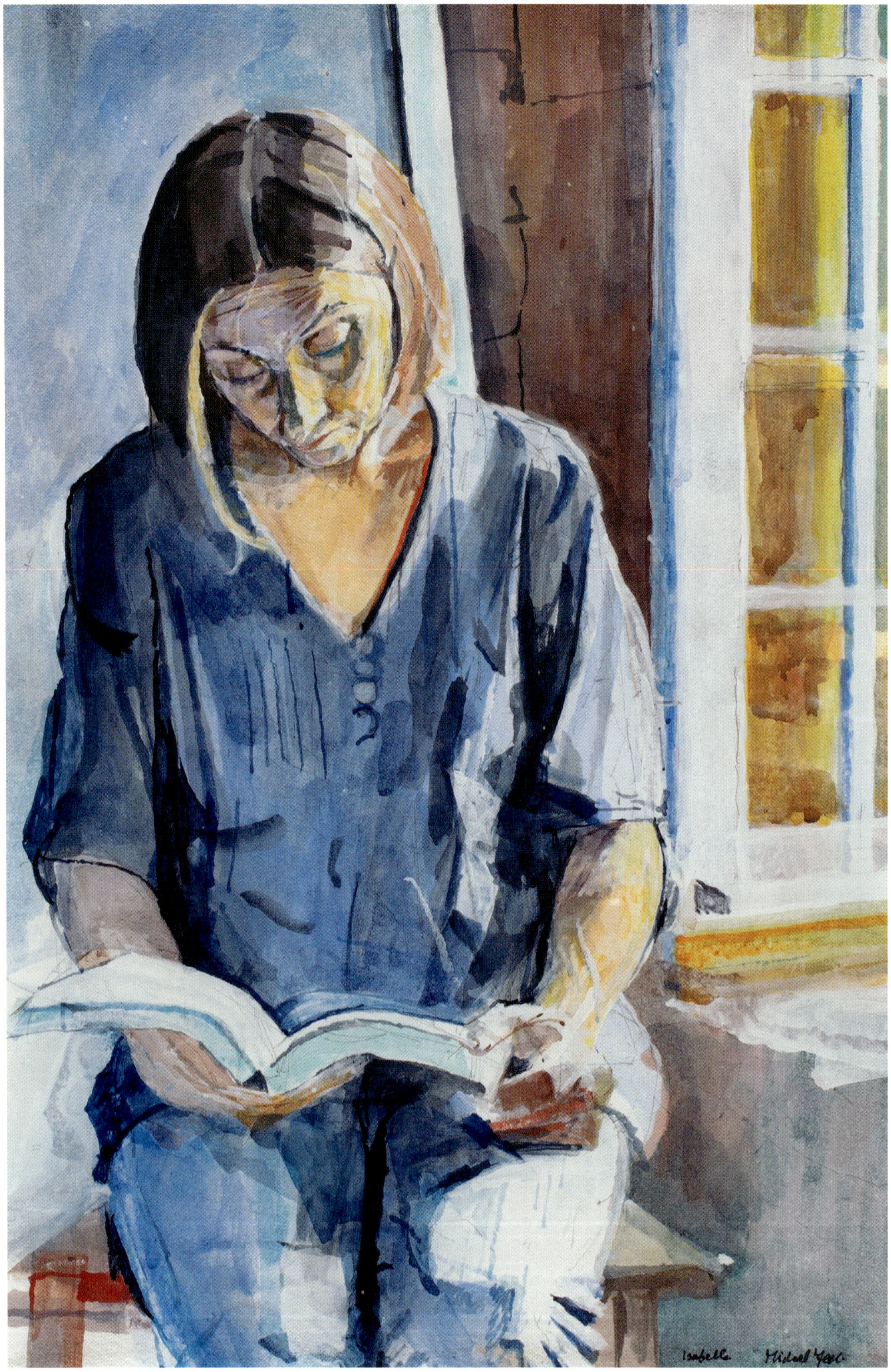

24. *Isabelle reading*, 2007, watercolour, 41.9 x 27.1 cm

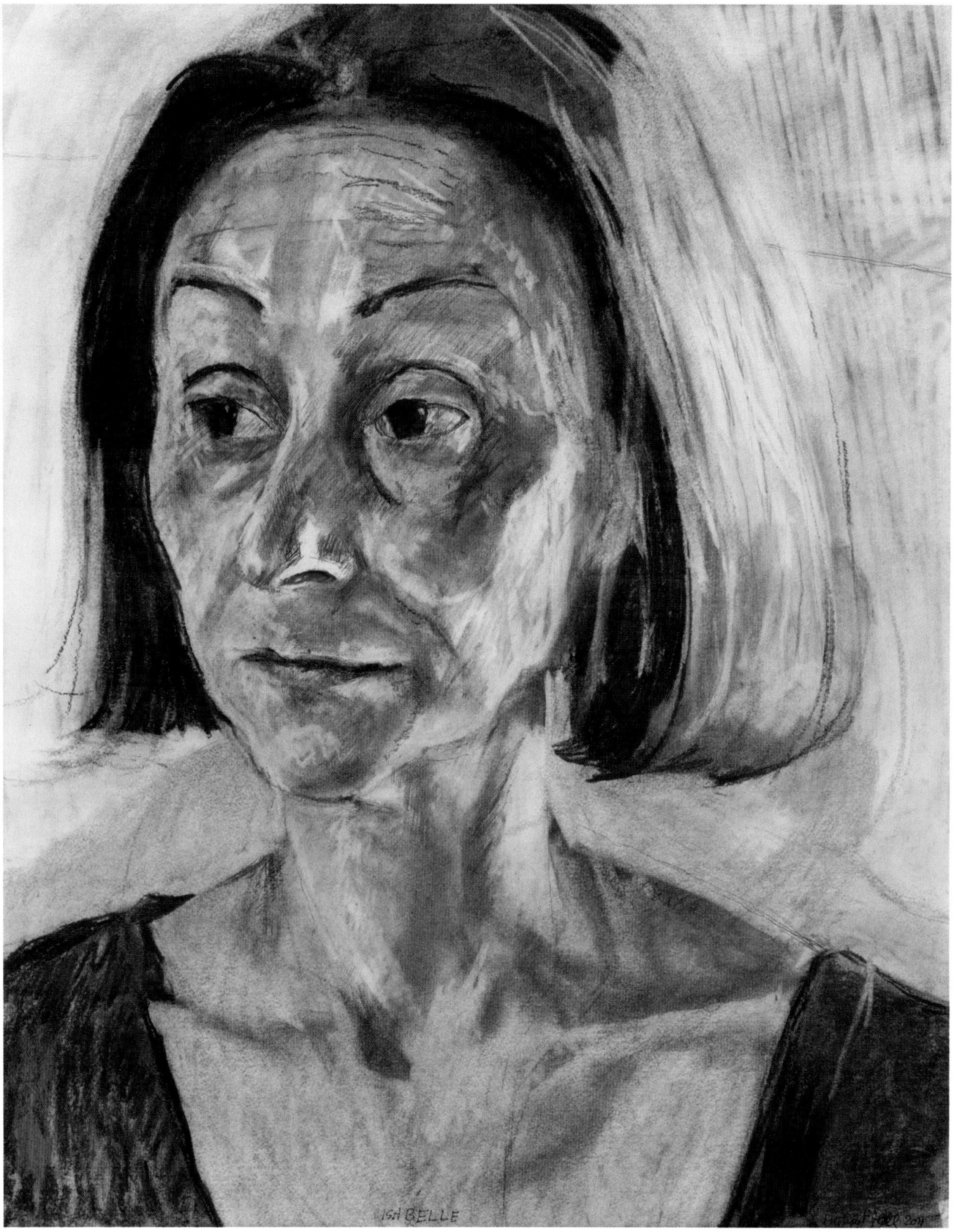

25. *Isabelle*, 2011, charcoal, 75 x 59 cm

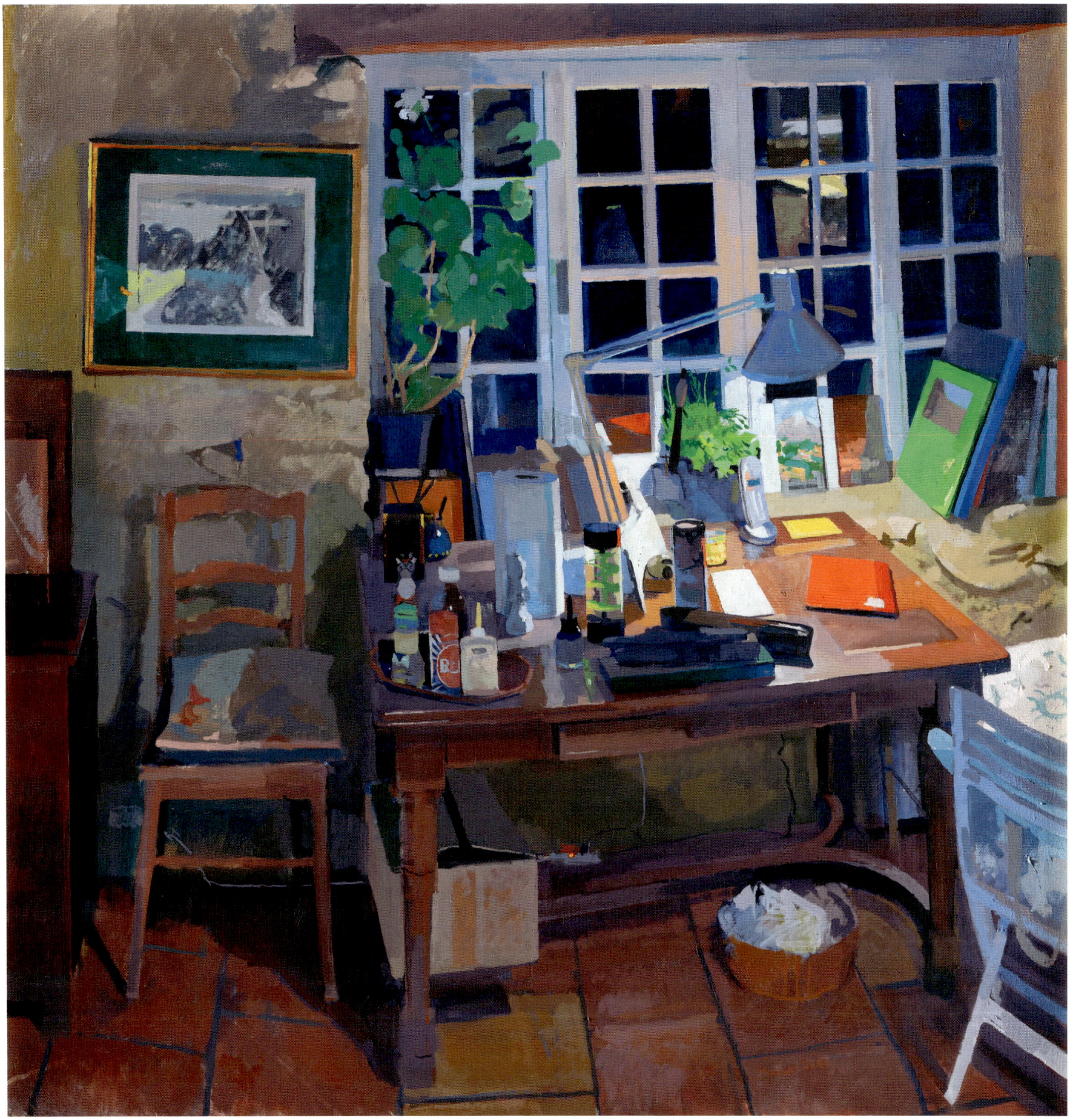

26. *My Desk*, 2000s, oil on board, 89 x 89 cm

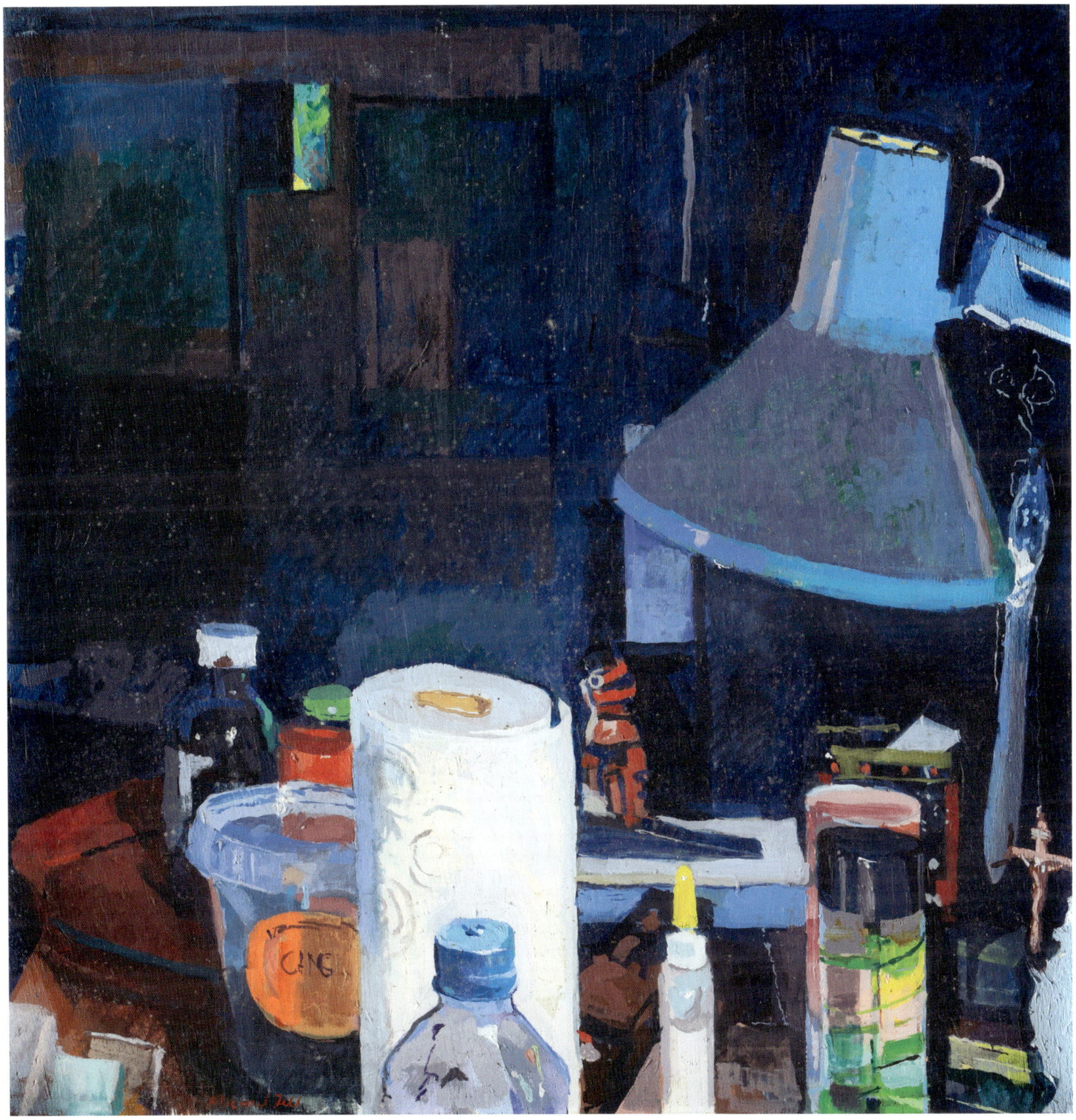

27. *View from my Desk*, 2016, oil on board, 45 x 45 cm

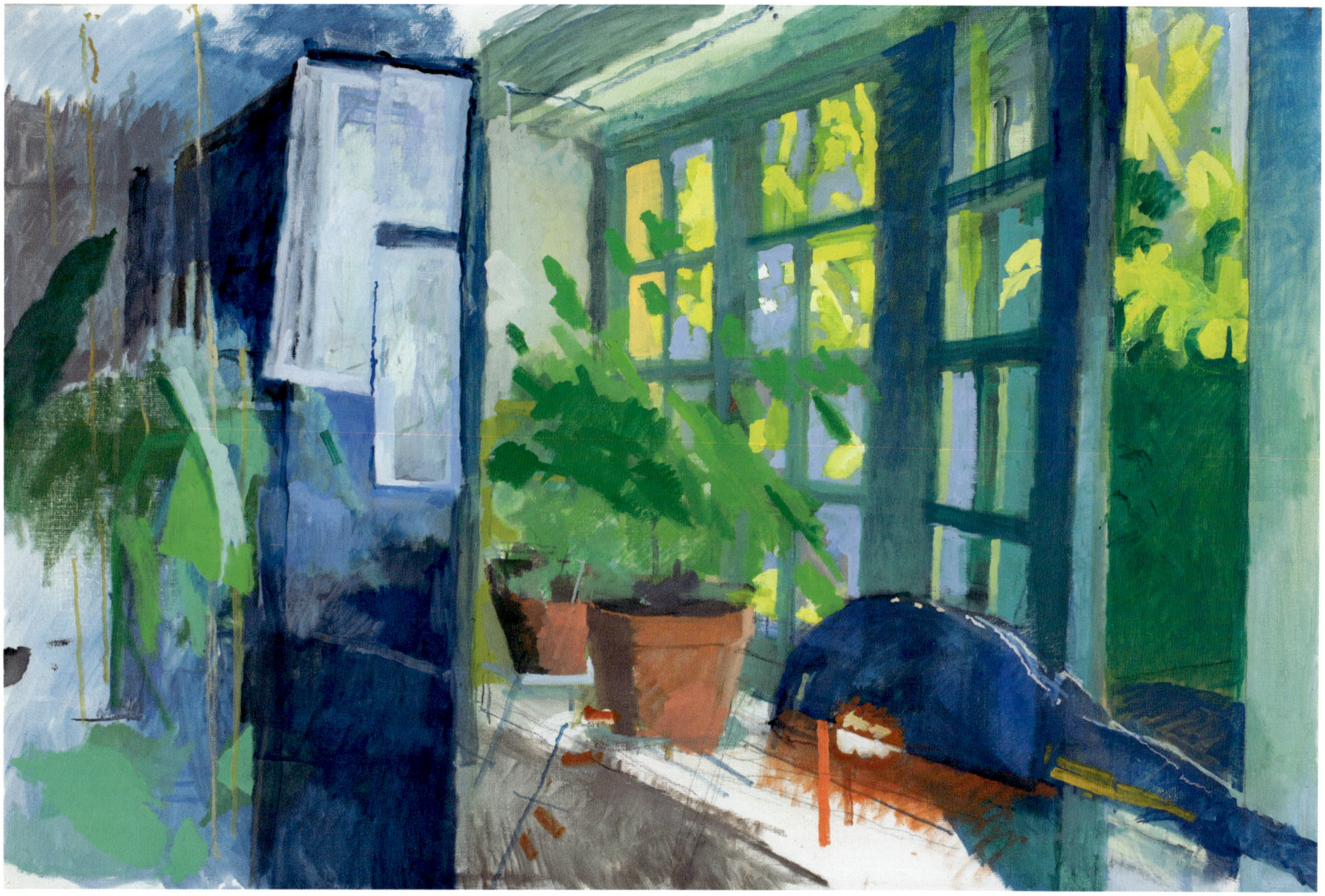

28. *Window at my Studio*, 2020–21, unfinished, oil on canvas, 60 x 92 cm

Printmaking

Printmaking

Adrian Bartlett

Michael Fell studied painting and printmaking as a mature student at the City & Guilds of London Art School in Kennington. He subsequently returned there in 1973, this time as a tutor, becoming Head of Foundation from 1985 to 1996, and a part time tutor of etching.

He had enrolled in 1965, as a painting student, but also soon started going into the print department, primarily interested in etching, although he also did some lithography and wood engraving.

Henry Wilkinson ran the print department, with the assistance of Daphne Casdagli, until he retired in 1976.

New students of etching were given a zinc plate to be bitten by nitric acid. When more experienced they would use copper plates, more expensive and a harder metal, bitten by Dutch mordant. This is hydrochloric acid with potassium chlorate as an oxidising agent. It has the great advantage over nitric acid of not producing gas bubbles, which tend to coarsen lines, and eating cleanly into the metal. It is so called because it was an attempt to reproduce as closely as possible the acid that Rembrandt had used.

All students of etching will have studied the prints of Rembrandt (1606–1669) and his way of creating areas of tone with delicate cross hatching, and Goya (1746–1828), one of the earliest artists to master the newly discovered way of making tone with aquatint. Fell would have looked at Piranesi and Morandi, Meryon and Meissonier, Samuel Palmer, Whistler, Sickert and Anthony Gross.

He was also interested in the powerful group of early 20th-century German printmakers loosely labelled as Expressionists, whose creative freedom was abruptly brought to an end in 1933 with the coming to power of the National Socialists. Of particular interest to him were Max Klinger, Lovis Corinth, Käthe Kollwitz and Max Beckmann, as we can see in the vigour of his drawing, manifest in his early studies of the Covent Garden workers [33–35].

His dedication to printmaking lasted throughout his life, and he was proud of the large printing press that he acquired and installed in the Music House at Bungay, celebrating it there in a large painting, *Robert at the Music House* [16]. This canvas compares the industry of his younger son doing his homework with the labour and passionate application that he himself applied to the production of prints all his life. At Barrère in Gascony he installed this same press side by side with another large one in an outdoor studio that became as important a workplace for him as the house itself.

Unfortunately Fell did not date his prints. The earliest that he exhibited were tiny needle drawings of Covent Garden workers – porters, dustmen, traders [33–35]. They are notable for their vivacity, strongly bitten. He shows his fascination with people and city life.

A much more ambitious composition worked on by Fell while still a student is *Victoria Station* [37], an experimental plate where he tries out different techniques. It captures the atmosphere of a busy mainline station in the rush hour – City workers in bowler hats, rough sleepers, queues for coffee, and a mysterious central figure. Is it an embrace of greeting or farewell? Or a man holding a child? There is a sinister black bird at his feet.

Several techniques have been used: hard ground, soft ground and aquatint. Hard ground is the basic traditional etching technique. The ground is the thin layer of wax which is laid over the metal plate. It is acid resistant, so the metal is bitten by the acid only where the artist has drawn into it with a needle or other sharp tool. It is composed of beeswax and a little bitumen to colour it. The plate is warmed sufficiently for the wax to be spread evenly over the surface. It is then suspended upside down and smoked with a candle or bunch of tapers. The wax is softened by the flame and absorbs the carbon in the smoke, giving a hard dark surface when cool.

In *Victoria Station* there are some ruled lines with some cross-hatched shading, but very lightly bitten. Then the outlines of the large foreground figures in their bowler hats have been drawn using a soft ground. For this a thin sheet of paper is laid over the plate and the drawing is made firmly on the paper, which when lifted off pulls the wax off the plate where the pressure has been exerted, exposing the lines to the acid. Unfortunately more wax is often pulled off than intended, giving some foul biting. Fell has decided not to let this worry him, and it is probable that the little black figures started off as unwanted marks but have been manipulated into a curious little group, out of scale with the rest of the composition. It is as though the artist has rather revelled in the power of the acid.

There have also been some changes of mind. The outline of one of the large male characters in the centre left foreground has been left transparent, revealing the rough sleepers in the background and the little black figures. The other businessmen have been given more solidity with aquatint, which is also used for the very dark band across the top. There are signs that this is beginning to break down and lose its strength, but there remains a rich variety of tones, textures and movement. All in all, a strong image of the haphazard swirl of humanity.

Aquatint is a method of creating a shape rather than just a line. It was devised in the mid-18th century and pioneered by Goya, among others. Powdered resin is shaken over the surface of the plate and then melted to make it stick. The acid bites the tiny spaces in between the little grains of resin. A slightly later work by Fell is an interior of St Anne's Church in nearby Vauxhall [36], which makes great use of aquatint, and shows greater technical control. This was presumably done while he still had access to the press at the art school [11]. After this he left the school, and spent some time travelling around Europe.

The prints we see from the mid-1970s and 1980s are quite varied in the manner of their working; some very naturalistic, as in *The Gates of Heaven* [86, 87], a long narrow plate depicting not the great and the good waiting to be admitted but a typical English bus queue of ordinary people. Young children first, a woman pushing a pram, and an old gardener with a wheelbarrow (Adam?) bringing up the rear. A lovely direct image, the plate is very much Stanley Spencer's approach to Christian iconography. The companion piece to this work is *The Gates of Hell* [5], with a quote from Rabindranath Tagore, a much more elaborate composition of figures with some very fine use of aquatint.

Some other prints of about this time are much more in the Expressionist vein. *Theatre People* [40] has a woman looking sympathetically at a wreck of an old actor, drawn with a touch of savagery but not without compassion, recalling Corinth or Beckman. *Last Train Home* [42] and *My Friends* [39] are drawn in a similar way.

By great contrast there is also *Riverscape* [29]. It shows masterly use of aquatint, and, unusually, hardly a soul in sight. It is an abstraction based on the London riverside architecture – Denys Lasdun's National Theatre, the dome of St Paul's, Somerset House, Waterloo Bridge, and the bowsprit of the *Cutty Sark*. It is not completely devoid of human figures. Are there a couple of tiny roller skaters outside the National Theatre? There is certainly a solitary figure leaning on the rail overlooking the river and a small shadow of him or her in the distance. The National

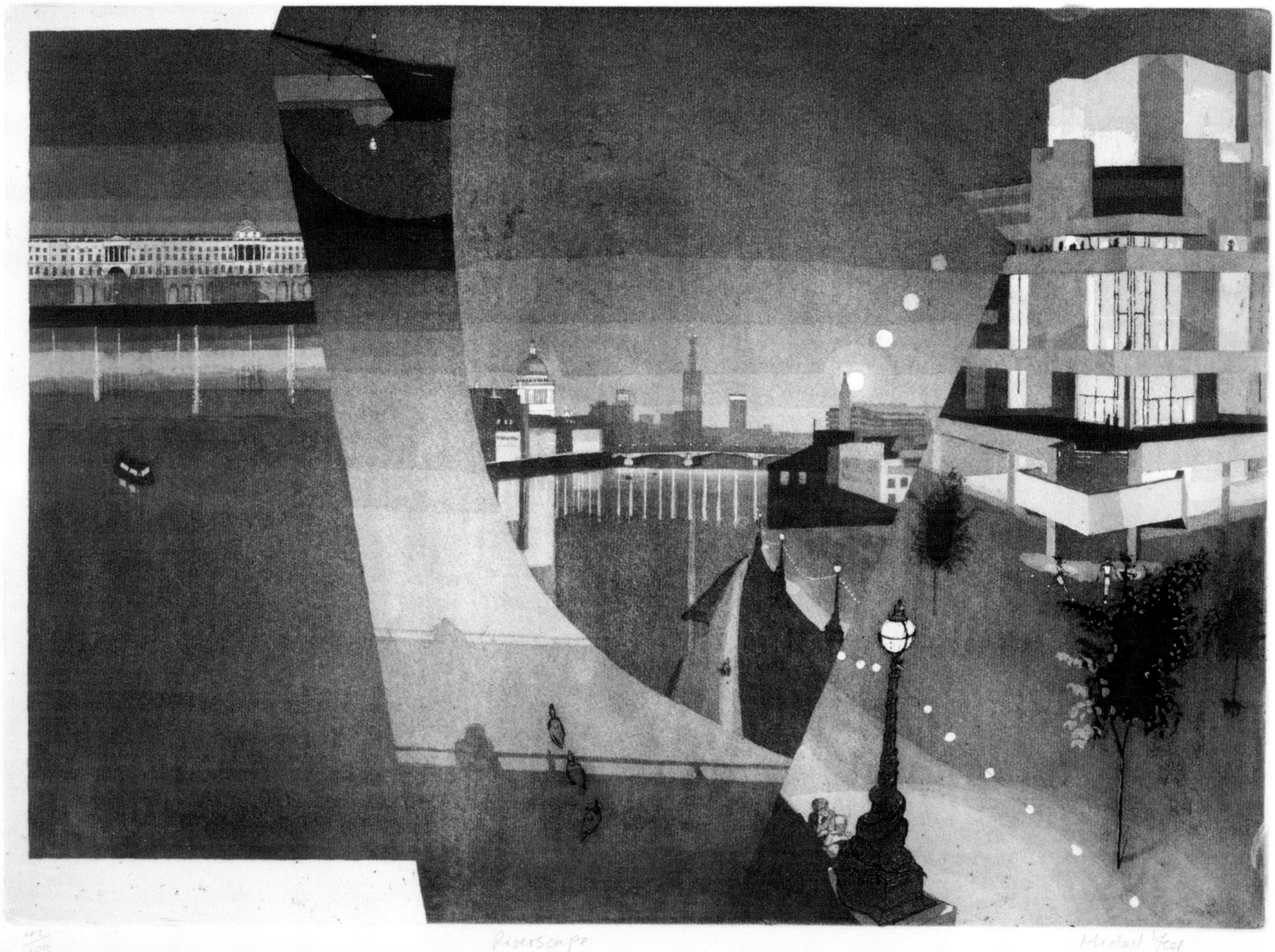

29. *Riverscape*, *c.* 1976, aquatint, 38 x 54 cm

Theatre was completed in 1976. We do not know the exact date of this print but it shows Fell in total control of the medium, with multiple tones of aquatint beautifully graded.

A lovely print of this time too is *Italian Café, New York* [30]. A frontal composition of the blank side wall of a building with a frieze of activity across the bottom – the café, a doorway, an unthreatening group of unemployed men, and a parked car. The bare wall above has birds and their shadows darting about. It is tinted with a very pale aquatint. And then looking up, a fine iron balcony with multiple shadows cast by many lights from behind us. The print gives a warm peaceful sensation.

A companion piece in feeling, from the same period, is *Travellers at the Elephant* [41]. The setting is a bus station. The frontal composition of slabs of aquatint, nearly all vertical and horizontal, creates a calm effect of the travellers waiting patiently – a distinct contrast to the earlier student work, *Victoria Station* [37], with its frantic activity. Here a silhouetted figure of a man sits on his suitcase. Behind him another little frieze of characters: a pram is pushed, a couple have a dog on a lead, man and dog are looking at a child resting on the floor against a pillar.

From the late 1980s or early '90s there are two prints composed of many tiny plates: *Canterbury Tales, The Prologue* [43], comprising many line drawings of lively faces, the characters on the pilgrimage, most of them given added form with aquatint shades; and *A Simple Easter*, many scenes of the Christian Easter story (see the section on 'Religion', pp. 111–18).

There are some quiet studies of individual people: the *Librarian* [38] and *L'étudiante* [46]. Also a rare lithograph of the medieval stone rose window in the ruin of the west wall of the Great Hall of Winchester Palace in Southwark [4]. Lithography, unlike etching, where all the marks to be printed are bitten below the surface of the plate, is a technique where the image is drawn or painted directly onto the surface. It was originally done on slabs of a stone with a very fine grainy surface which, when dampened, would hold the water evenly. The drawing is made with an oily or greasy crayon or ink. Oil and water do not mix, so the printing surface is divided between areas which will accept the printing ink and those that will not. Many lithographers now use zinc plates, which have a grain imposed on them, instead of stones, for obvious reasons of portability. Working on a lithograph can be more direct and spontaneous than etching, but the range of possible marks is perhaps more limited.

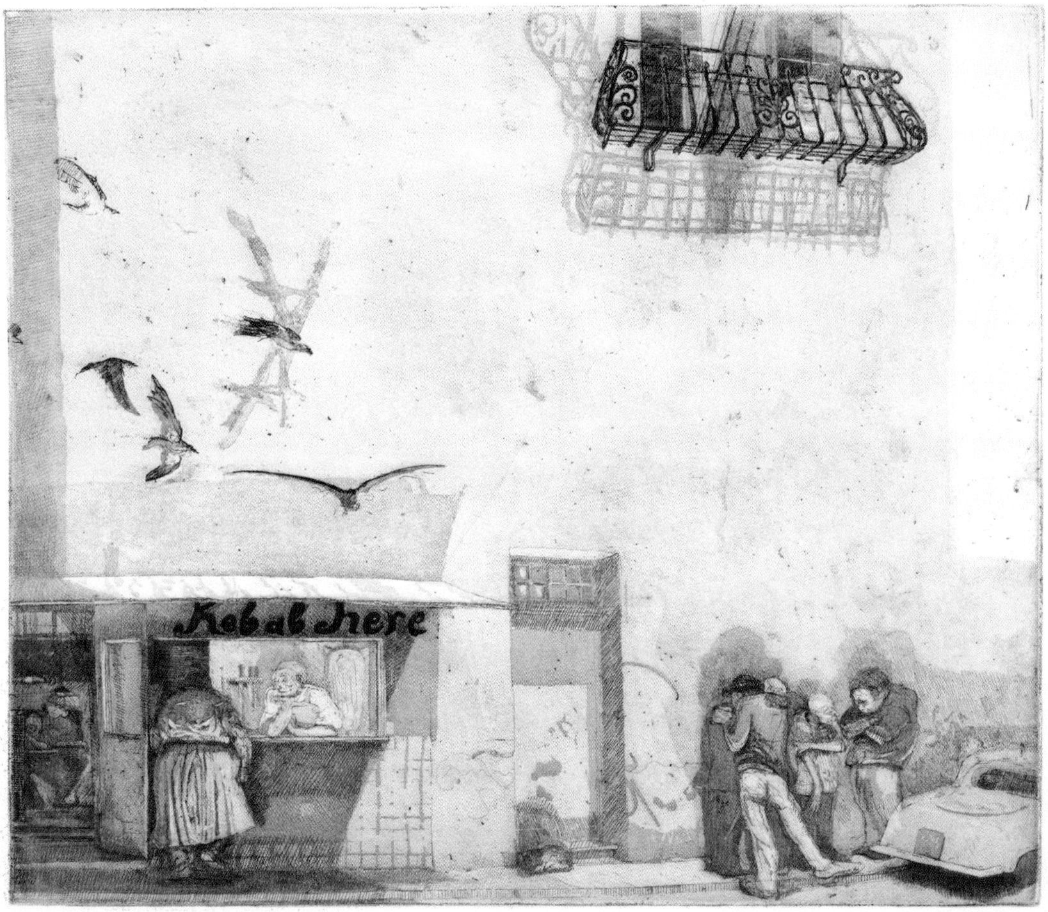

30. *Italian Café, New York*, 1980s, etching and aquatint, 30.7 x 36.7 cm

One of Fell's colleagues at the City & Guilds who became a friend was the typographer Berthold Wolpe, who taught calligraphy and lettering and lived nearby. He sat for a portrait which became a compelling composition, a print of strong tonal contrasts [31]. We see Berthold in ruminative mood. Wearing a cravat, he sits behind a Rococo column with a pair of callipers in his upturned palm. He was a colourful character, a collector, not of one particular sort of object but as a magpie. He wore large heavy jackets with many large pockets; he might suddenly produce from one of these a strange bit of ironwork, for example, and say 'I bought this this morning. I think it's Byzantine. What do you think?'

In the bottom left corner of the etching is the name 'BERT' in the Albertus typeface that Wolpe designed. A shadow of some lettering plays across his chest. There are some more baroque-looking objects in the background. It is a good likeness, but bear in mind that while we see the sitter's right cheek, the artist would have drawn the face from the left, the printing producing the mirror image. Berthold died in 1989. Fell left the art school in 1996.

Apart from the notable exception of the aquatint *Riverscape* [29], Fell's main subject matter was his fellow beings. The men are not heroes or villains or the women idealised madonnas. This remained the case when in 2000 he went to live permanently in south-west France. There he exchanged the big railway stations and city streets as his backdrops for French village life. He draws the people he sees immediately around him: his friends, a local choir, a group at a funeral, people on bicycles, motorbikes and in cars.

Two of the larger works from this later period of his life show well his love of his community in France. First, a village street scene, full of life, *Moto-Experience* [47]. A curious black shape confronts us. On inspection it becomes three motorcycle helmets on a round café table. Beside that, to give a dramatic tonal contrast, are two more round café tables, but these are in bright sunlight on the pavement away from the awning's shade. Three men sit in the shade to the right of the helmets, drinks on their table: the bikers are in town. Along the sun-filled street passes a truck, nudging pedestrians and cyclists out of its way. Another arrival struggles to remove his helmet. Within the dark café customers jostle and glasses are raised. It is a fairly chaotic scene, but an exhilarating chaos, a riot of human activity.

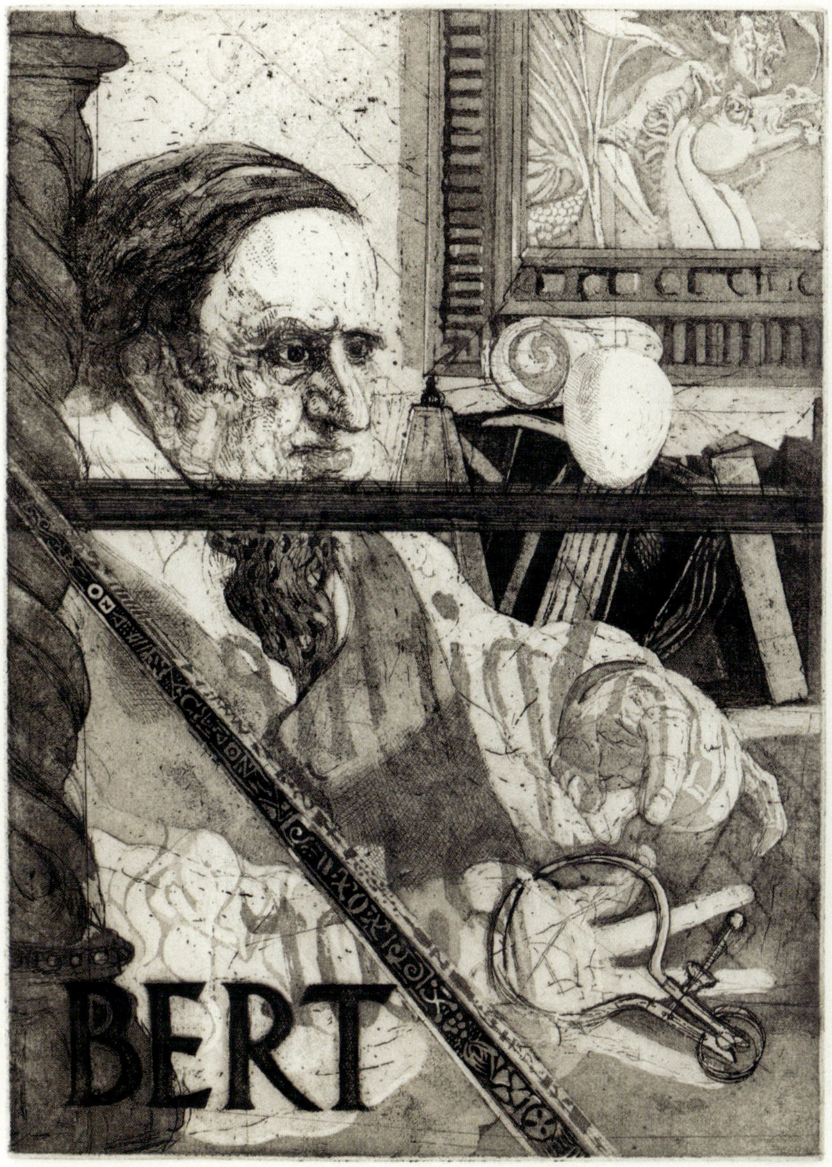

31. *Berthold Wolpe*, 1980s, etching and aquatint, 30.5 x 22 cm

The artist has only used line in this print, cross-hatched to create the dark shapes. His desire to make really black areas has led him to bite the plate for almost too long: there are warning signs of the surface beginning to break down, to become *crevé*. This is when the rich black areas begin to become a dull grey, fortunately not seriously enough here for the image to suffer. It is interesting to note that Fell has thought that the simple traditional technique of line drawn into a hard ground was perfectly adequate for his purpose.

The other important work of this later period is *Katie's Wedding* [32]. The post-ceremony dance is an ideal vehicle with which to express Fell's positive view of the world. The plate is full of exuberant, finely drawn dancing figures. He uses aquatint on top of the line drawing, as a means of dramatising the two groups of figures in the background. There is a tunnel of raised arms with a couple fighting their way into it, and a formal group of brightly lit dancers. Energetic movement pervades the scene.

From the time Michael Fell started learning to etch in the 1960s, print workshops were springing up all over the British Isles. These were an excellent way for artists to share the cost of expensive presses and equipment, and to share the solving of technical problems. Anthony Gross (1905–1984), an artist Fell admired, tried out the use of colour, of photo-etching, and a variety of other means of mark making. Fell seems not to have been tempted into technical experiment outside the repertory of etching, aquatint and lithograph, methods he used with wide-ranging originality. He had a clear view of what he wanted his work to express: an unsentimental but altogether positive love of life. He proved that this could be realised with relatively simple means.

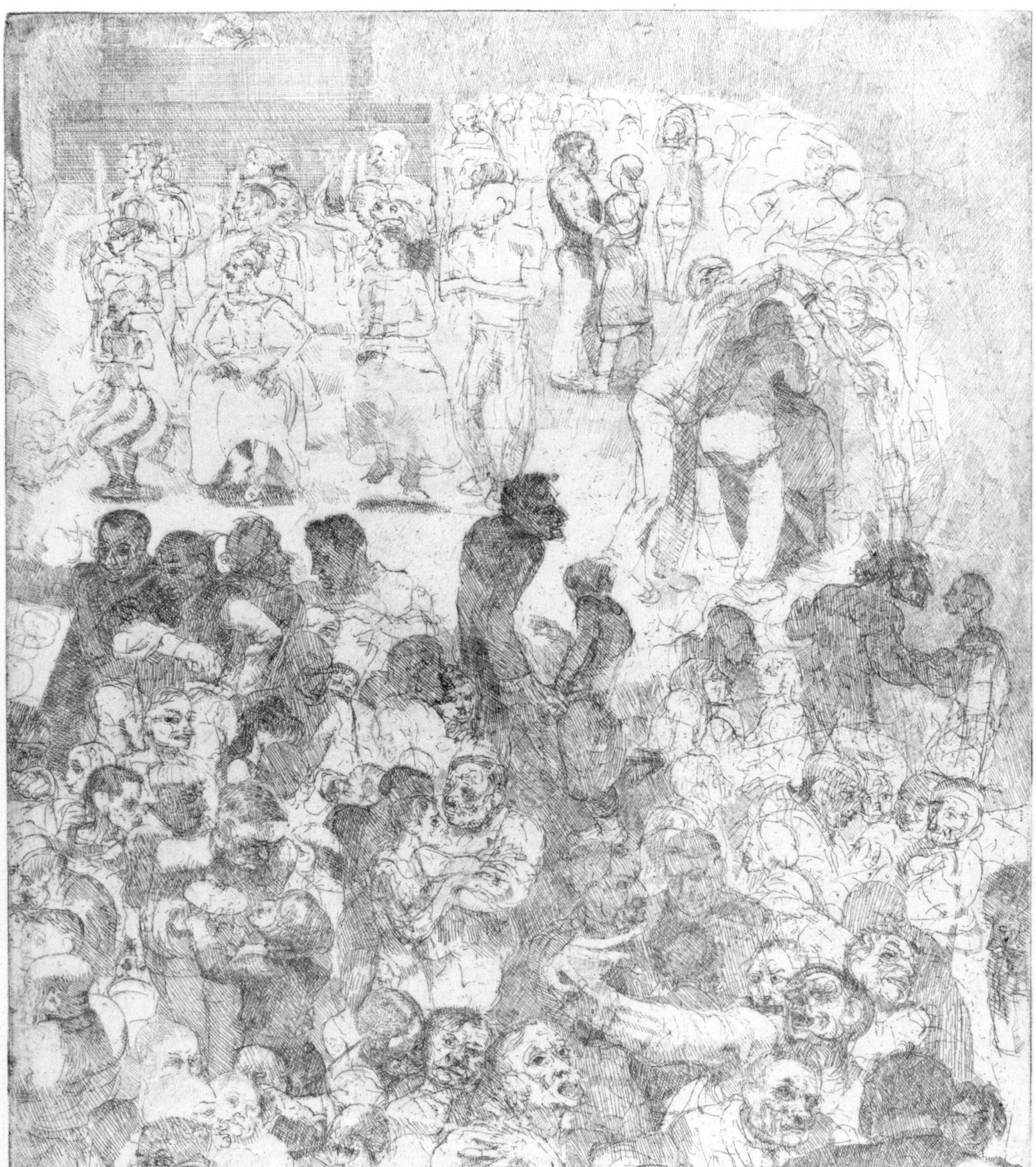

32. *Katie's Wedding*, 2007, etching and aquatint, 33.9 x 29.8 cm

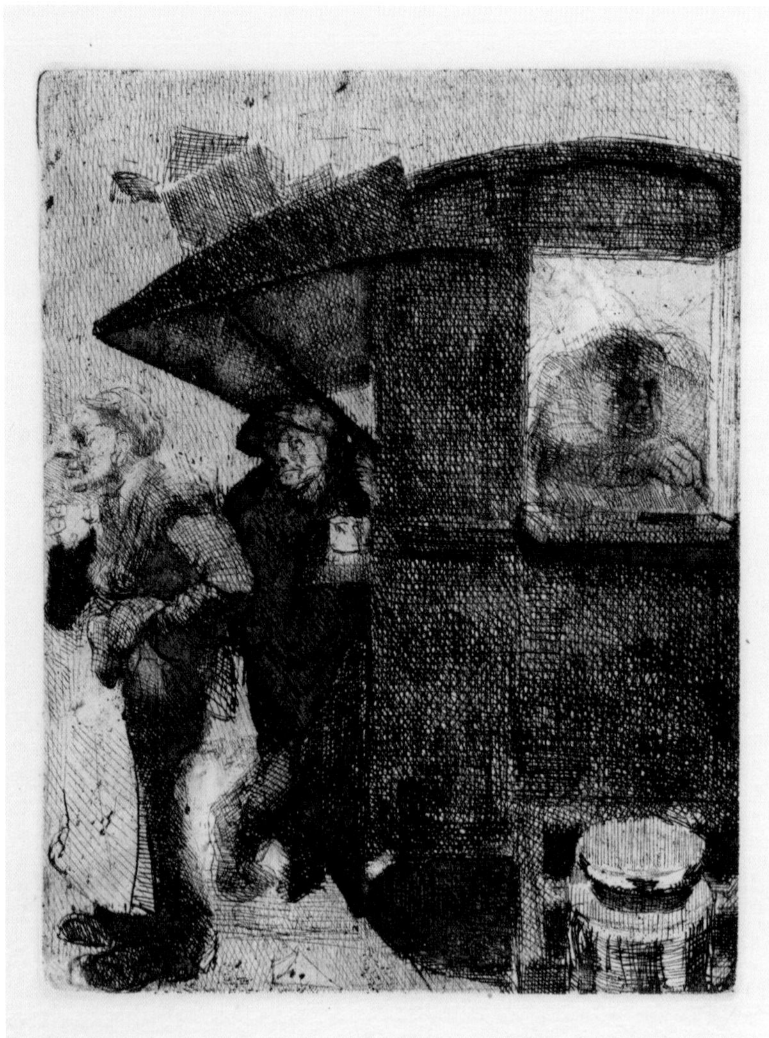

33. *Covent Garden – early morning*, 1968, etching, 14 x 11 cm

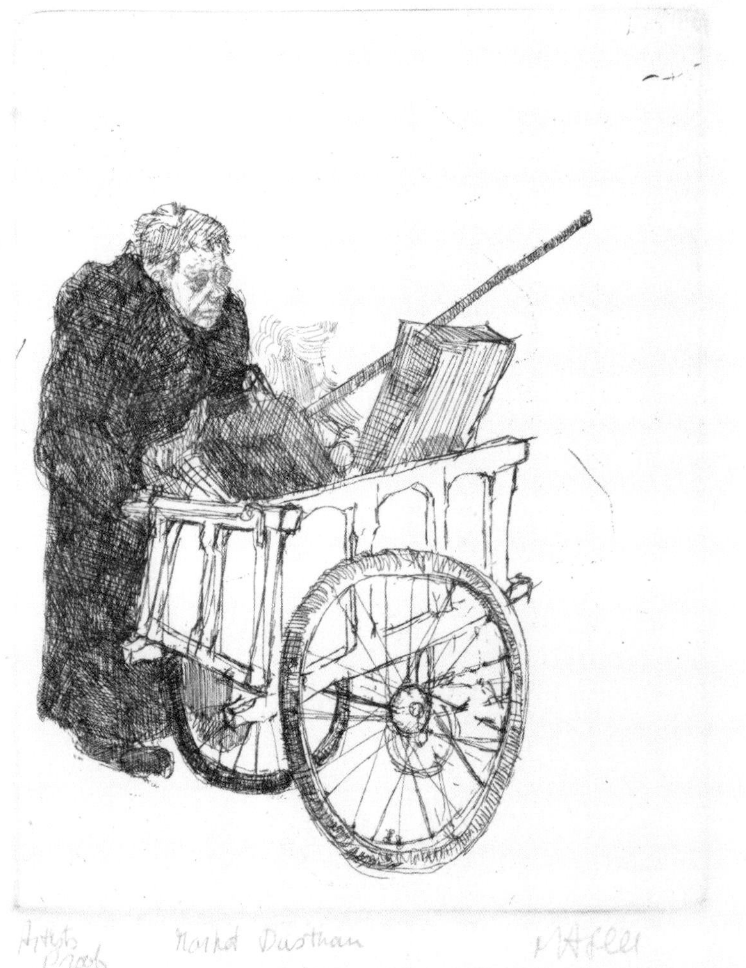

34. *Covent Garden – market dustman*, 1968, etching, 14 x 11 cm

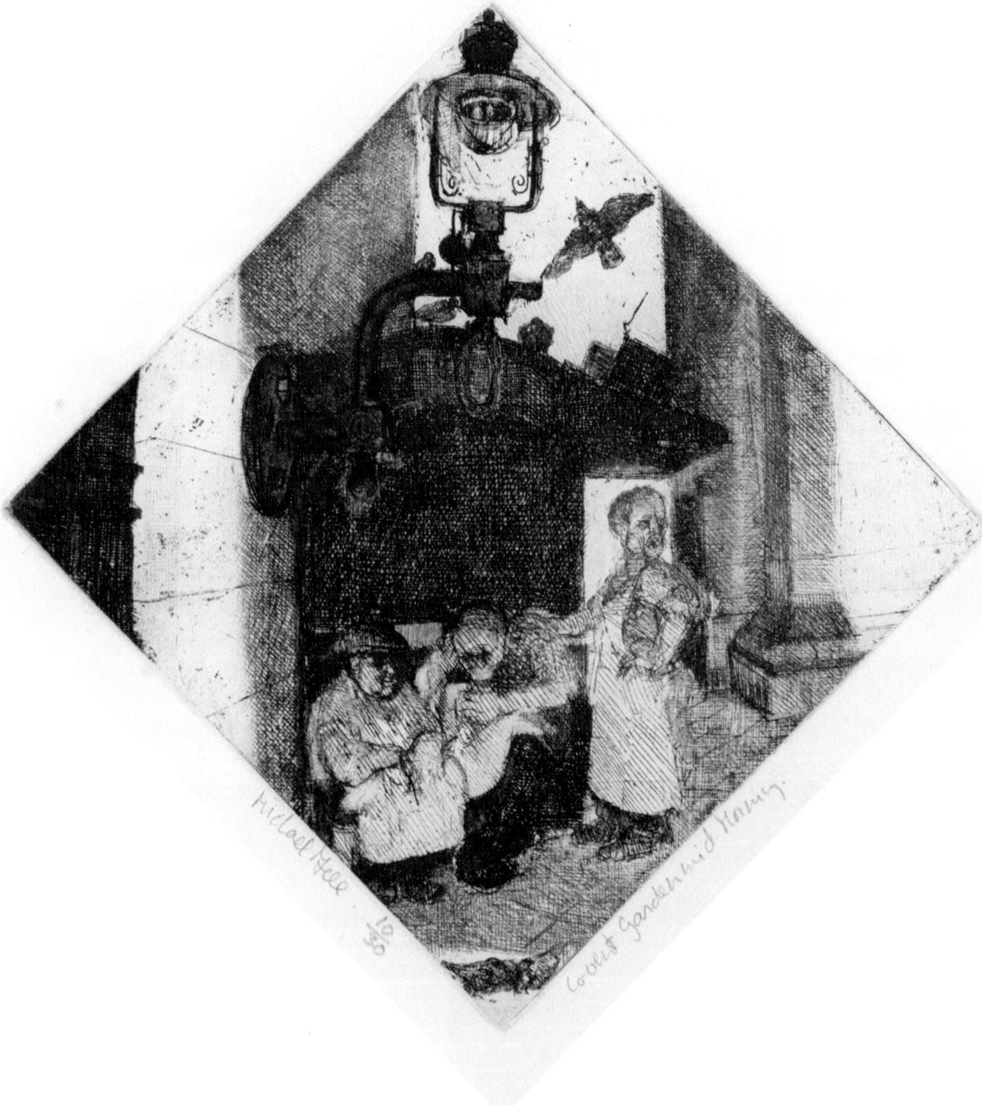

35. *Covent Garden – late morning*, 1968, etching, 14 x 13.5 cm

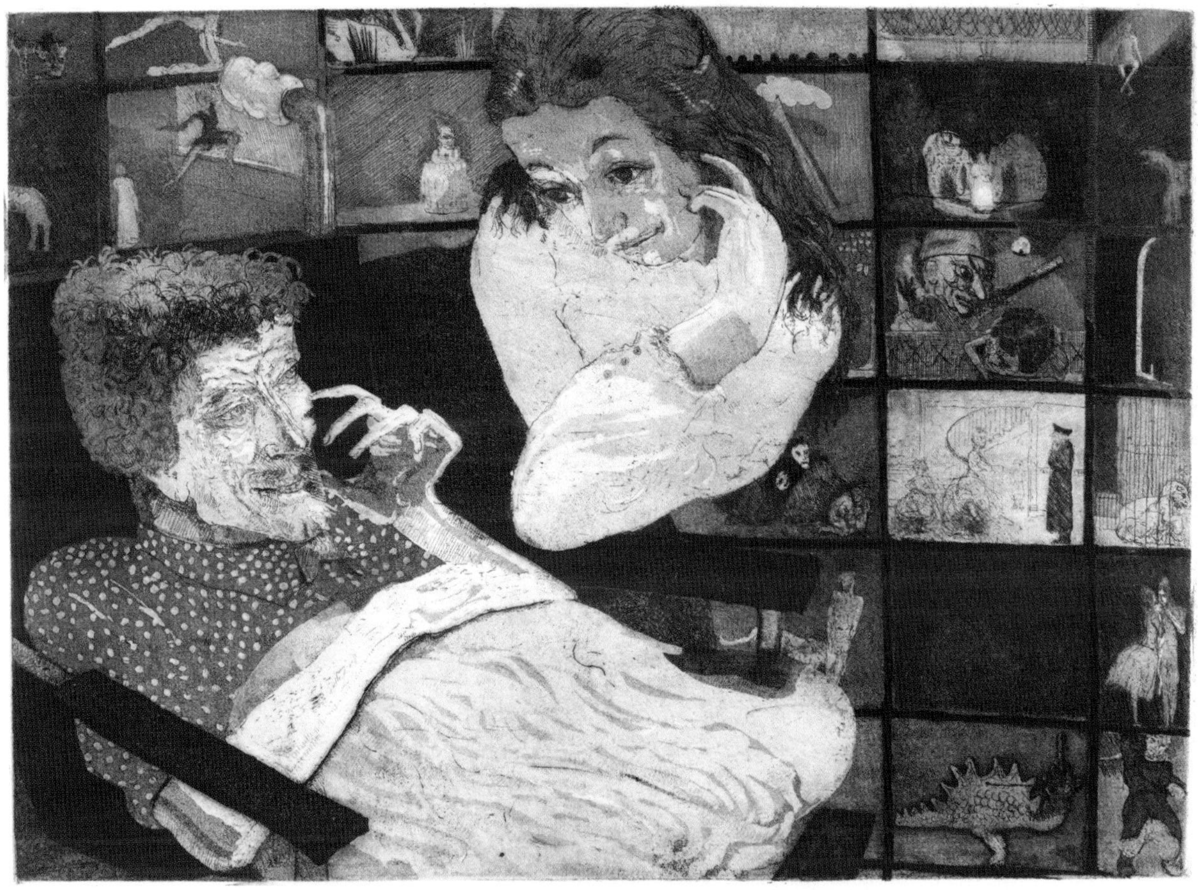

40. *Theatre People*, 1980s, etching and aquatint, 28 x 40 cm

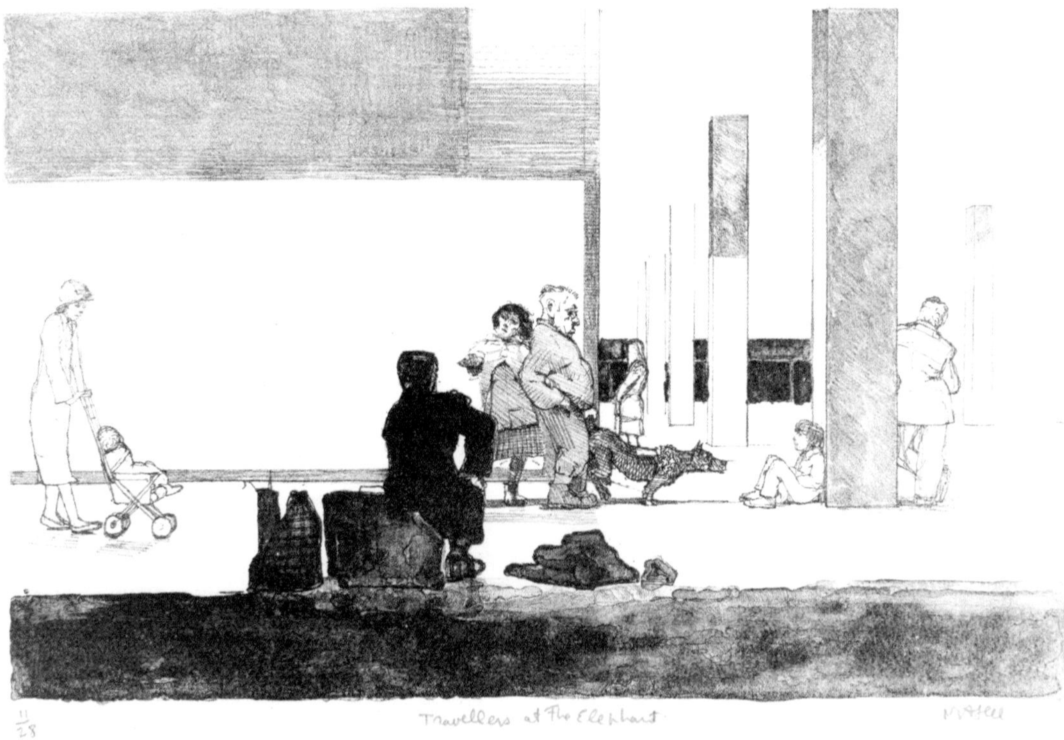

41. *Travellers at the Elephant*, 1980s, etching and aquatint, 18.5 x 29.5 cm

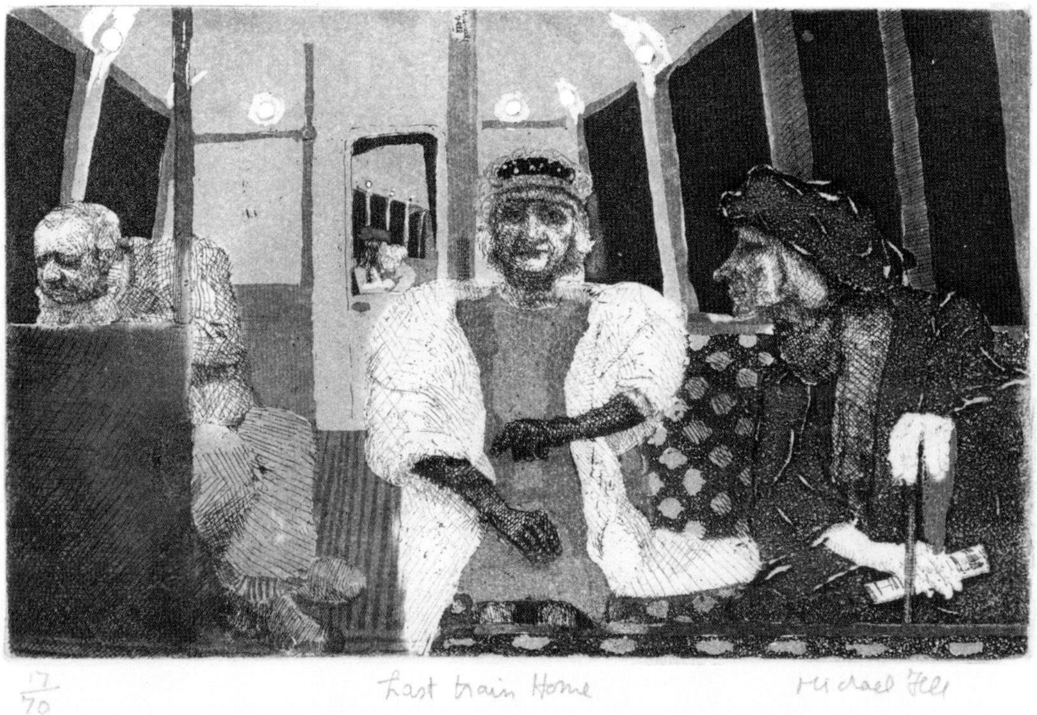

42. *Last Train Home*, 1990s, etching and aquatint, 11 x 17 cm

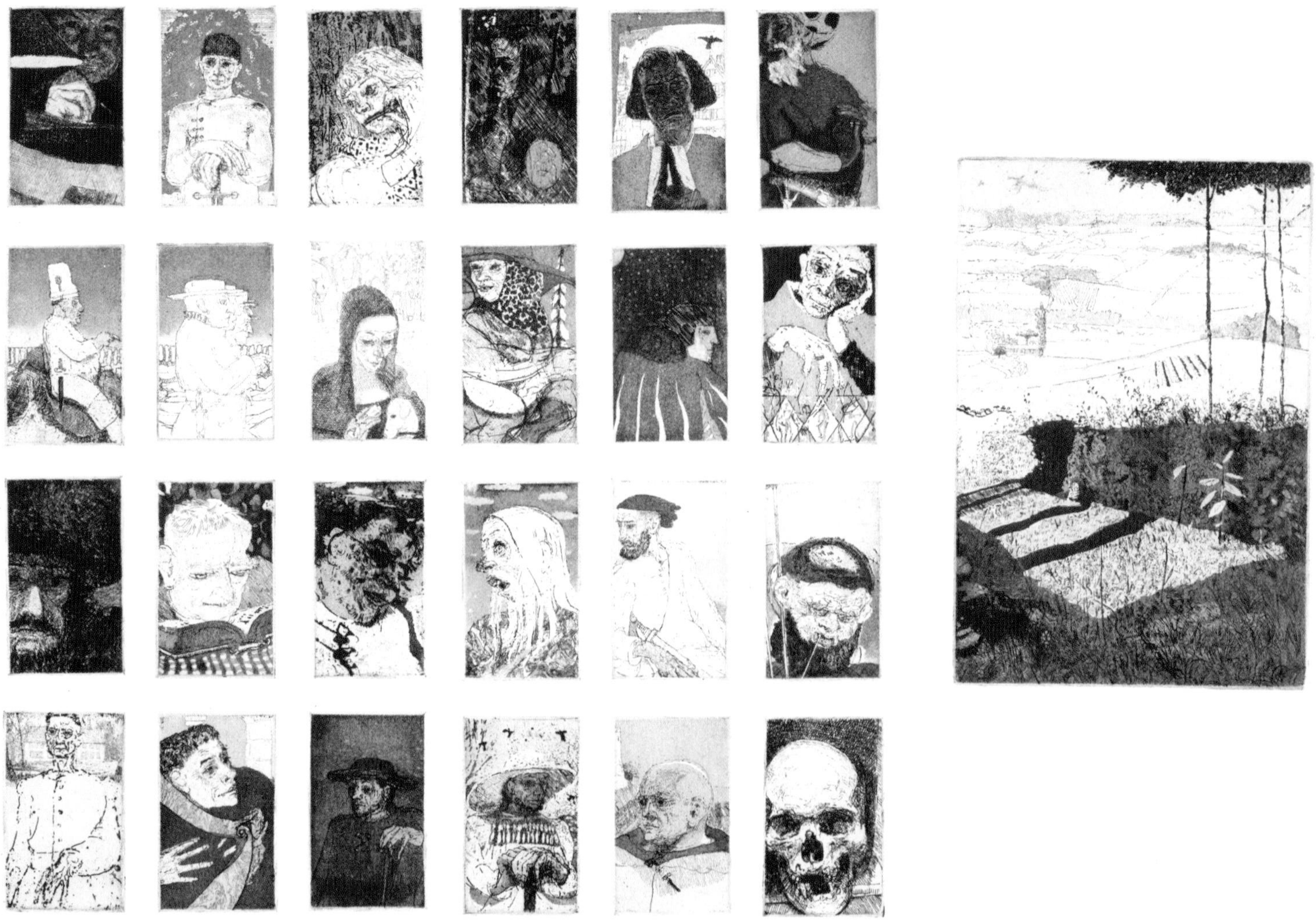

43. *Canterbury Tales, The Prologue*, 1990, etching and aquatint, 60 x 77 cm

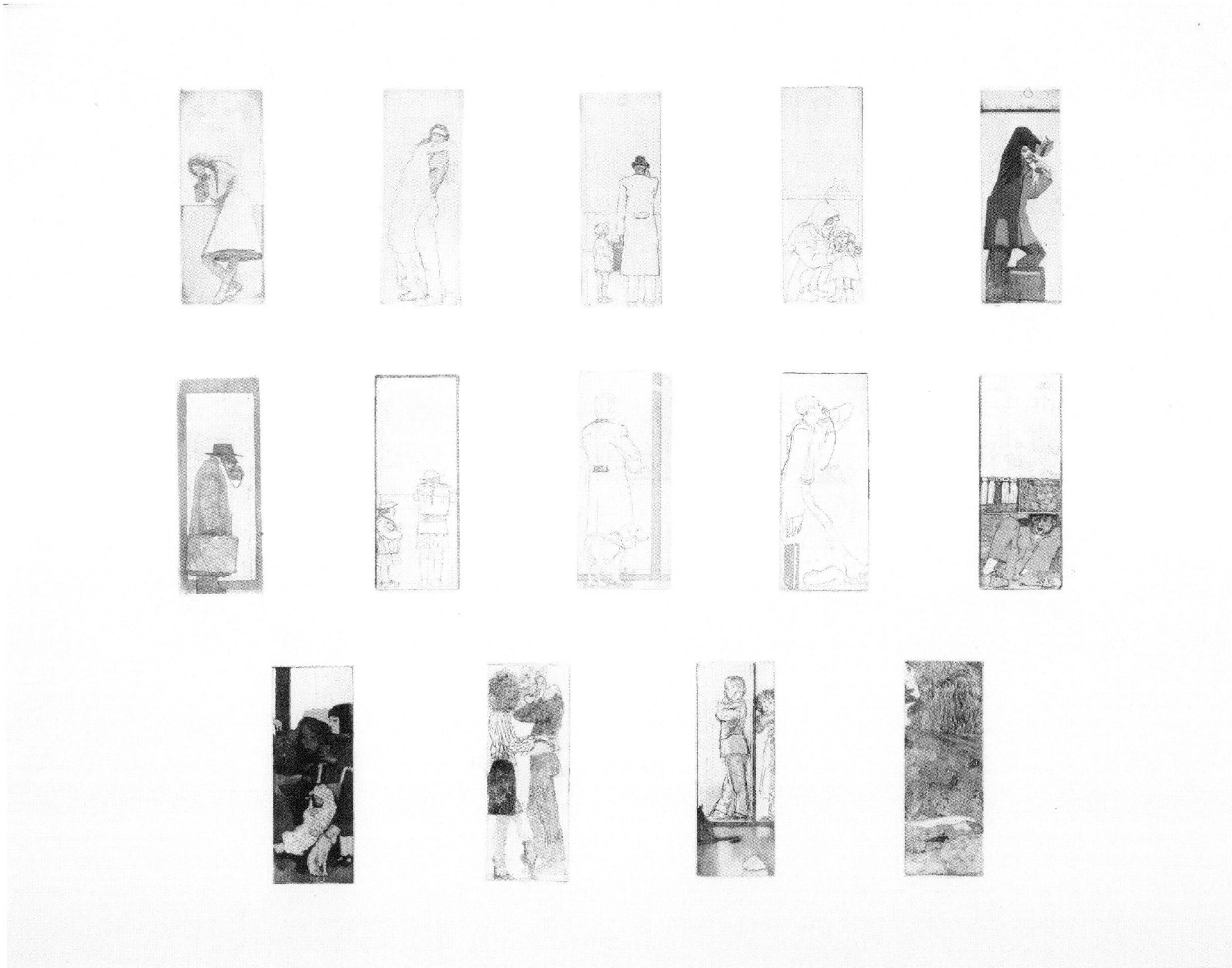

44. *Telephones*, early 1990s, etching and aquatint, 60 x 77 cm

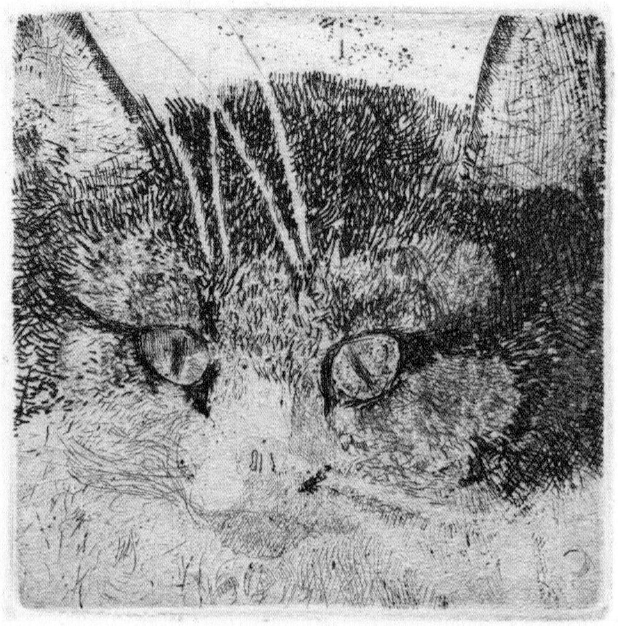

45. *Cat*, *c.* 2000, etching, 6 x 6 cm

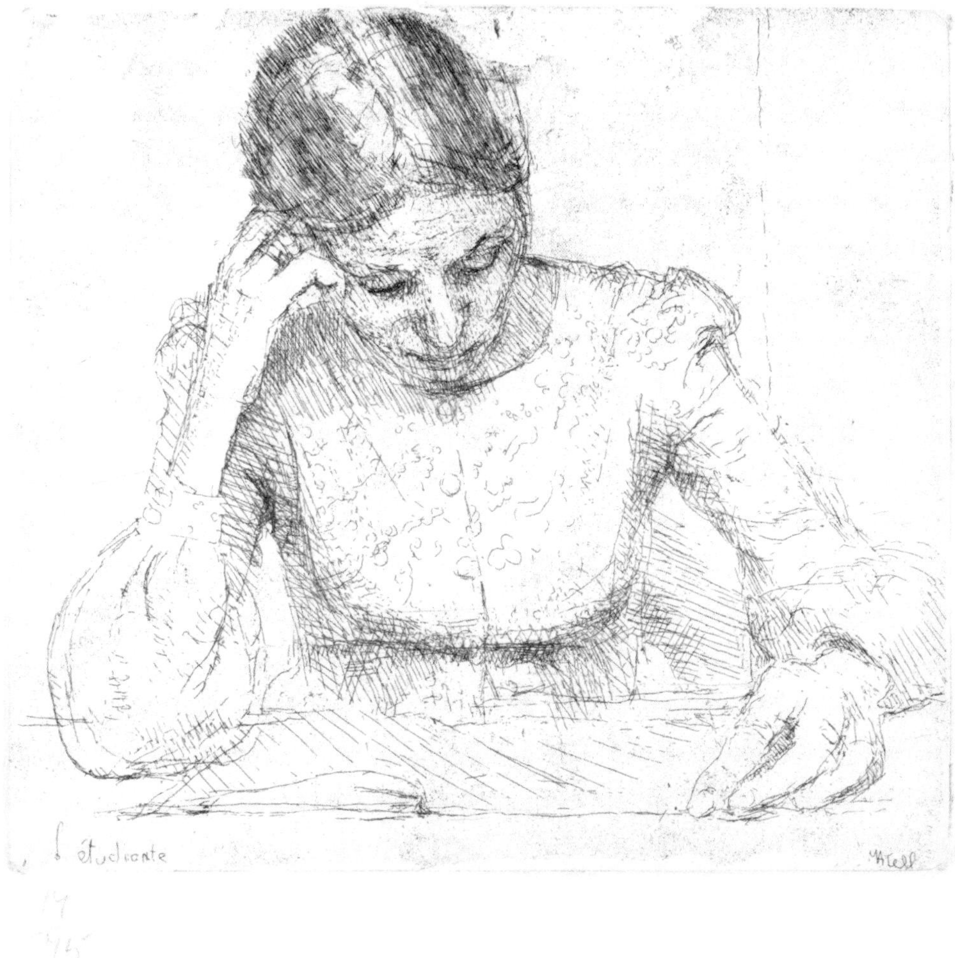

46. *L'étudiante*, *c.* 2000, etching, 11.5 x 12.5 cm

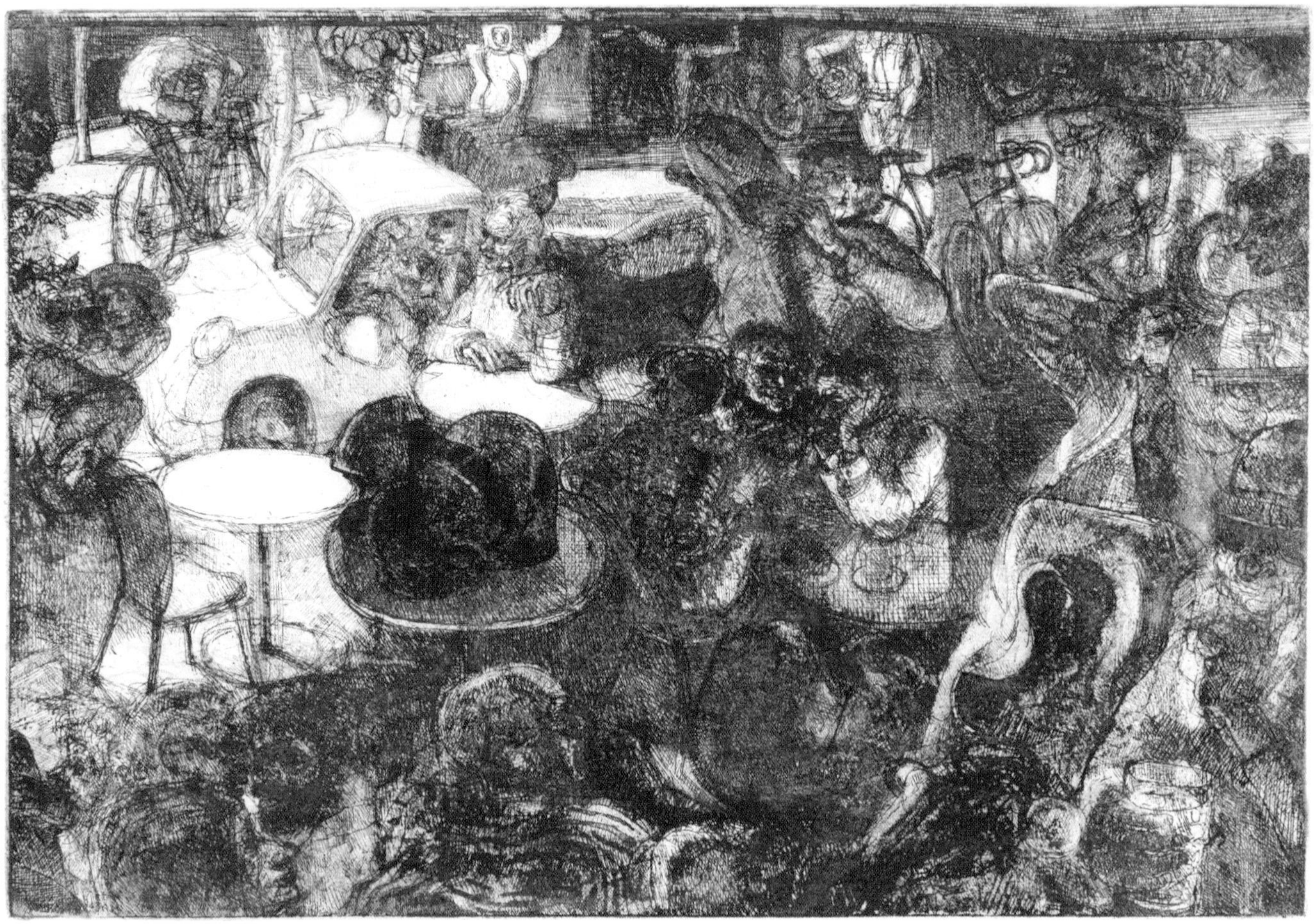

47. *Moto-Experience*, 2007, etching, 27 x 40 cm

Gascony

Gascony

Katie Alice Fitz Gerald

> The fertile core of Gascony is inviting but unimposing: a hodgepodge of oddly shaped farm plots, forest remnants, vineyards, oak and hawthorn groves, shrubby hedgerows, irrigation ponds, orchards, grazing pastures, and miles and miles of paved and unpaved farm roads – some 7,000 kilometres of them in all – extending across the Gers like fine capillaries, plus many more miles of footpaths, including a segment of the Chemin de Saint Jacques pilgrimage route to Compostela.[1]

In 1972 when Michael and Maureen Fell first laid eyes upon the Gers landscape it was mostly untouched farmland, having remained an undisturbed corner of France with very little interference from outsiders. However, as the artist spent an increasing amount of time in the Gers and became familiar with the local community (which over time would become more international), his work also moved naturally towards including the region's people and spirituality. These two elements had always formed an integral part of Fell's practice as both painter and printmaker. His portrayal of the local people and the verdant scenery across the region was steeped in his own spiritual beliefs. The discovery of the Gers' Arcadian vistas, where humanity and spirituality can be said to meet,[2] had a huge effect on Fell's way of thinking about the depiction of landscape.

Fell absorbed the world around him into his work, monumentalising his familial life and this forgotten part of France where the untouched beauty led him to feel he had stumbled upon a portion of heaven on earth. In his painting *The Family* [48] we see an example of this: his two sons Mark (standing) and Robert (seated alongside) are depicted inside their house, Barrère, against a backdrop of the Gascon countryside. Mark gazes towards the window which is open to reveal the brilliant light of the outside world. The mood in both spaces is polarized: the inside shadowy, subdued and quiet, the outside luminescent and exuberant. The lighting pierces the scene, cascading in from the window at top right of the painting, bathing Robert, the playful cat and the top of the counter in bleached colours and leaving the rest of the scene cast in a shadowy blue. The clear use of chiaroscuro adds Baroque drama to an otherwise simple scene and gives a sensuous display of the Gascon heat as embodied by the sun outside and the coolness of the interior.[3] Fell places himself as a tiny figure outdoors, involved in painting *en plein air*, where he could capture accurately the colour, light and intensity of the heat. The window

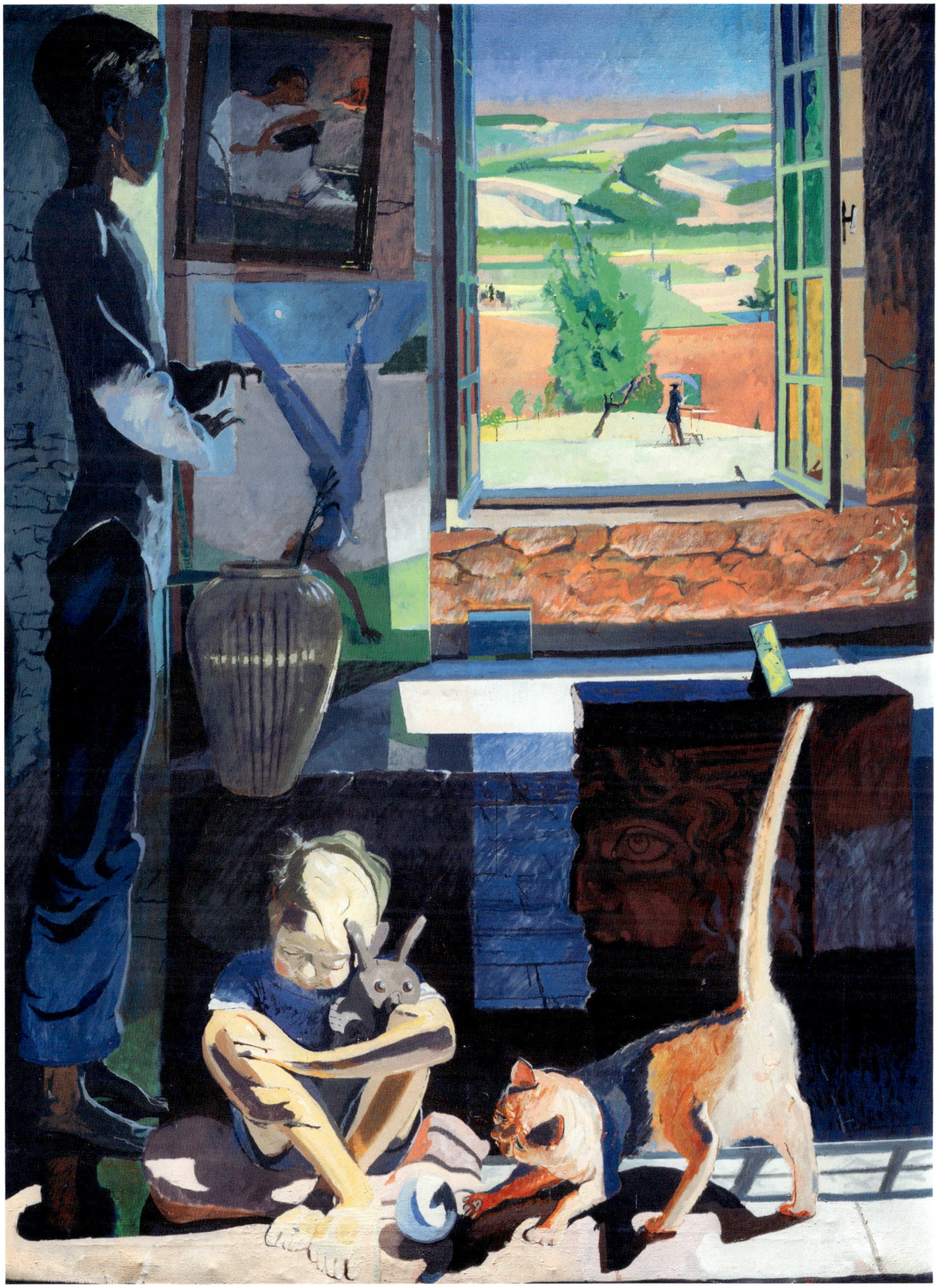

48. *The Family*, *c.* 2000, oil on canvas, 121 x 90 cm

becomes a portal into Fell's contemporary reality: his life as a painter in the Gers, immersed in the land, the light and the colour.

We can see the symbolism of the distance between the artist and his family (around this time he separated from his wife) both literally and figuratively depicted through the distinct difference in lighting as well as the indoor/outdoor interplay. He was experiencing detachment from his faith, and ultimately the physical separation from his two sons who continued to live in England. It was often through painting that Fell would work through his moods and emotions. They were direct reflections of his internal impulses. Fell, although reticent about discussing his work, also poured himself into his imagery, and the joy he felt in his new life in the Gers was countered by sadness at the dispersal of his family.

There is a magical assimilation of human figures and the represented world around him which meets with the flattened forms or the line divisions that interrupt the depicted scenes. The *Fête at Rozès* of 1996 [49] is an important work which comprises myriad varying elements woven into the scene. Fell was asked once by a student admiring the painting what was the purpose and meaning of the rainbow line separating the top two thirds from the bottom. His response: 'Well it's a line.' This wry refusal to elaborate on any further imposition of meaning on his work, or discussion around it, is something that Fell was known for. Meeting with his assertion of this being simply 'a line' we understand it as such: a delineation between one thing and another. We can also put this into context with his work as a printmaker and draughtsman, where line is the essential form to construct the image. Understanding that the line creates separation, in the *Fête at Rozès* we see it used as a demarcation of an indoor scene and an outdoor scene showing night-time revelries. The local *fêtes* take place across the Gers during the warmer months of the year. Each village, Rozès included, proudly celebrates with its own mini festival. The celebrations include all the highlights from the region: Gascon food, plenty of wine, traditional dances and music, and, of course, everyone from the local community. Fell depicts this spirited event with all its energy and chaotic *joie de vivre*. Beside the local characters and their interactions, we find more abstract formal elements creeping in. The large diagonal blocks at the top and bottom of the painting help to translate perspective, and the thin lines of the horizontal railing and vertical skinny trees also divide up the space. These flattened forms give

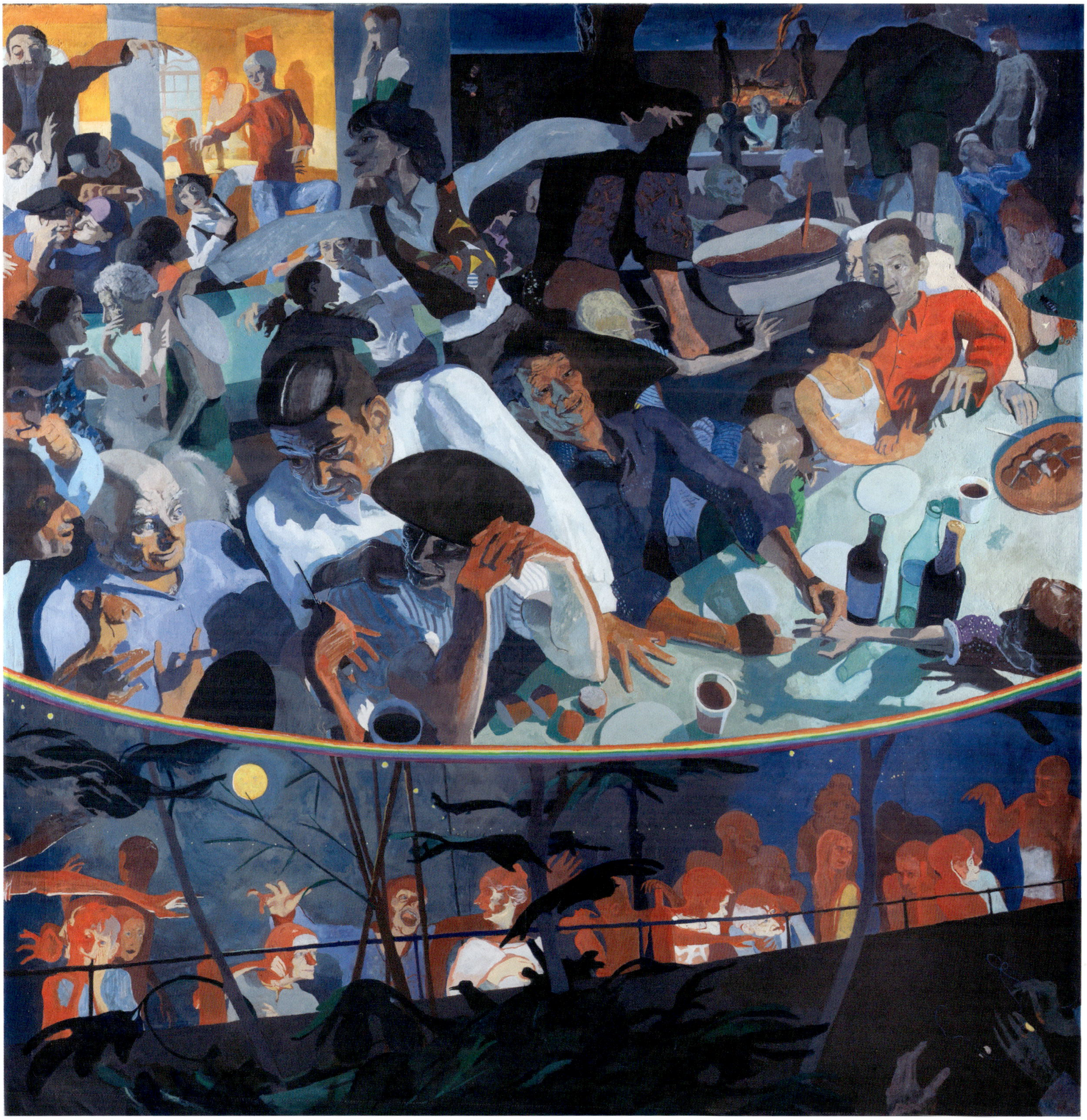

49. *Fête at Rozès*, 1996, oil on canvas, 182.1 x 182.5cm

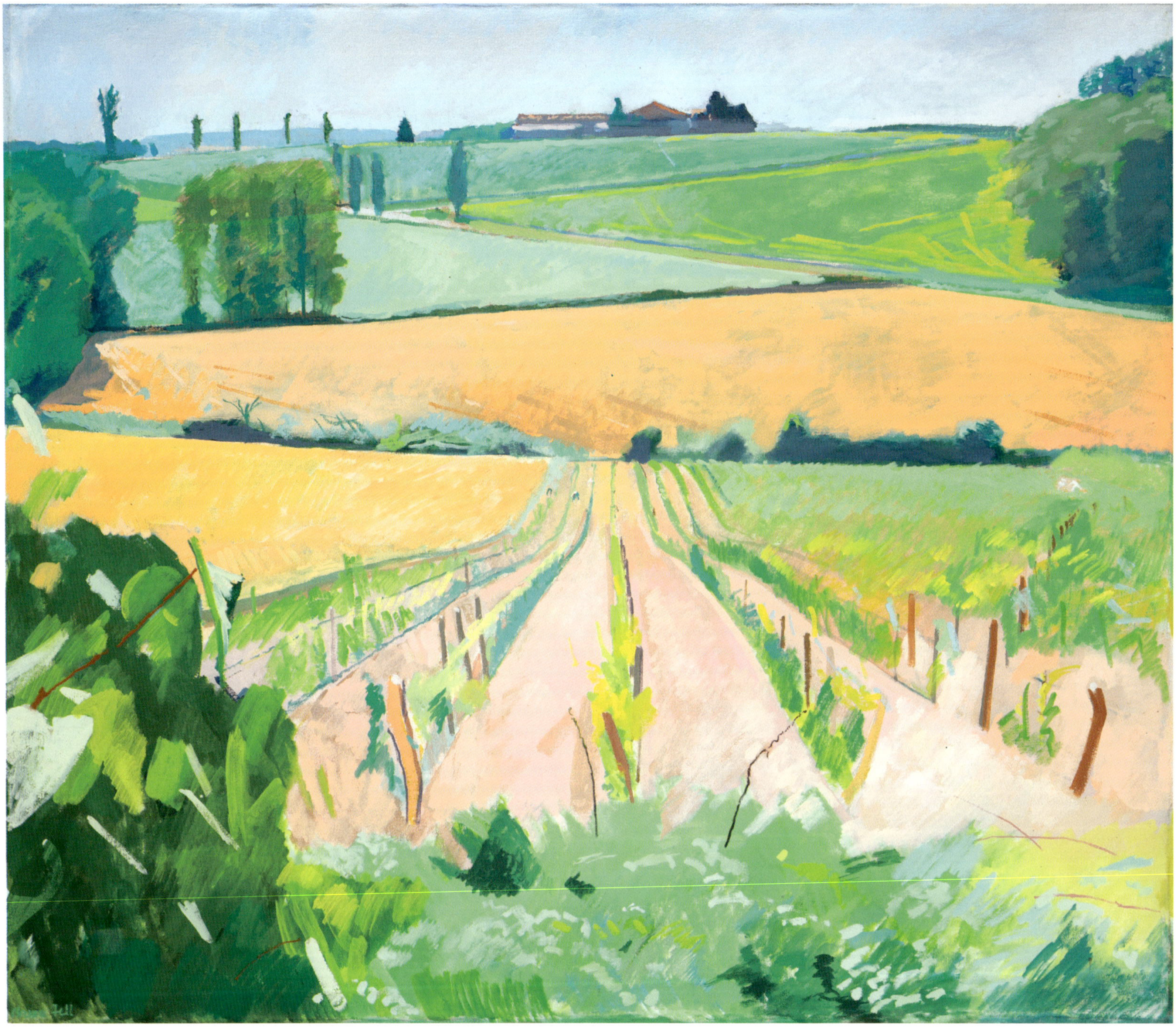

50. *Vineyards at Routgès*, c. 2000, oil on canvas, 75.8 x 90.9 cm

a nod to the decorative arts, craft and design. Fell was Chairman of the Society of Designer Craftsmen in the late 1980s, and throughout his career as teacher and Head of Foundation at the City & Guilds he championed the inclusion of the applied arts as of equal importance to the so-called 'fine arts' of painting and sculpture.

The most important influence of the Gers on Fell as an artist was the unique landscape, a never-ending source of inspiration to him as he returned to painting these lush scenes again and again throughout his life. He would block out the chequered fields in works such as *Vineyards at Routgès* [50] or *Valley of the Baïse – morning* [64] where swathes of colour are interrupted by precisely observed detail of trees, hedgerows and buildings. While his palette would be drawn most often to the diversity of greens and yellows, the landscape also offered the rich ochres, burnt umbers and burgundy reds of the earth set against the dazzling blues of the skies, which were reminiscent for him of Renaissance depictions of the Madonna. The quality of light he found across the Gers countryside was a key element in transmitting life, movement and colour to his landscapes. We see these open scenes where squares of even colour are placed side by side emphasising the patterns of the farmland. The flat blocks of scorching colours are immediately recognisable as the Gers countryside.

The southwestern sunlight was particularly alluring to him in the summer months as it would help transform the colours from the flat browns and yellows of the agriculture to brilliant gemstone hues of ultramarine and cerulean blues, emerald greens and strident cadmium yellows. The variety of colours he would see in the Gers through the summer months is particularly evident in the painting *Afternoon from Barrère* [56]. The diversity of tone in the abundant foliage in the foreground highlights numerous greens, lime, veridian, chartreuse, which then give way to the warm yellow fields and the purplish grey mountains in the far distance. The three planes dividing foreground, middle ground and background all pull the perspective in different ways, the foreground from right diagonally down, the fields from top left down and the mountains marking out the horizon line. The interaction in these contrasting geometries is interrupted by the leafy trees shielding the larger view. They pull the viewer's gaze back to the harmonious composition as a whole which adheres to traditional landscape composition.

The village of Rozès, near where Fell lived, is located in a particularly beautiful part of the Gers. It sits in the hills surrounded by three valleys which would be the subject of many of his paintings. He would set up his easel and oil paints in different parts of his sloping garden which overlooked the valleys below. From that spot he operated a disciplined routine, working religiously often on one painting in the morning and another in the afternoon, according to the changes of light. Despite the appearance of his work capturing a moment from a specific time of day, Fell's process was slow and calculated and would often force him to set paintings aside till the following year when he could continue in the same light conditions. While he became most often associated with the bright and bold colour palettes found in the heat-soaked summer paintings, he was also drawn to the winter landscapes of the region, where the light would soften and the colours would assimilate into a soft haze. *Rozès in February* [51] shows a winter scene, where the sun and the snow coalesce, creating a subtle harmony of pale corals and pinks broken by shadows of trees made up of purples, blues and greens. Wide vistas of delicate peach tones top and tail the articulated landscape. In the winter tableau Fell's brushwork is minimal and efficient, avoiding overworking the details created through the sparse shapes of buildings, trees and fields. With his confident single strokes or dabs Fell calls on the viewer's visual perception to read the clues he offers. On the left side we find the texture of water in the thinning blue paint meeting vitality in the foliage where the solid colour and paint mark out buildings in the negative space. Fell returns to the exact same viewpoint in another canvas, *Bright Light, early a.m.* [67]. The repeated vista is bathed in a cool wash of pale buttery yellows and lurid greens. These higher toned colours, along with the floral spray creeping in at the left corner, suggest that the season is now spring, as Fell gives us an insight into his own life's trajectory, showing the different seasons, times of day and weather.

The interplay of shape and colour drives many of Fell's paintings, and his return to the same view or subject would become the perfect foil to work through these formal puzzles. The subject where he could really play with such geometric conundrums was his lily pond. The rectangular pool of water, home to goldfish, frogs and waterlilies, was an architectural feature of Barrère, sitting directly underneath his studio window. Fell's paintings of his lily pond push the boundaries of perspective, bending

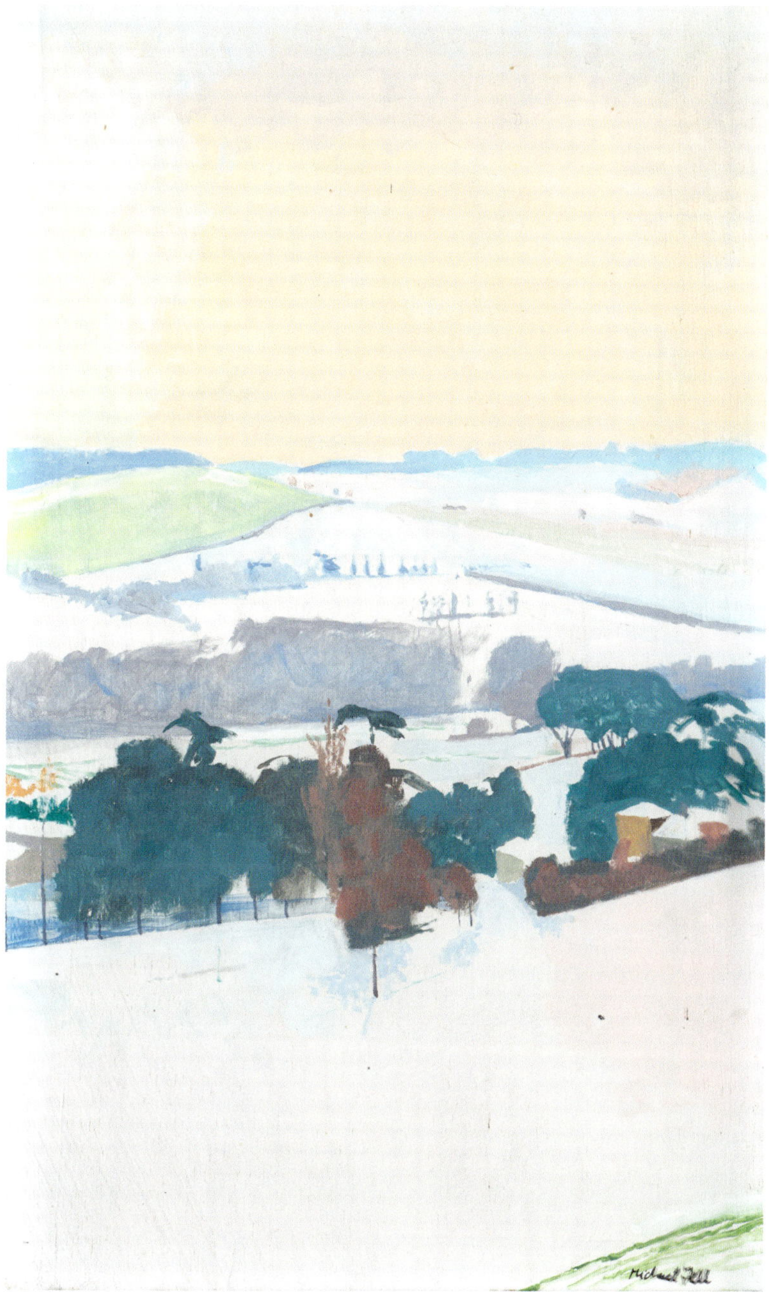

51. *Rozès in February*, 2010, oil on board, 35.1 x 21.4 cm

viewpoints and toying with stylisation and realism. His intention was to emphasise what was *seen*, rather than what was there. These paintings are some of Fell's most sophisticated compositions. He saw them as an opportunity to combine formal traditions of representation alongside experimentation in colour, line and geometry. They gave a backdrop for him to home in on the detail which would be different depending on his position, the light, and the flora and fauna in the pond itself. The three works *My Pond* [54], *Lily Pond* [60] and *My Fish Pond* [61] are representative examples of this. *My Pond* shows the painstaking attention to detail given to the architecture of the pond itself, the cracks and crevices of the structure giving character and nuance to the fields of ochre in the wall and the reflection. *My Fish Pond* offers an alternative perspective, where the foliage – the broad flat lilies and the tumbling ivy – interrupt the close attention paid to the water and the changes in colour from direct sunlight to shade. As in many of his works, chiaroscuro is applied in the stark contrast of the colours in the water, emphasising the sunlight and the dark shadows of the building. Using Michael Baxandall's shadow theory,[4] questioning how shadows are an integral part of creating shape and form, we can see Fell's own experiments along the same lines of inquiry: how do differences in light affect perception of objects and scenes along with what we see in colour? *Lily Pond* becomes more of an investigation in colour changes through light and shadow – the lilies moving from yellow to orange when shown in direct sunlight to a greenish blue and grey in the shade.

Fell's landscapes and treatment of this corner of rural France comprise one of the most attractive aspects of his output. They are bold experiments, by which he could move between colour theory, draughtsmanship and the application of paint. One of his last paintings is a self portrait painted in his Gers studio [68]. Here we see all aspects of Fell as an artist. The scene of the studio is a vehicle for the communication of truth which comes through the use of paint. The crosshatch markings and single outlines suggesting frames or stacked paintings encourage the viewer to understand the full spectrum of Fell's practice as printmaker, painter and formal draughtsman. It is the connectedness of all these elements that provides the gateway into his whole practice, underpinned by the pervading gentleness of his character and sympathy for other people. As he expressed it, 'I believe in the translation of the physical impulse that one gets from things seen, felt, or imagined. The creative bit is to hang onto that spark and go on reinventing it until everything sings the same tune.'[5]

[1] David McAninch, 'Hills and Valleys', from *Duck Season: Eating, Drinking, and other Misadventures in Gascony – France's last Best Place* (New York: HarperCollins Publishers, 2017, p. 129.

[2] In his seminal book *The Discovery of the Mind* the German writer Bruno Snell describes Arcadia as a place where 'the currents of myth and empirical reality flow one into another; gods and modern men stage meetings': Chapter 13, 'Arcadia: The Discovery of a Spiritual Landscape', *Discovery of the Mind: Greek Origins of European Thought*, trans. T. G. Rosenmeyer (Oxford: Basil Blackwell, 1953), p. 283.

[3] Chiaroscuro is a technique first used in Renaissance art but it has become most famously associated with the 18th-century Baroque artist Caravaggio. The Italian term references the extreme contrasts of lighting used within a work to create a specific atmosphere of drama and intimacy and to add depth to the modelling of what is depicted. The concept of chiaroscuro in relation to both cognitive science and theories surrounding visual perception in the 18th century is discussed in depth by Michael Baxandall in his book *Shadows and Enlightenment* (New Haven/London: Yale University Press, 1995).

[4] Baxandall, cit. at n. 3.

[5] From 'A Taste of Armagnac and the comfort of friends', written by Michael Fell to accompany his exhibition *A Taste of Armagnac* at the Grosvenor Gallery, March 1996.

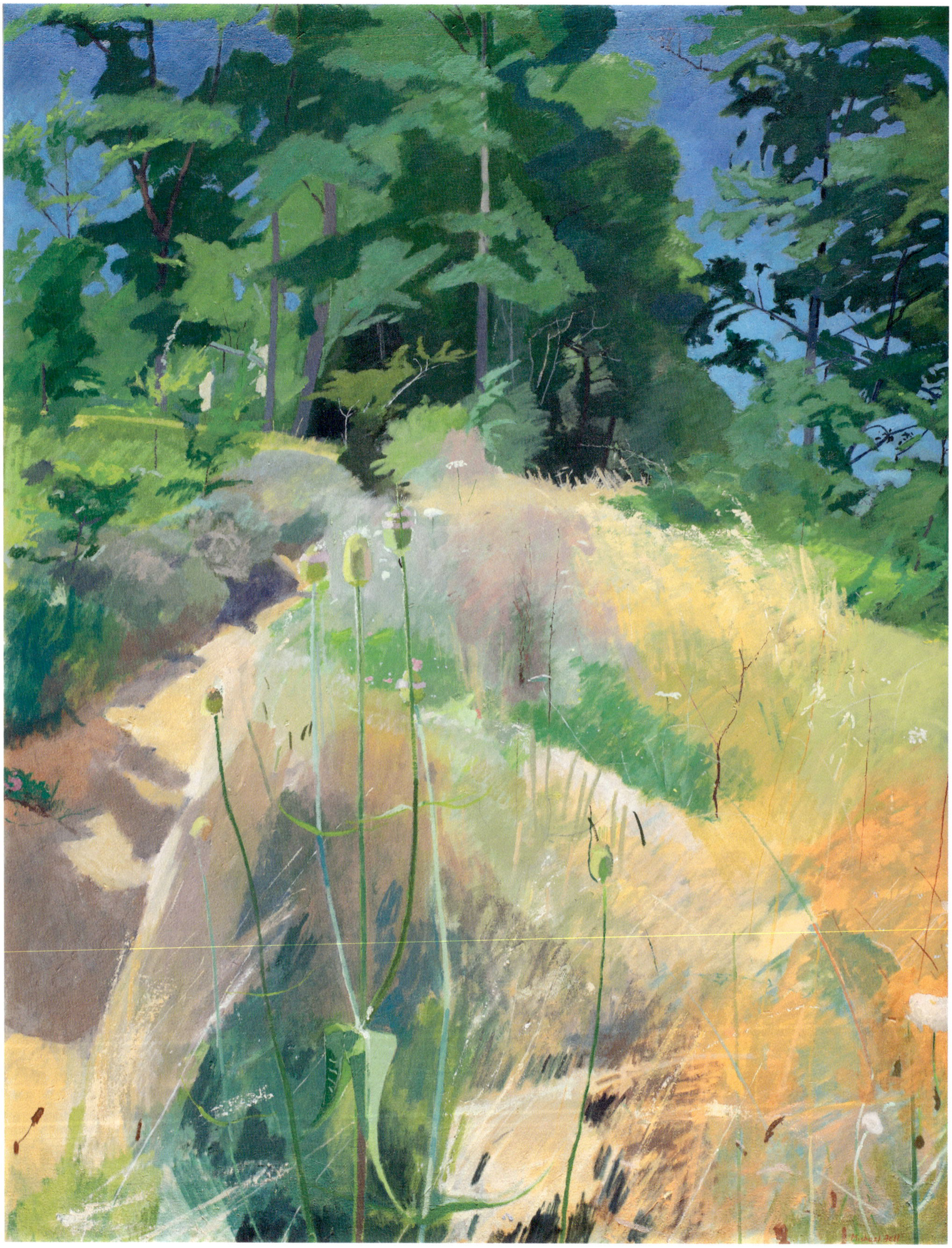

52. *Hillside at Barrère*, 1980s, oil on canvas, 118 x 93 cm

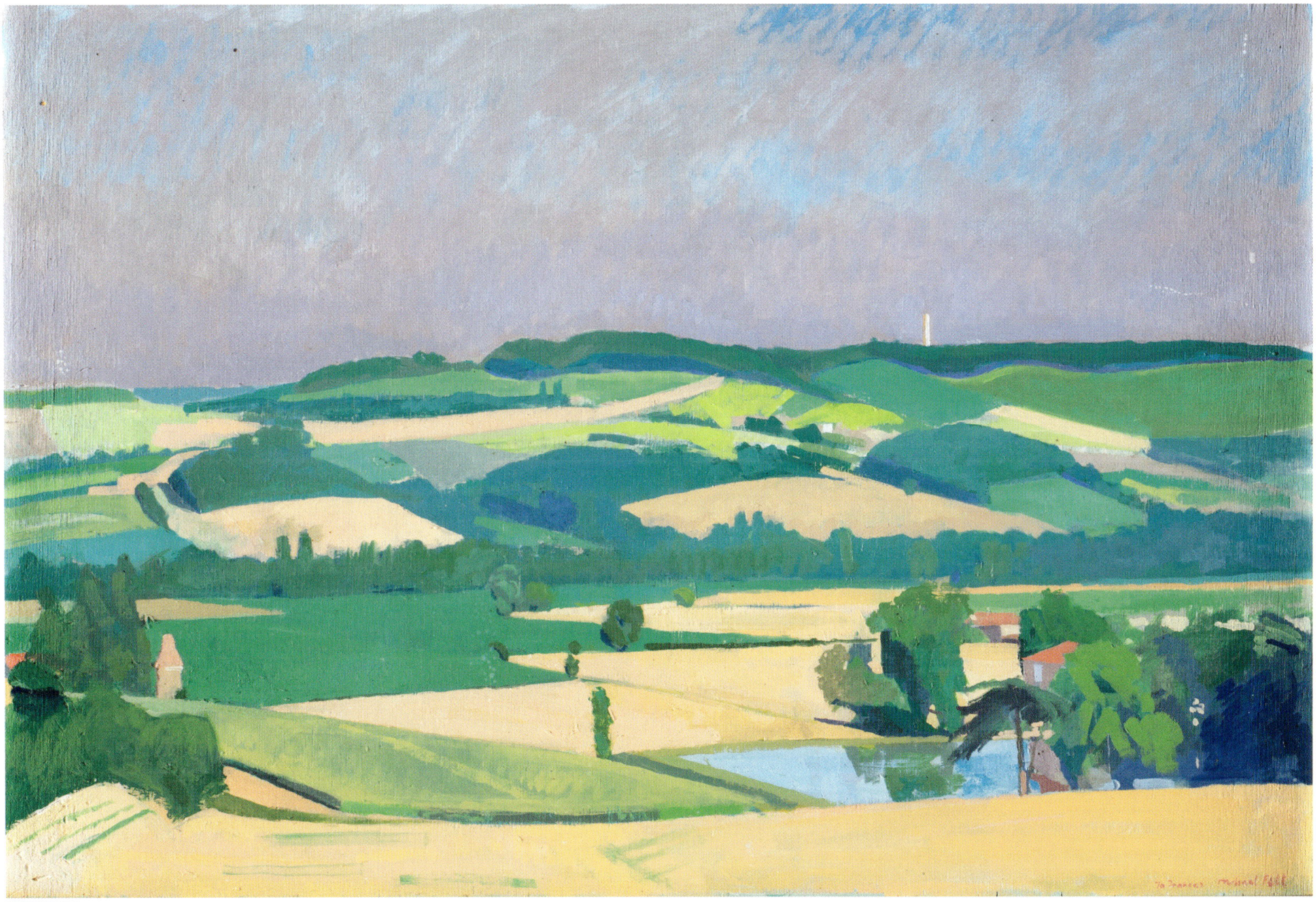

53. *View from Barrère*, 1980s, oil on board, 40 x 50 cm

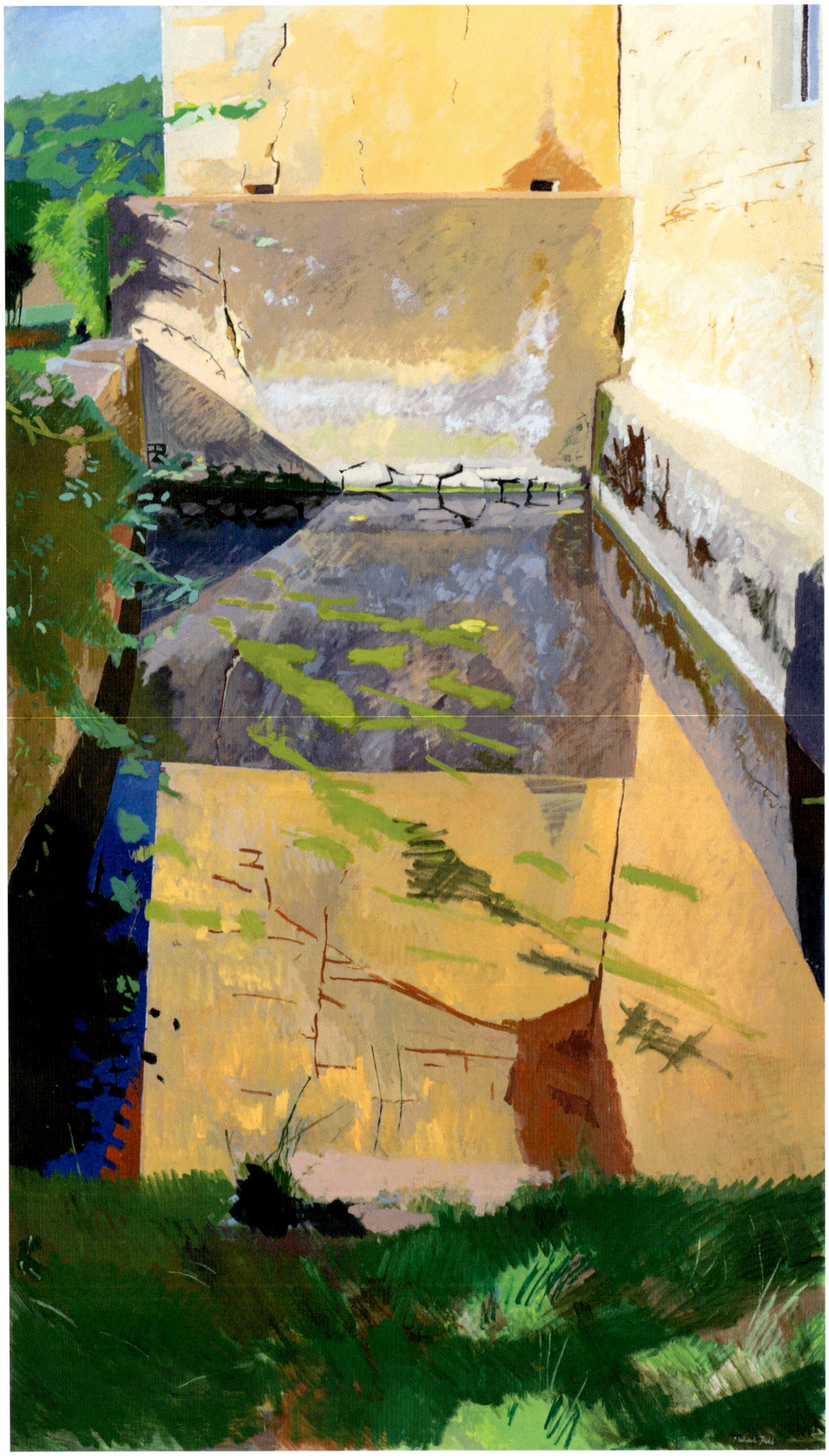

54. *My Pond*, mid-1990s, oil on canvas, 172.1 x 101.4 cm

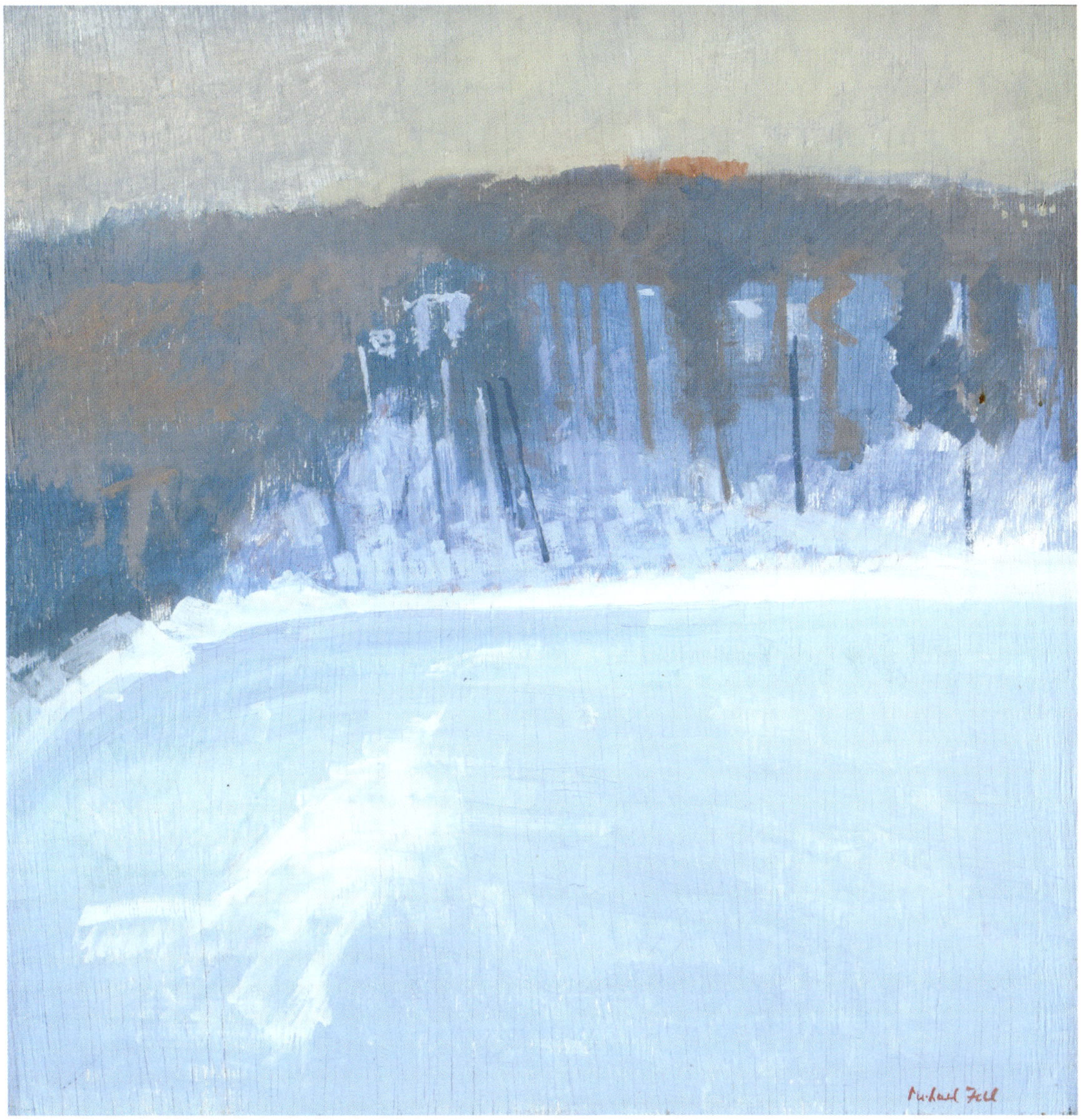

55. *Winter in Gascony*, late 1990s, oil on board, 29 x 29 cm

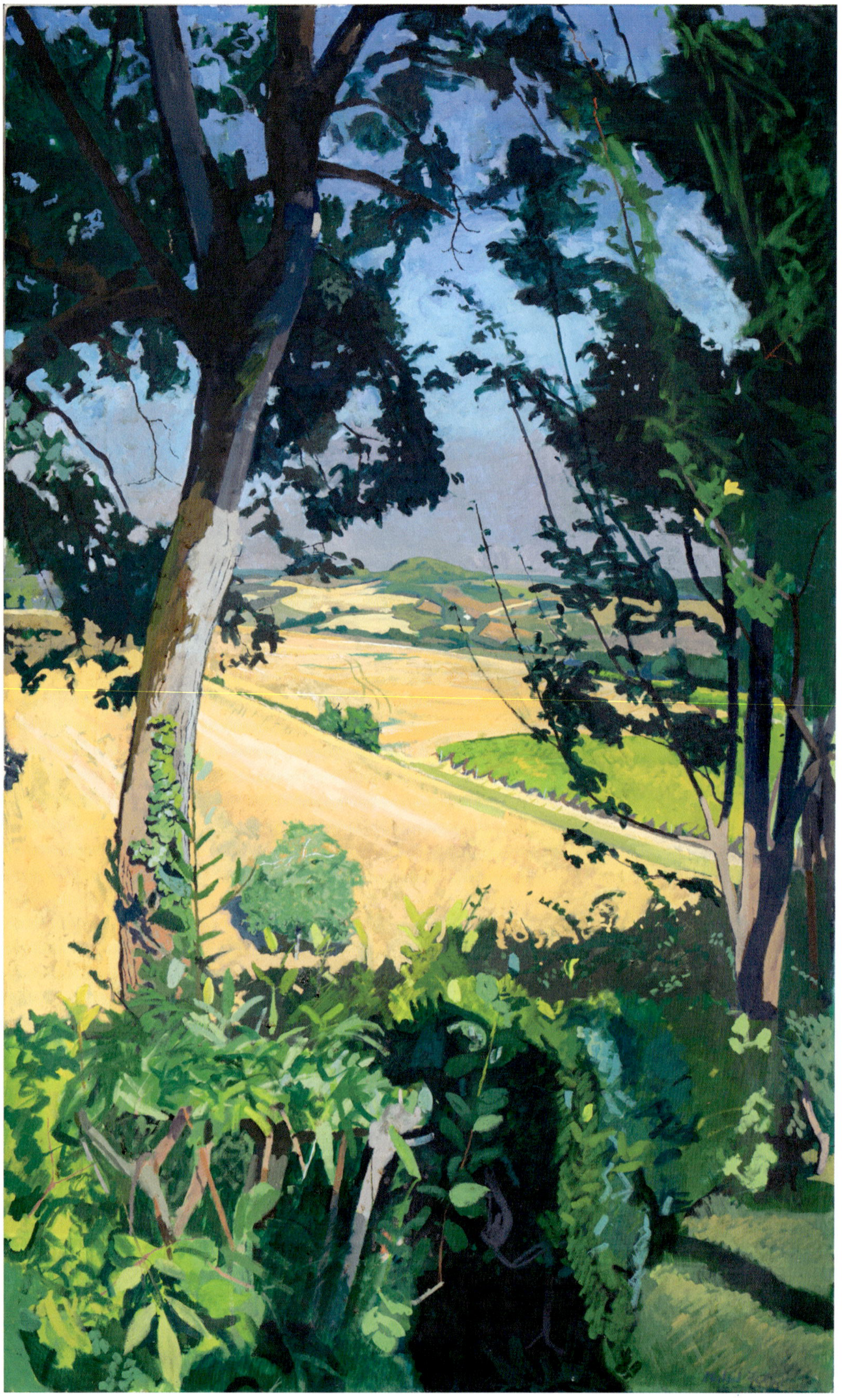

56. *Afternoon from Barrère*, *c.* 2000, oil on canvas, 122 x 76 cm

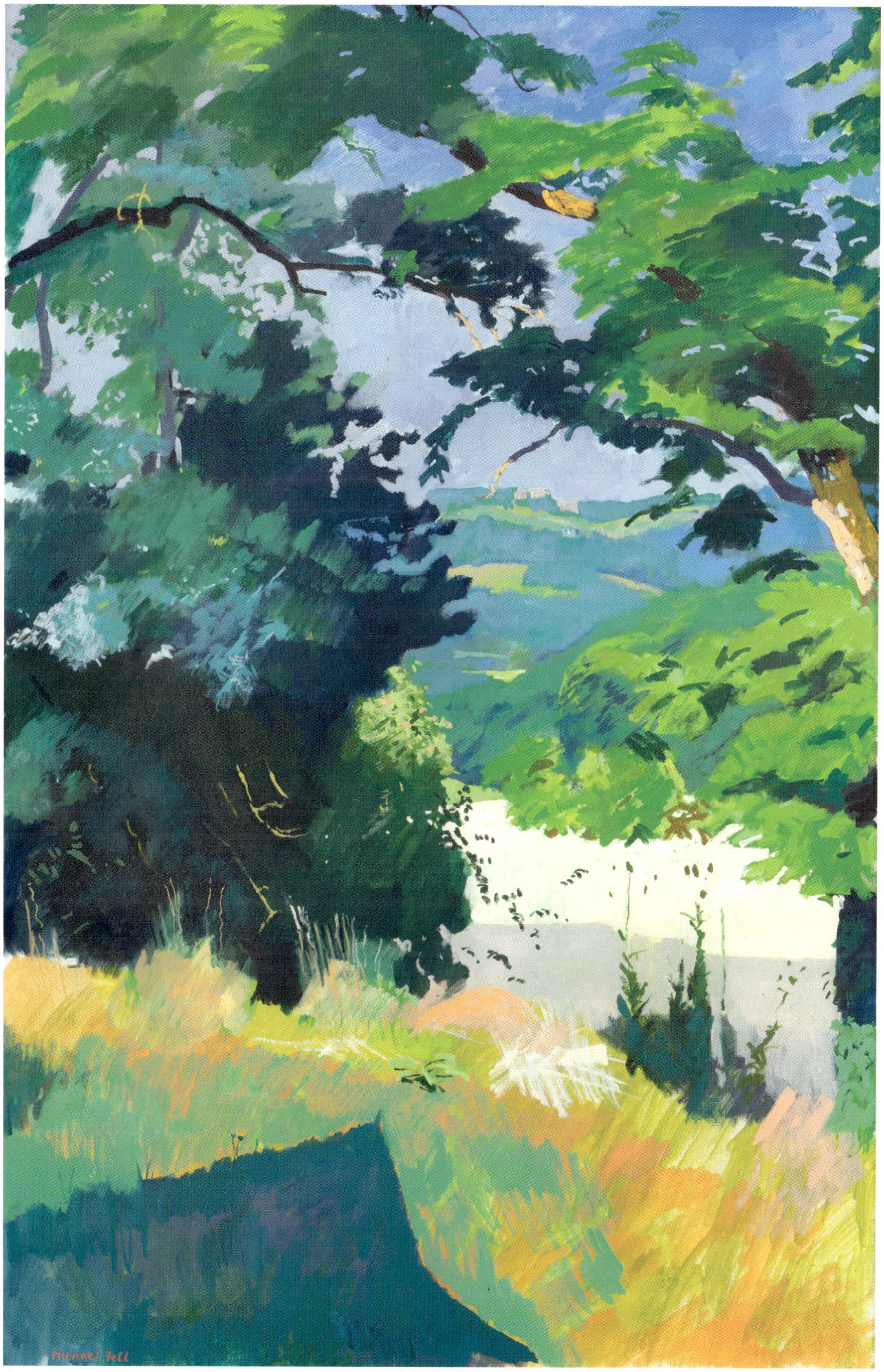

57. *A View (Routgès)*, *c.* 2000, oil on canvas, 90.5 x 60 cm

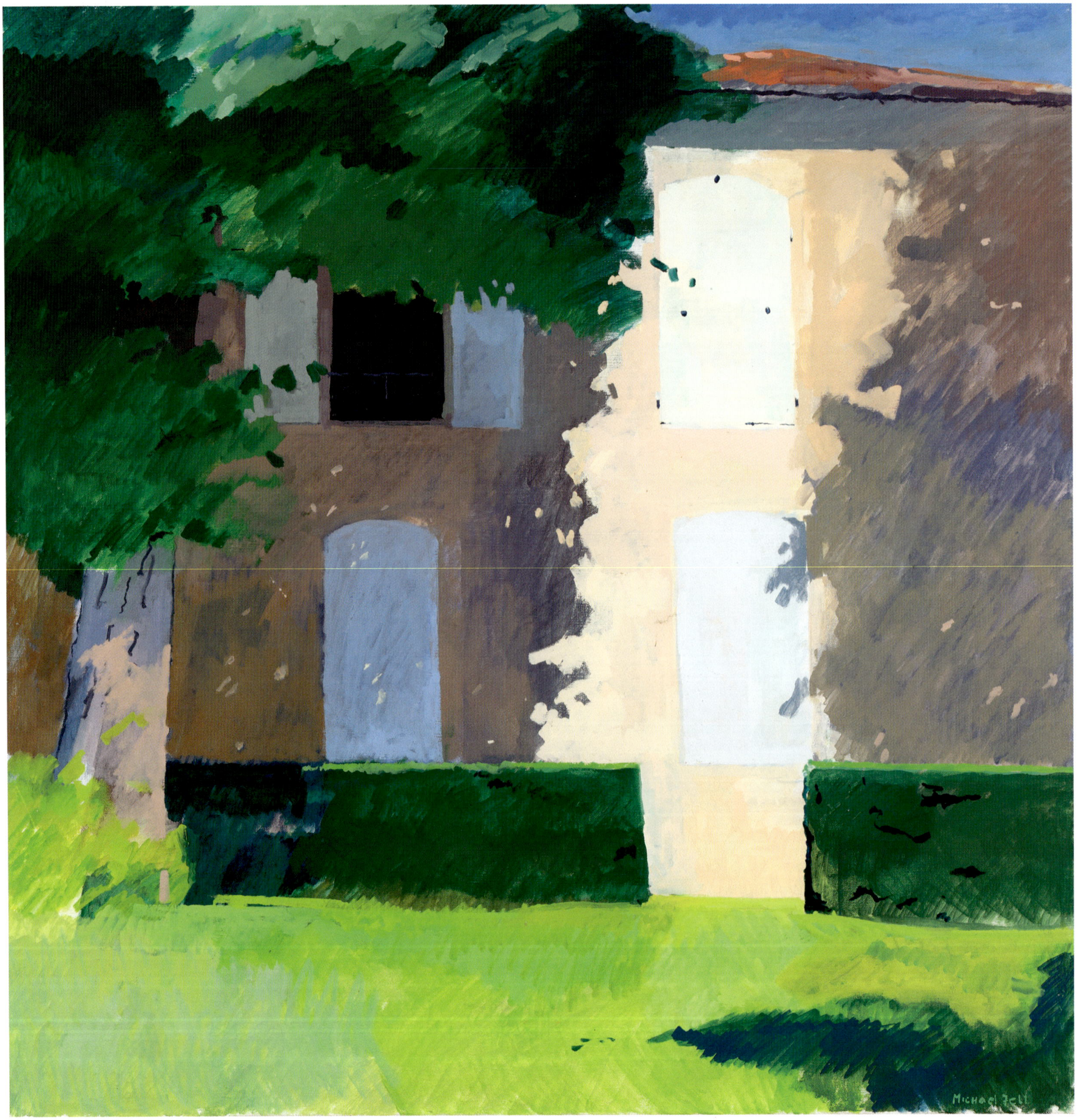

58. *Routgès*, *c.* 2000, oil on canvas, 75.5 x 75.5 cm

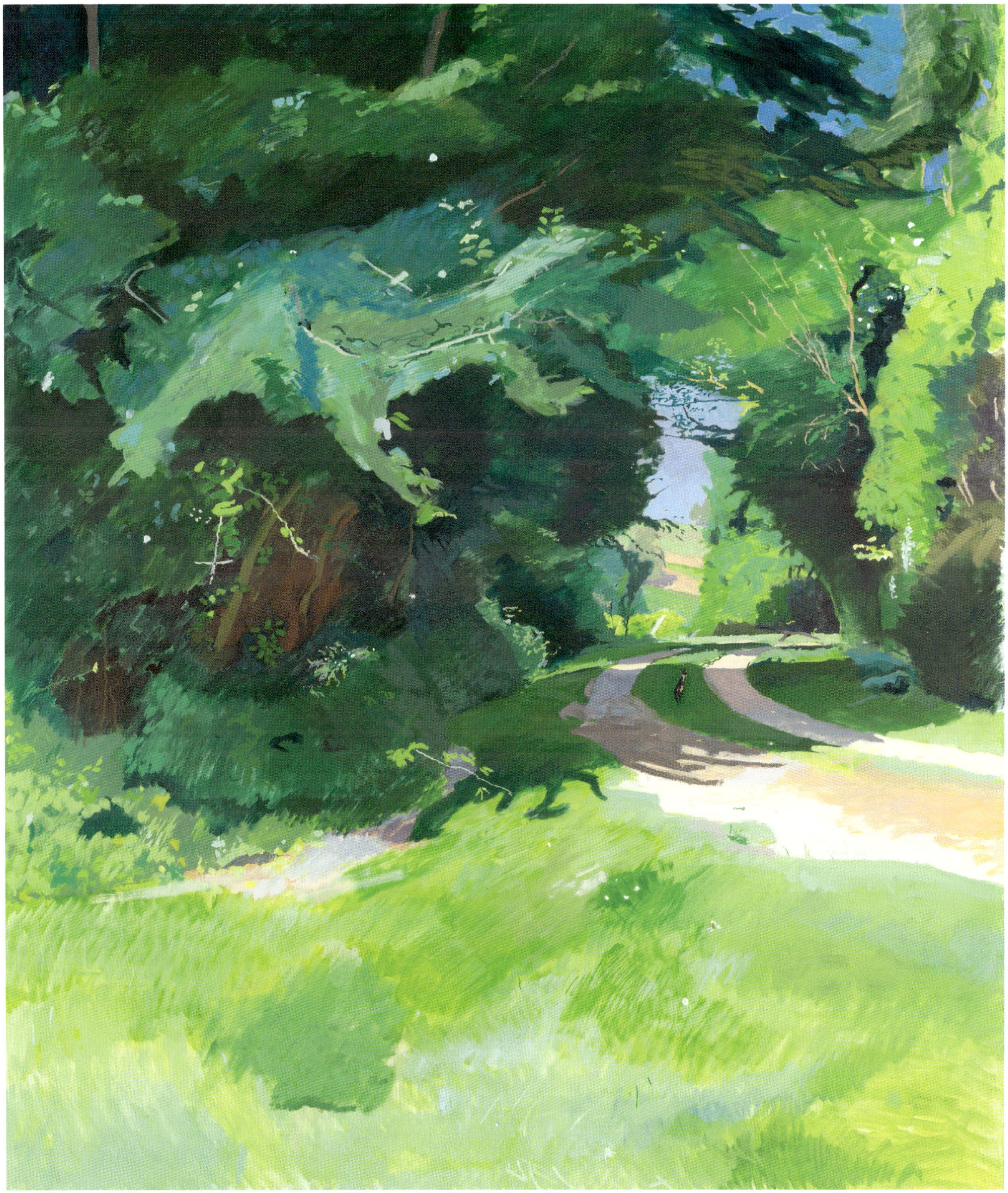

59. *Drive at Routgès*, *c.* 2000, oil on canvas, 104 x 91 cm

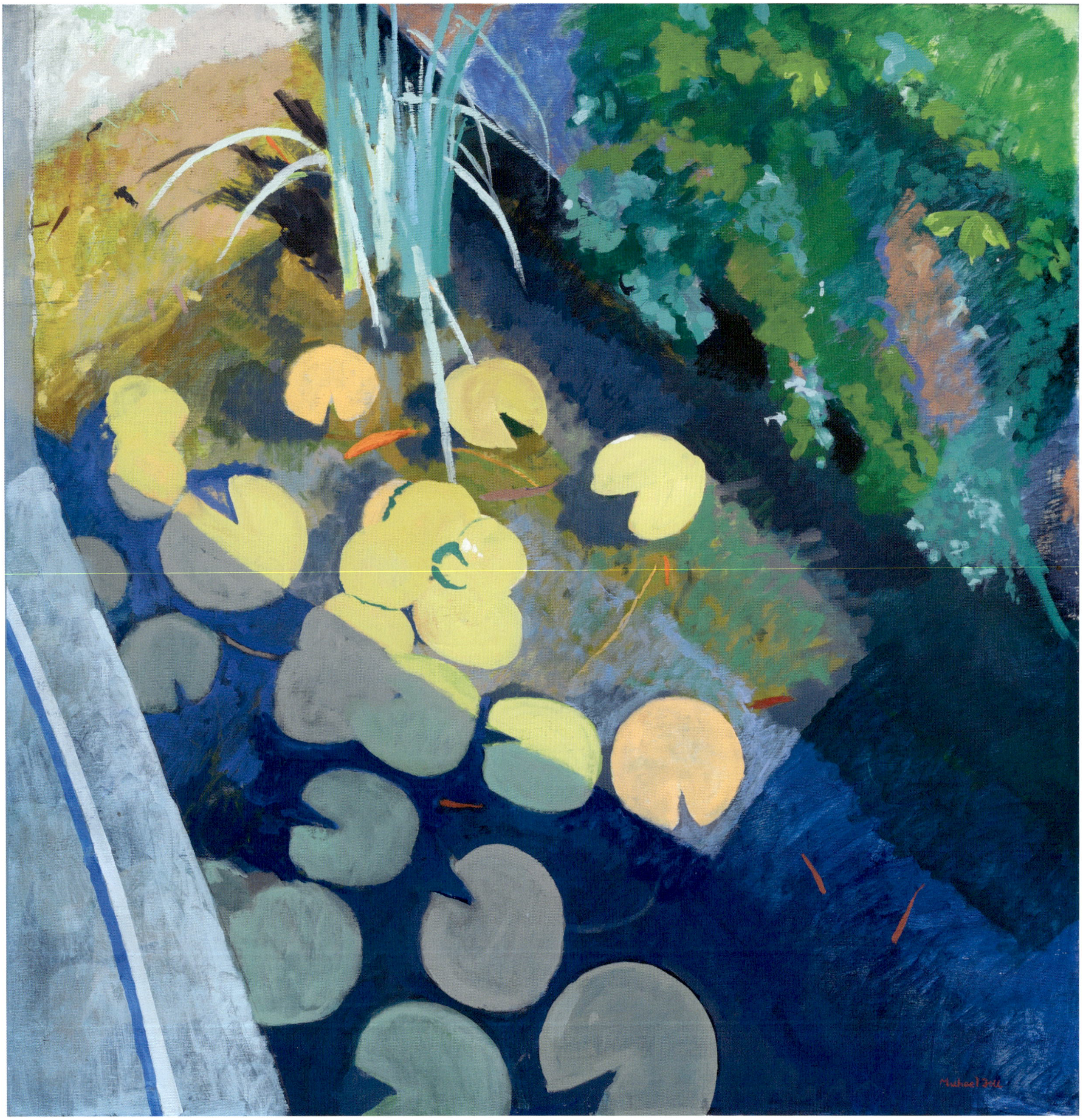

60. *Lily Pond*, 2000s, oil on board, 60 x 60 cm

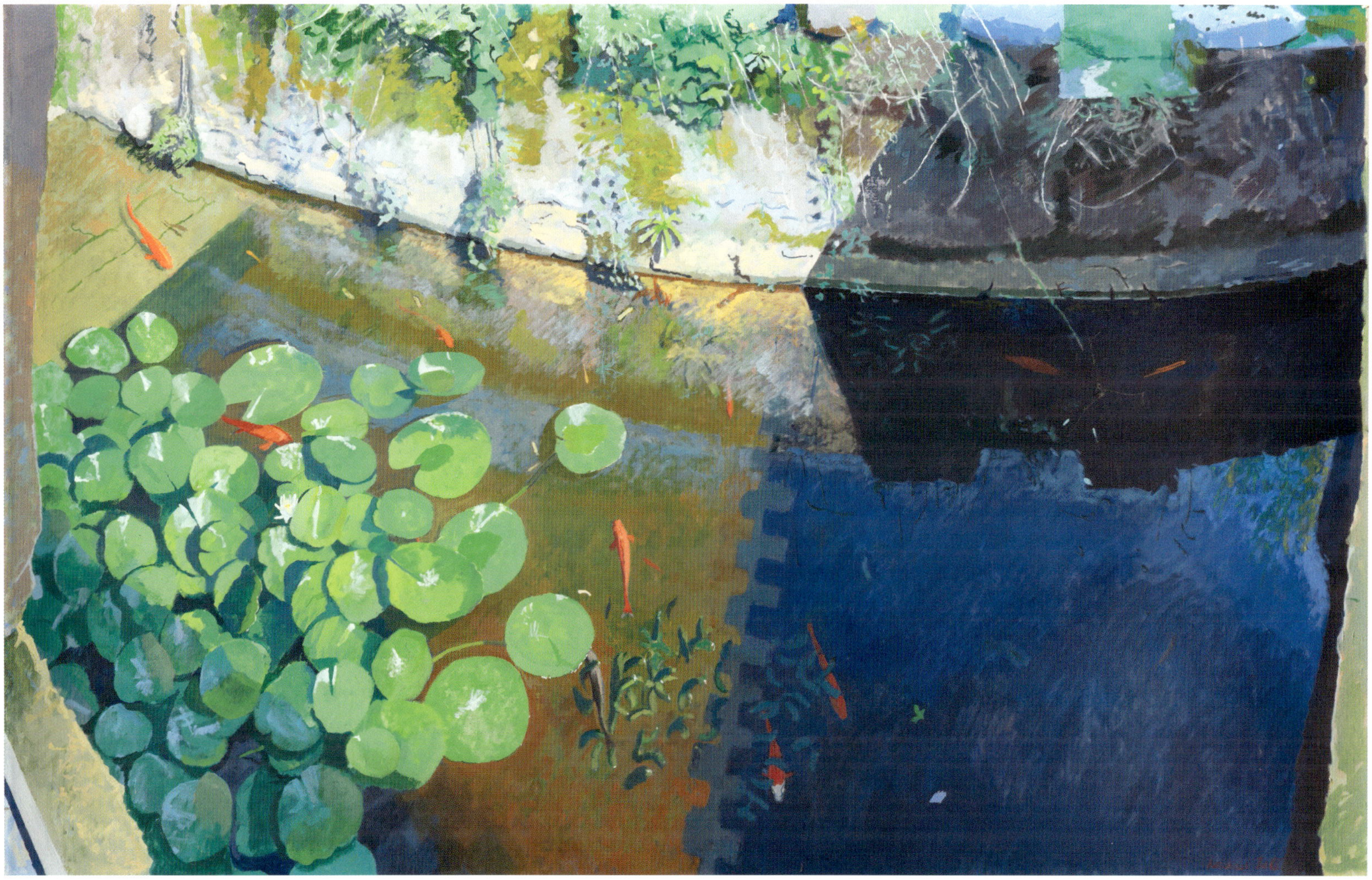

61. *My Fish Pond*, 2000s, oil on canvas, 75.3 x 121 cm

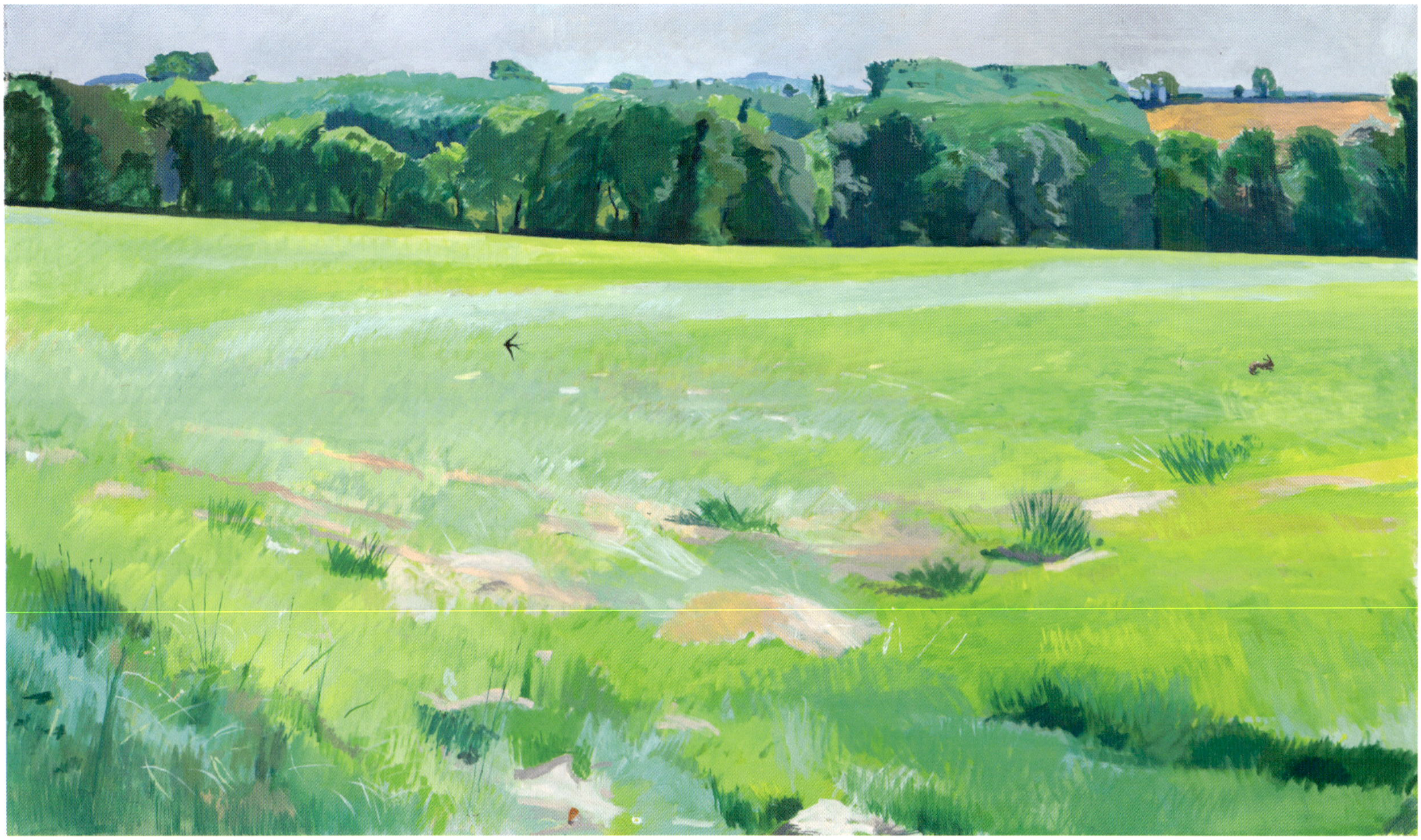

62. *Field at Routgès*, *c.* 2000, oil on canvas, 104.5 x 180.8 cm

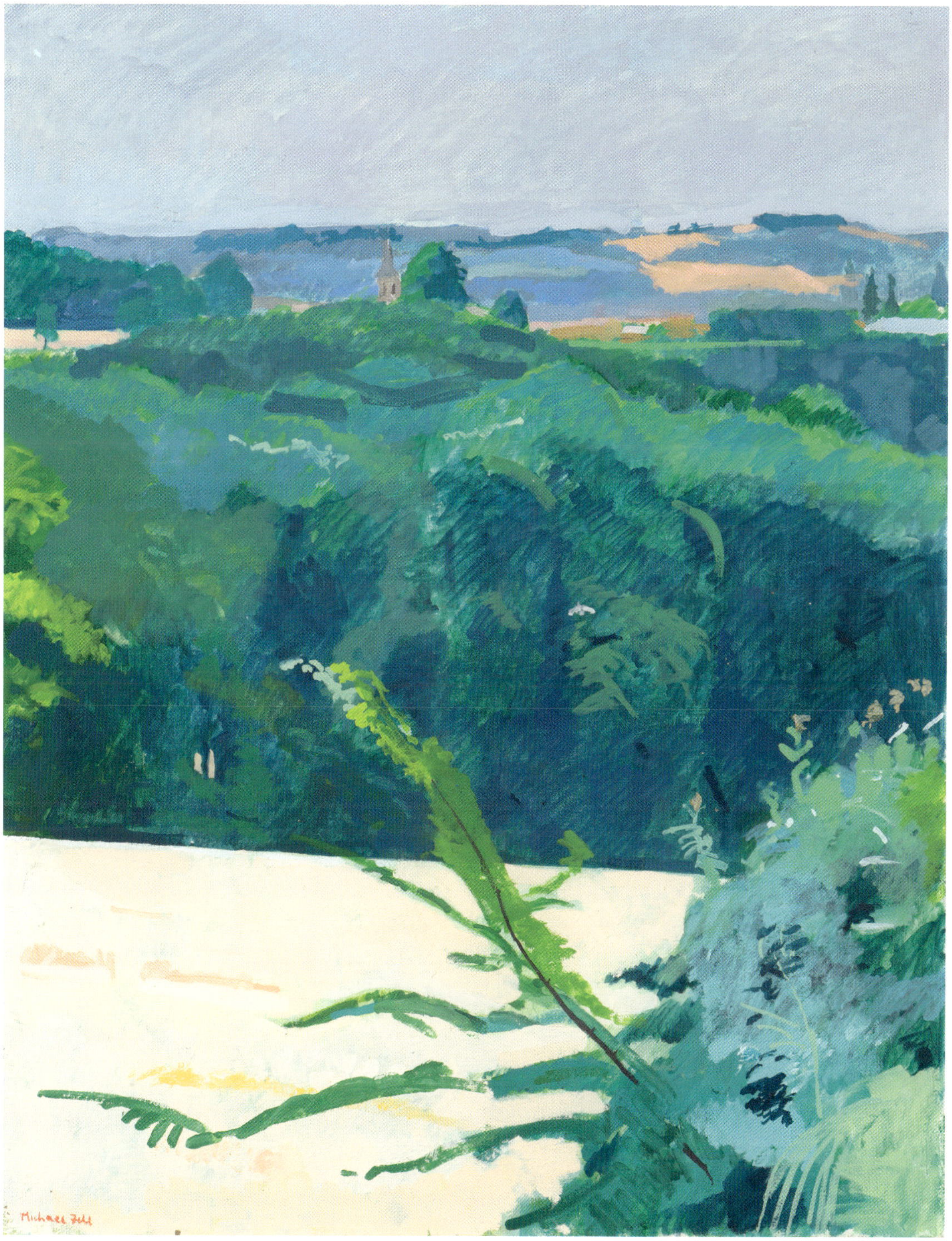

63. *View at Routgès*, *c.* 2000, oil on canvas, 62.6 x 49.6 cm

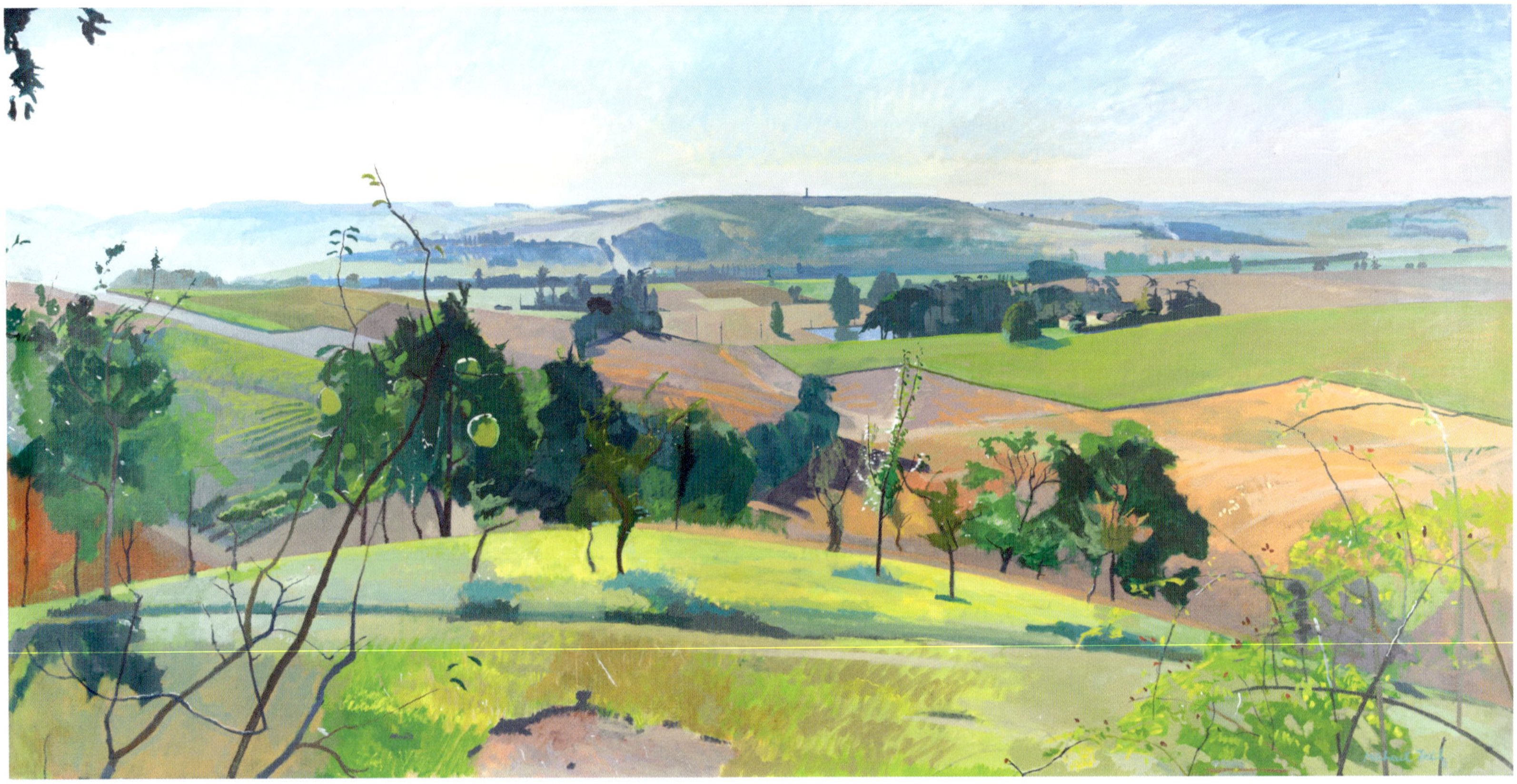

64. *Valley of the Baïse – morning*, c. 2000, oil on canvas, 74 x 151 cm

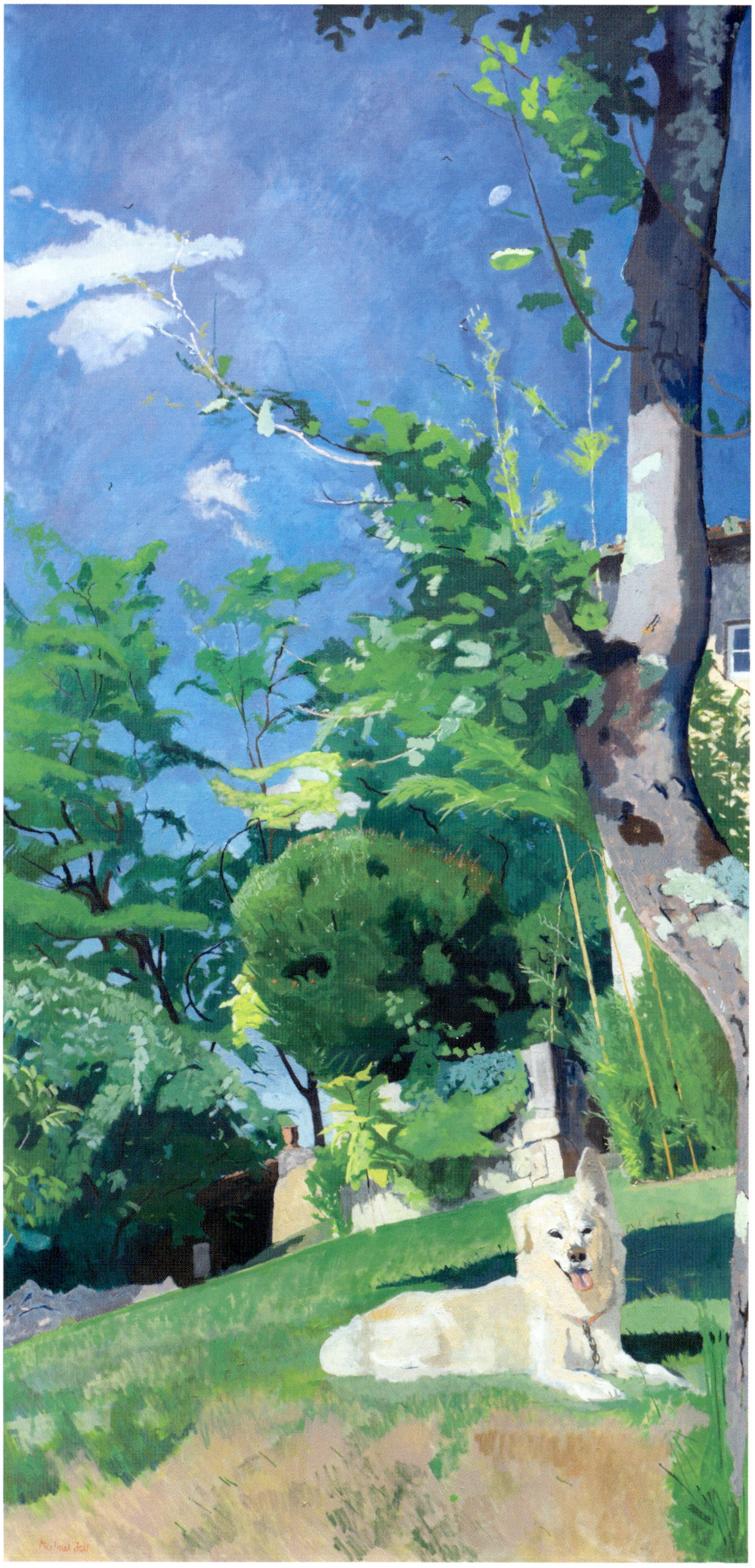

65. *Charlie*, *c.* 2000, oil on canvas, 155 x 83 cm

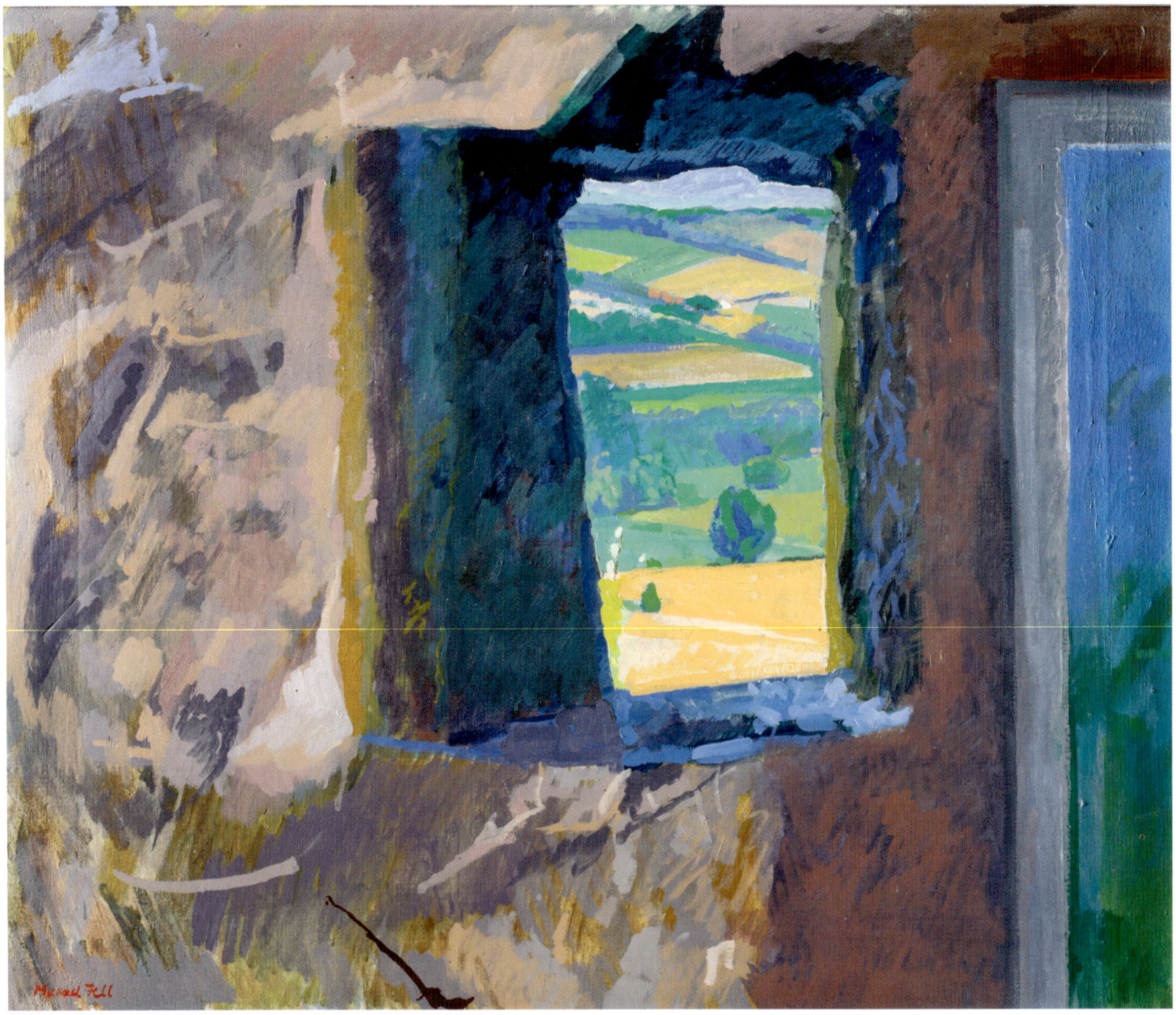

66. *View from a Window*, *c.* 2000, oil on canvas, 49.7 x 60 cm

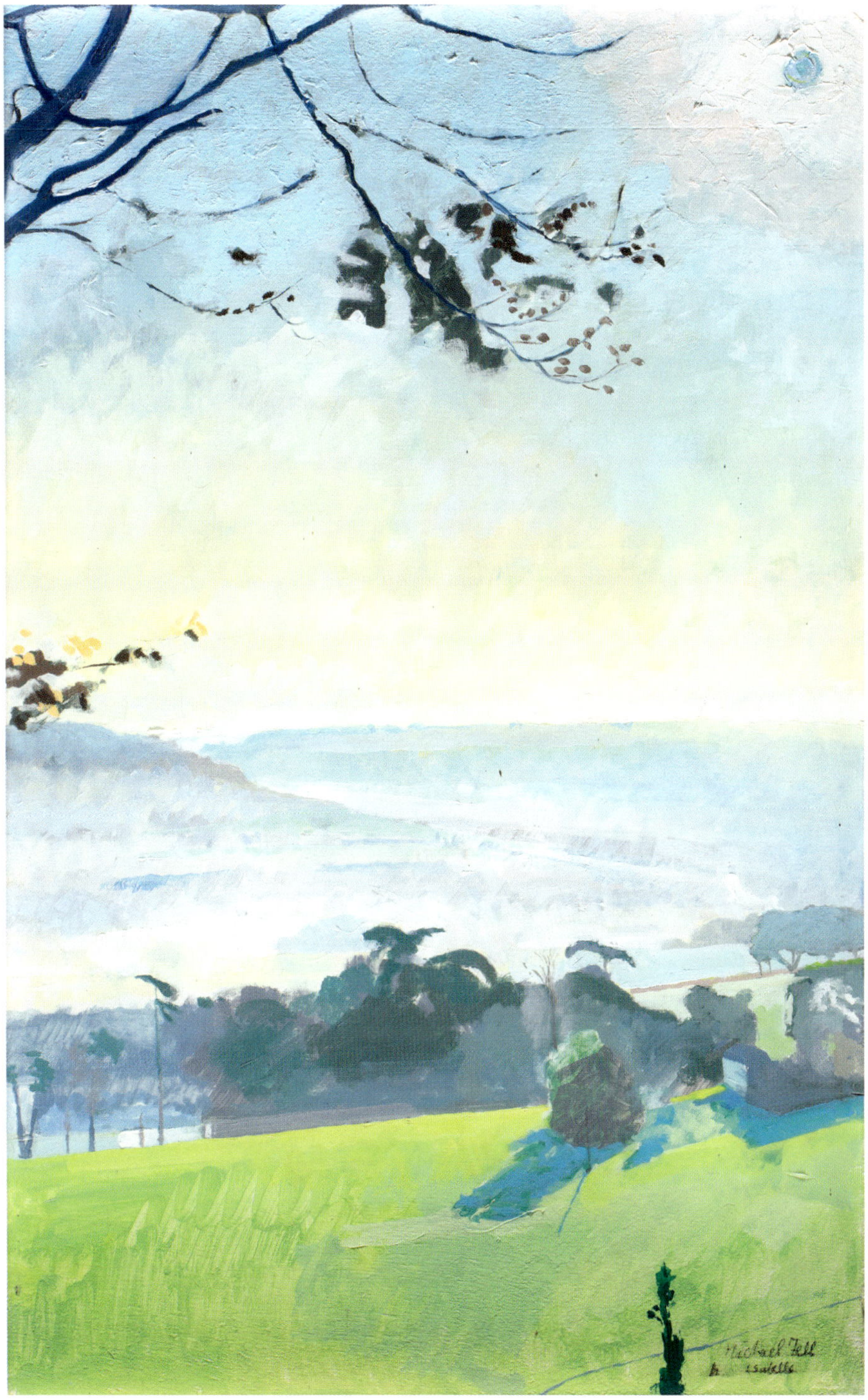

67. *Bright Light, early a.m.*, 2010, oil on board, 40.3 x 25.4 cm

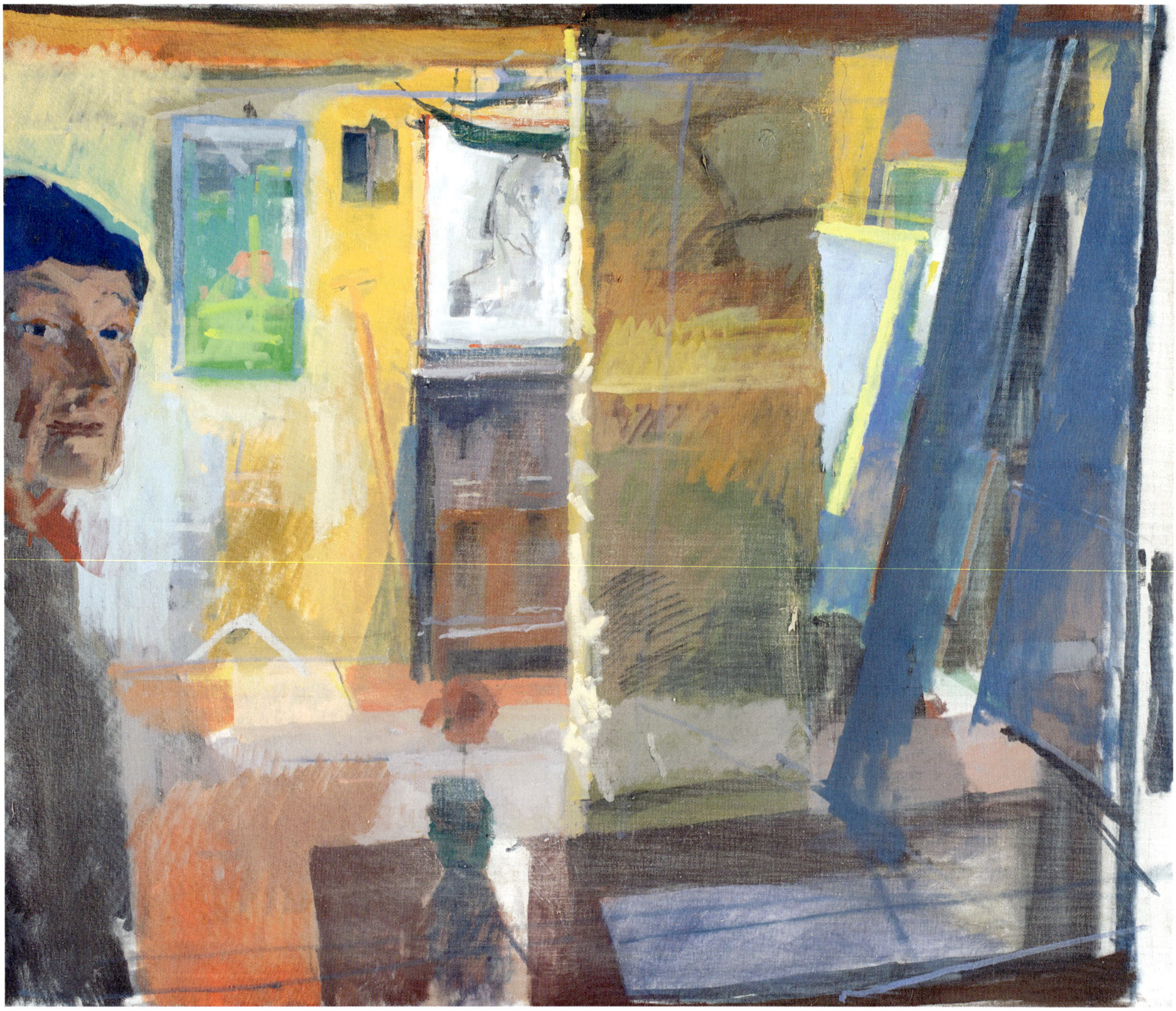

68. *Self Portrait*, 2023, oil on canvas, 75 x 90 cm

Religion

Religion

Revd John Summers and Andrew Wilton

As a pious English Catholic Fell took a great interest in, to the point of identifying with, the martyrs who were victims of the Protestant Reformation in Elizabeth I's reign and later. He paid tribute to them in the set of illustrations he made for *The Burning Babe* [18, 19] a mystical poem that meditates on an apparition of Christ on Christmas night. The large oil painting of *St John Southworth in Westminster Cathedral* [69] is a more extended celebration of the subject. It shows the mummified body of John Southworth in the Chapel of the English Martyrs, with the great building opening out behind him, beyond a metal screen.

After the Emancipation of Roman Catholics in England in 1828, nearly three hundred years after they had been suppressed under the Tudors, many new churches were needed and built. Westminster Cathedral had been planned since the middle of the century: a new building was commissioned by Cardinal Vaughan, and executed between 1895 and 1903 by the architect John Francis Bentley (1839–1902). It is remarkable as a notably successful essay on a large scale in the Byzantine style, deliberately avoiding the Gothic of Westminster Abbey and the Classicism of St Paul's. The division of the vast space into areas with different character, from the small side chapels to the high domed vaults, makes for an exhilarating composition as Fell brings all these elements together into a single pictorial idea, centred on the body of the martyr.

John Southworth was born into a recusant Roman Catholic family in 1592 and ordained in 1618. Arrested for heresy in 1627, he was hanged, drawn and quartered in 1654, having been engaged, when permitted, in pastoral work among the Catholic poor in London. After his death his body was purchased from the executioner by the Spanish Ambassador, with permission from Oliver Cromwell, for fifty guineas, reintegrated, embalmed and taken to France where it was interred in the English College at Douai. A cult developed around him. Having been hidden by students under the College's bakery floor during the French Revolution, the body was returned to England when Douai was demolished in 1927 and in 1930 placed in Westminster Cathedral. As one of the forty English martyrs of the Reformation he was canonised in Rome by Pope Paul VI in 1970. The body with its gold mask and hands was placed in its current position in the Chapel of the English Martyrs in 1930.

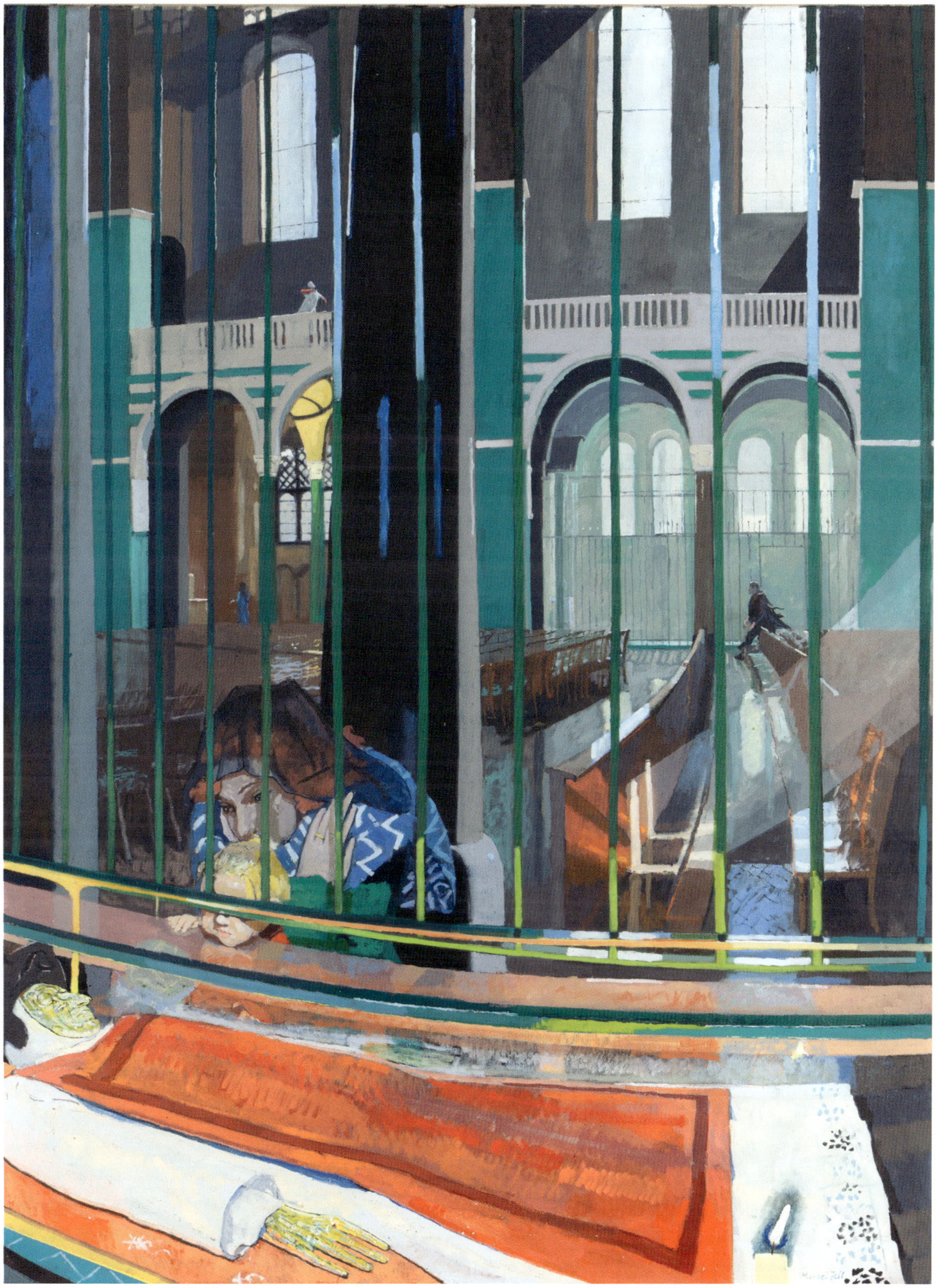

69. *St John Southworth in Westminster Cathedral*, 1980s, oil on canvas, 122 x 91 cm

Fell places the saint's body in its scarlet chasuble and Canterbury Cap at the bottom of a soaring view through the upright bars of the screen, with their varied reflections, across the Cathedral nave with its parallel rows of bare seats to the far arcade between tiers of round-headed windows that illuminate the whole space. He makes little attempt to record the scene in any kind of topographical detail: even the colours of the famous marble cladding are altered in an imaginative reinvention of the building. Although it is almost empty, it contains enough figures to animate it along with the bright light. Immediately in front of us at the end of an empty row of chairs, a man strides purposefully along the north wall (where in fact the chapels of St Andrew and St Patrick stand). Two other figures are almost lost in the expanse of the nave and the balustered gallery above. And in the immediate foreground a woman wearing a mantilla is gazing over the head of a small boy at the metallic face of the martyr.

Her face is expressive of intense meditative devotion. The child's blond hair is caught in the light that partially illuminates her as well as the whole of the saint's body with its two candles; but a bar of the metal screen falls across the boy's eyes so that his expression is obscured. Perhaps he is thinking what his mother has told him to think – a difficult cognitive feat for a small child, one would imagine; perhaps he is simply intrigued by the strange mummified object in front of him. These are questions that hardly detain us in the splendid context of the great Cathedral and the ambiguous patterns that Fell conjures out of the monumental architecture, and yet they embody the central mystery of the whole canvas: what do we as visitors to this awe-inspiring building think as we contemplate it and its highly charged contents?

A Simple Easter

The sequence of fifteen small plates grouped under the title *A Simple Easter* constitute perhaps Fell's most heartfelt expression of religious feeling. Most striking about them is the way in which that feeling is embodied in the technical exploitation of etching and aquatint which are used almost as if they were ink and paint: the artist's homage takes the form of a display of his mastery of the medium. The concentration of expressive power in these miniature compositions is an apt vehicle for the ideas and emotions that they convey. Parallel displays of virtuosity are rare in the history of etching: Goya's *Disasters of War* (1810–20) are a powerful precedent.

Fell himself doesn't seem to have finalised the order in which the prints are to be read, though he gave most of them titles (indicated by quotation marks), and it is perhaps best to take them in sequence as illustrations to the narrative of the Passion.

'Palm Sunday' [70] The plate with that title is a rich pattern of two or more tones of dark aquatint in a network of black or paler streaks that at first seem to make little sense. The puzzle resolves itself into a close-up view of an ass's head, among a rain of stems that must be the leaves and branches of palms: we are reminded of G. K. Chesterton's poem *The Donkey* (1914), in which the beast on which Christ rode into Jerusalem itself speaks:

> When fishes flew and forests walked
>   And figs grew upon thorn,
> Some moment when the moon was blood
>   Then surely I was born.
>
> With monstrous head and sickening cry
>   And ears like errant wings,
> The devil's walking parody
>   On all four-footed things.
>
> The tattered outlaw of the earth,
>   Of ancient crooked will;

Starve, scourge, deride me: I am dumb,
  I keep my secret still.

Fools! For I also had my hour;
  One far fierce hour and sweet:
There was a shout about my ears,
  And palms before my feet.

'Agony in the Garden' [71] A rich design of heavily bitten stems and leaves with a lightly etched face among them. The image of the garden will be a recurring motif in the series.

'Lord, is it I' [72] The plate consists of lightly bitten studies of heads with some aquatint: it looks like a set of rapid portrait studies taken during a meeting or a meal by one of the participants. Jesus has just prophesied that one of them will betray him, and each asks the anxious question. The artist imagines himself a participant at the Last Supper.

'Pilate's troubles' [73] A breastplate and helmet, with medals, cup and plate. Emblems of Pilate's authority as the Roman governor of Palestine, and the utensils with which he 'washes his hands' of responsibility for Christ's death: 'He took water, and washed his hands before the multitude, saying, I am innocent of the blood of this just person' (Matthew 27:24). There is perhaps also a reference to Pilate's wife's nightmare prompting her to warn her husband to have nothing to do with Jesus (Matthew 27:19). There is a noticeable heightening of tension in this plate.

'The Sanahdrin' [*sic*] [74] The Jewish legislature, sitting in the Temple at Jerusalem. Fell uses an ornate mitre and embroidered collar to signify their authority. Inscribed in the plate is the name of Barabbas, the criminal convicted of sedition and murder (Luke 23:25), whose name Pilate suggested as an alternative candidate for the punishment of crucifixion. It was not the Sanhedrin but Pilate himself who asked the people to decide between the two men.

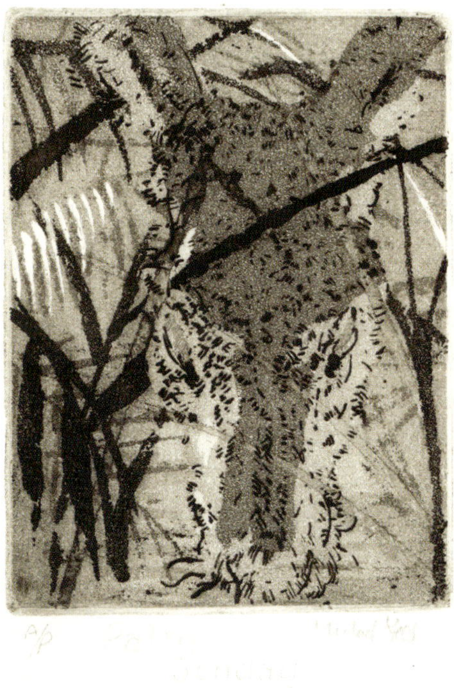

70. *'Palm Sunday'* (from *A Simple Easter*), 1991, etching and aquatint, 10 x 7.5 cm

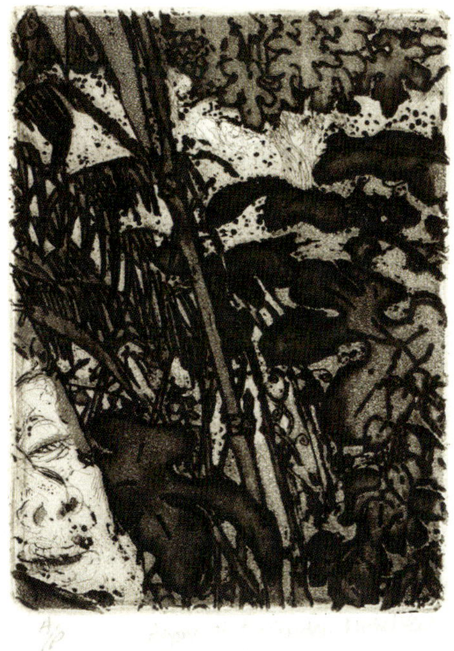

71. *'Agony in the Garden'* (from *A Simple Easter*), 1991, etching and aquatint, 10 x 7.5 cm

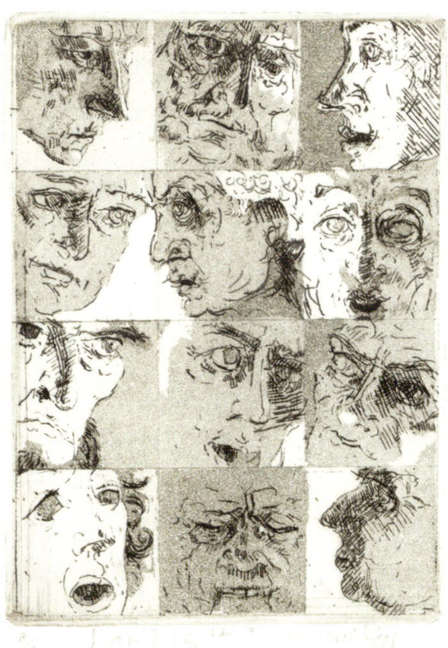

72. *'Lord, is it I'* (from *A Simple Easter*), 1991, etching and aquatint, 10 x 7.5 cm

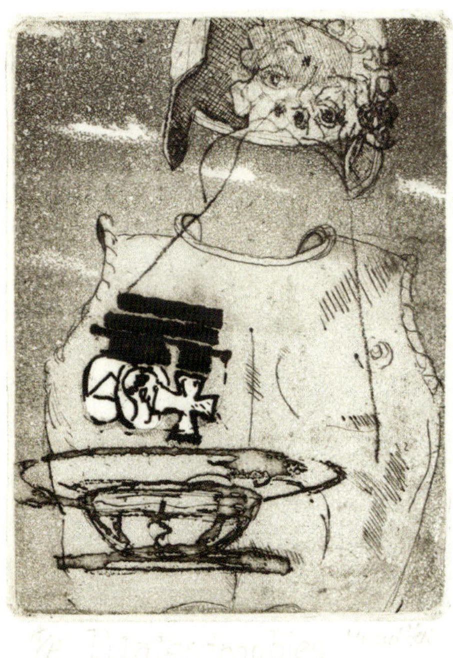

73. *'Pilate's troubles'* (from *A Simple Easter*), 1991, etching and aquatint, 10 x 7.5 cm

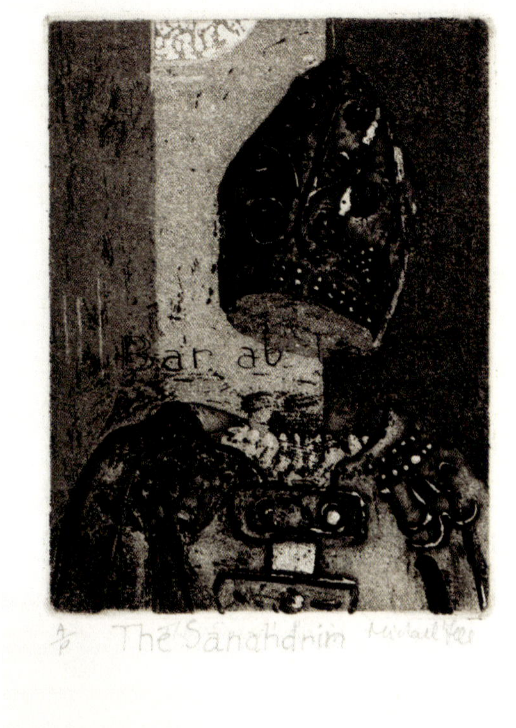

74. *'The Sanahdrin'* [*sic*] (from *A Simple Easter*), 1991, etching and aquatint, 10 x 7.5 cm

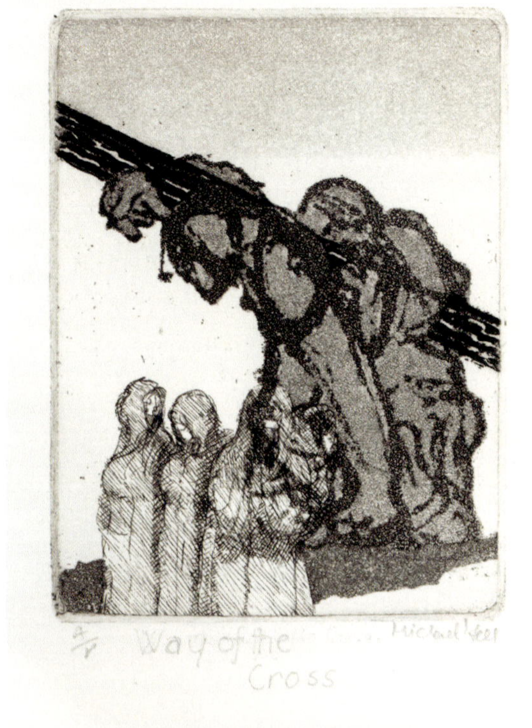

75. *'Way of the Cross'* (from *A Simple Easter*), 1991, etching and aquatint, 10 x 7.5 cm

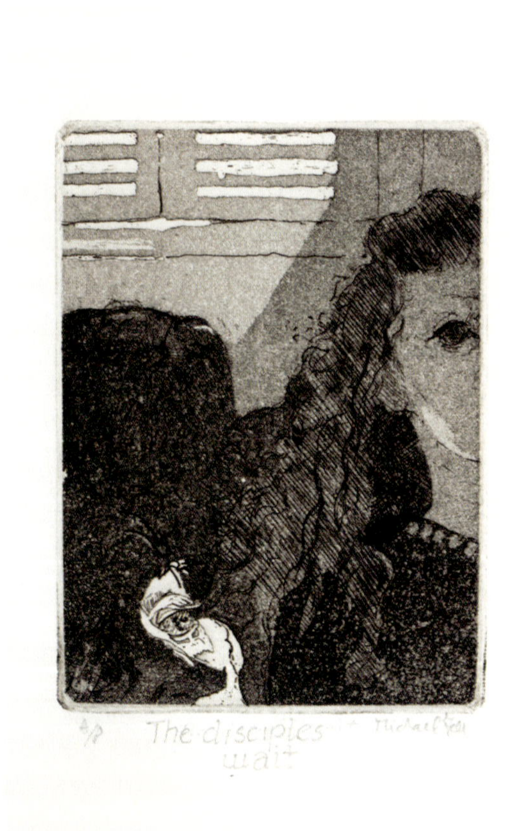

76. *'The disciples wait'* (from *A Simple Easter*), 1991, etching and aquatint, 10 x 7.5 cm

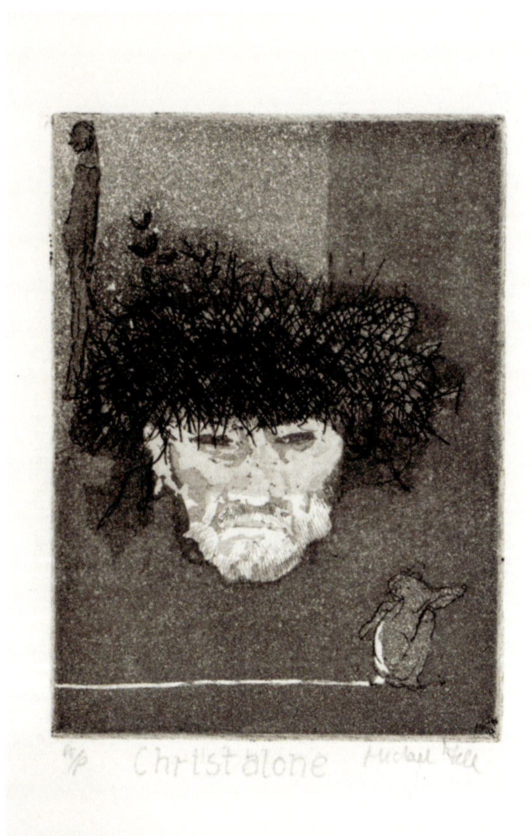

77. *'Christ alone'* (from *A Simple Easter*), 1991, etching and aquatint, 10 x 7.5 cm

'Way of the Cross' [75] A wonderfully strenuous portrayal in very heavily bitten aquatint of Christ struggling under the weight of the cross as he makes his way past onlookers to Golgotha, 'the place of the skull'.

'The disciples wait' [76] In a dark room, a shutter admitting strips of bright light. Conspicuously, one of the disciples is a woman, which conforms to the Gospel accounts. The plate dramatizes the anxious suspense in which Jesus's followers were held immediately after his death on the cross.

'Christ alone' [77] The most dramatic of the series: a brooding, Beethovenesque head illuminated against a dark aquatint ground, the crown of thorns a tangle of heavily bitten etched lines. This might more plausibly be a portrait of St Peter, repentant after having denied Christ three times, and therefore having emphatically abandoned him at this crisis. Neither interpretation explains the odd little animal outlined to the right of his head.

The Tomb [78] A cave in the rocky wall of a garden, with someone sitting on a bench outside it. The huge circular stone is to be rolled in front of the entrance (and subsequently rolled away). In a darker strip below, figures running. This seems to represent the Garden Tomb – the site of 'Gordon's Calvary,' just outside the Damascus Gate of Jerusalem, which General Gordon (of Khartoum) believed to be the true site of the Crucifixion. That has an upright rectangular opening. Fell offers an alternative version, with a lower entrance, on a second plate [79].

The Tomb [79] Alternative design, the entrance much lower and wider.

'The Tomb' [80] A tumbled shroud in a dark, stony cave.

'Jesus dies' [81] The plate cut in two, an agonized head divided on the halves.

'God's despair' [82] Inscribed in the plate 'Eil Eil leama [*sic*] sabachthani'. A distant view of the hill of Calvary with four crosses at its summit and

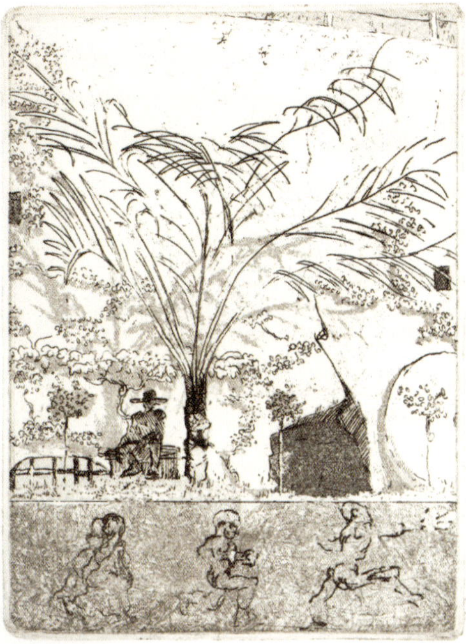

78. *The Tomb* (from *A Simple Easter*),
1991, etching and aquatint, 10 x 7.5 cm

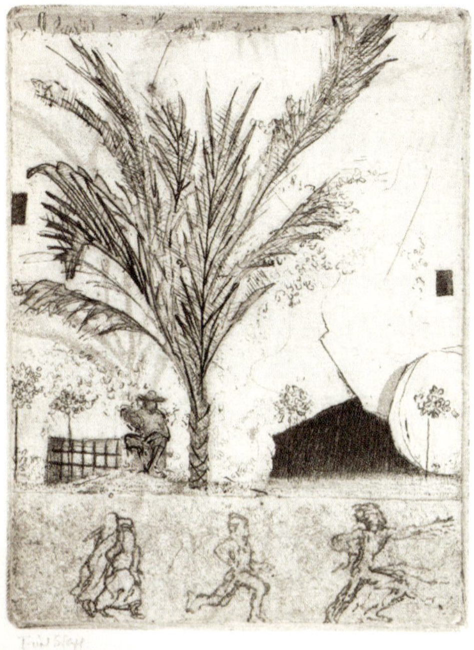

79. *The Tomb* (from *A Simple Easter*),
1991, etching and aquatint, 10 x 7.5 cm

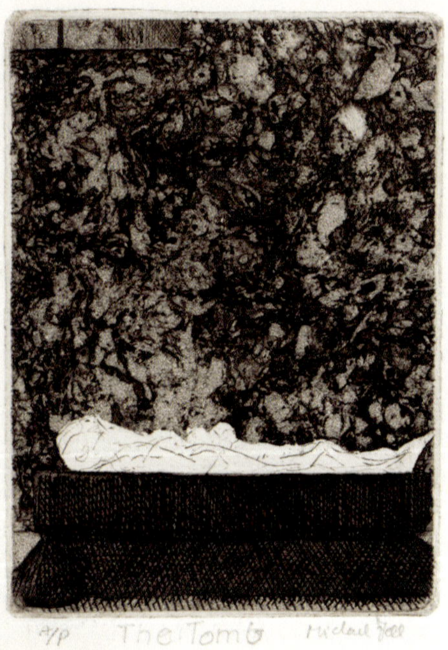

80. *'The Tomb'* (from *A Simple Easter*),
1991, etching and aquatint, 10 x 7.5 cm

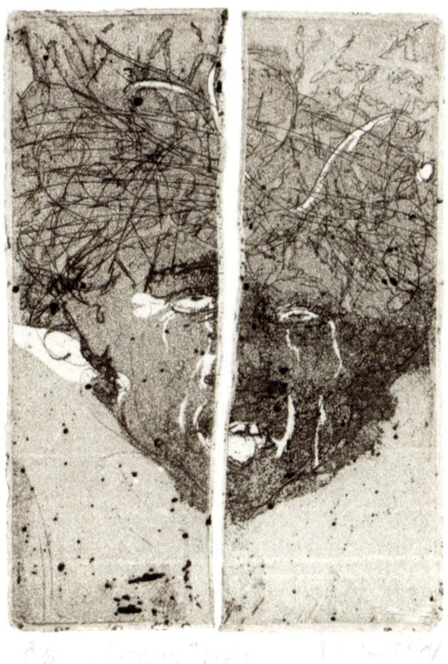

81. *'Jesus Dies'* (from *A Simple Easter*),
1991, etching and aquatint, 10 x 7.5 cm

a crowd of people. In the foreground a pair of figures, male and female, huddled in attitudes of despair. These are perhaps Mary, Christ's mother, and St John, 'the disciple whom Jesus loved', who are described as standing at the foot of the cross in John's Gospel (John 19:23, 26), and often shown like that in representations of the scene.

Christ's cross is traditionally shown between the two crosses of the pair of thieves alongside whom he was executed. The deeply personal and meditative tone of the whole series lends plausibility to the idea that the fourth cross is for the artist himself. The misspelling of the inscription must be simply a mistranscription of 'Eli, Eli, lama sabachthani' ('My God, my God, why hast thou forsaken me?').

'A Simple Easter' [83] Three figures under trees on a road signed 'Emmau[s]' – a reference to the story of two disciples joined by Jesus after his resurrection. They do not recognise him until he breaks bread at the inn in Emmaus where they have supper.

'And He was parted from them' (Luke 24:51) [84] An enigmatic image: Christ leaves the disciples, having appeared to them after his resurrection. He seems to be disappearing as we look, half his face invisible. Incongruously, the outline of a dog and a pattern of leaves share the plate with this image.

'St Peter's Faith' [85] Not a part of the narrative sequence: an intimate image of Christ stooping compassionately to embrace the disciple, who is seen from above, only the top of his head and his arms visible, outstretched to embrace the Saviour. St Peter was the disciple whom he delegated to be the founder of his Church on Earth.

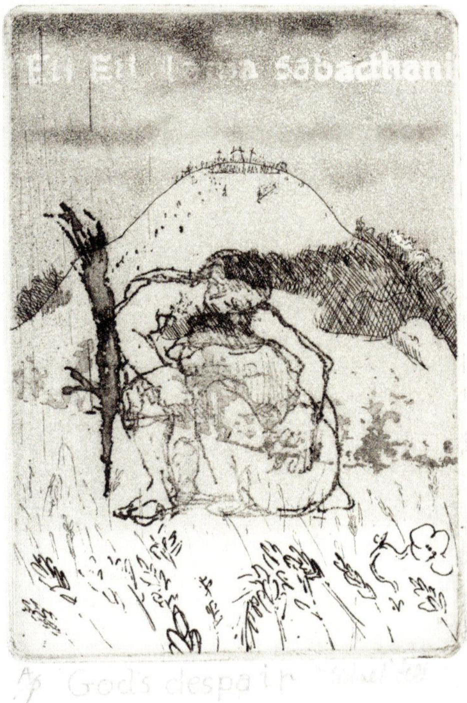

82. *'God's despair'* (from *A Simple Easter*), 1991, etching and aquatint, 10 x 7.5 cm

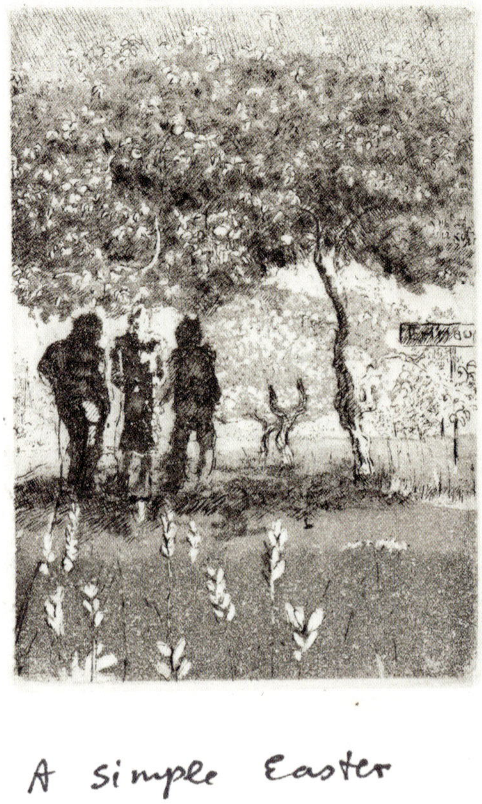

83. *'A Simple Easter'* (from *A Simple Easter*), 1991, etching and aquatint, 10 x 7.5 cm

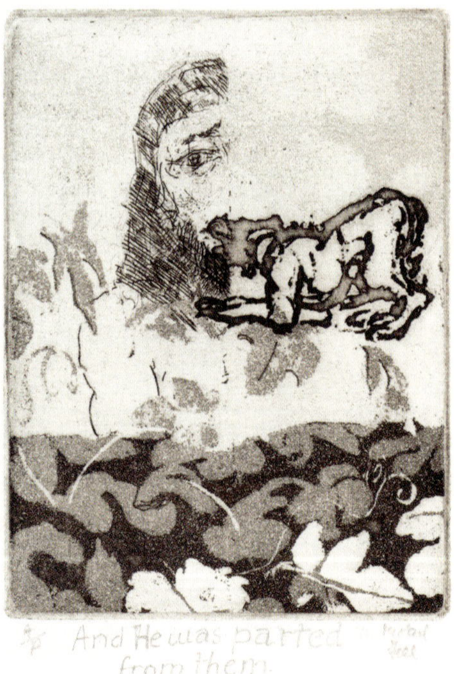

84. *'And He was parted from them'* (from *A Simple Easter*), 1991, etching and aquatint, 10 x 7.5 cm

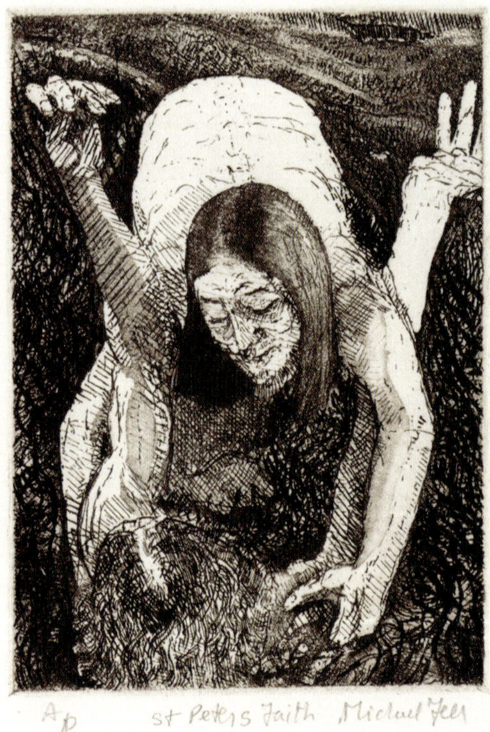

85. *'St Peter's Faith'*, 1991, etching and aquatint, 10 x 7 cm

The Gates of Heaven

This subject exists as a print in at least two quite different versions, one etching only [86], the other etching and aquatint [87]. The basic elements are the same in both: a straggling line of people, men, women and children, wait as if in a supermarket queue to be welcomed by a little old man, attended in one version by a tall winged figure (who resembles the artist himself), into an entrance lit, comically, by an old-fashioned electric light with a conical shade.

The entrance is a mere archway, a loop apparently of thin metal, with nothing beyond it. In the impression of the subject with aquatint there is beyond the arch a bright light that almost obliterates the tall winged figure – the Recording Angel? – who accompanies St Peter, and spills out on to the leading individuals in the queue. The subject etched with no aquatint has more even lighting throughout, and the angel, not quite so tall, is dark against it.

The people in the queue are different in the two impressions, and so cannot be reworkings of the same etching. They are clearly individualised: children playing, women chatting over a pram, men in trilbies and overcoats, a dog being pushed in a wheelbarrow. The randomness of the individuals is the point of the work, a synthesis, as it were, of all the chance observations recorded in Fell's early prints of London scenes. The format of the queue is a favourite of Fell's: he used it notably in *Olivier Stalls* [3], where a line of people wait to be admitted to the performance (a man is looking at his watch, and a young woman sits patiently in a burst of light), and the *Painting of the Priest* [6], which includes a colourful queue of communicants led by a young acolyte holding a tall candle. Whether waiting for an event or expecting divine succour, all humankind is, consciously or unconsciously, in a state of anticipation. If this seems to impose a benevolent purpose on our experience, Fell's *Crucifixus* [88] offers a very much more ambiguous interpretation of things.

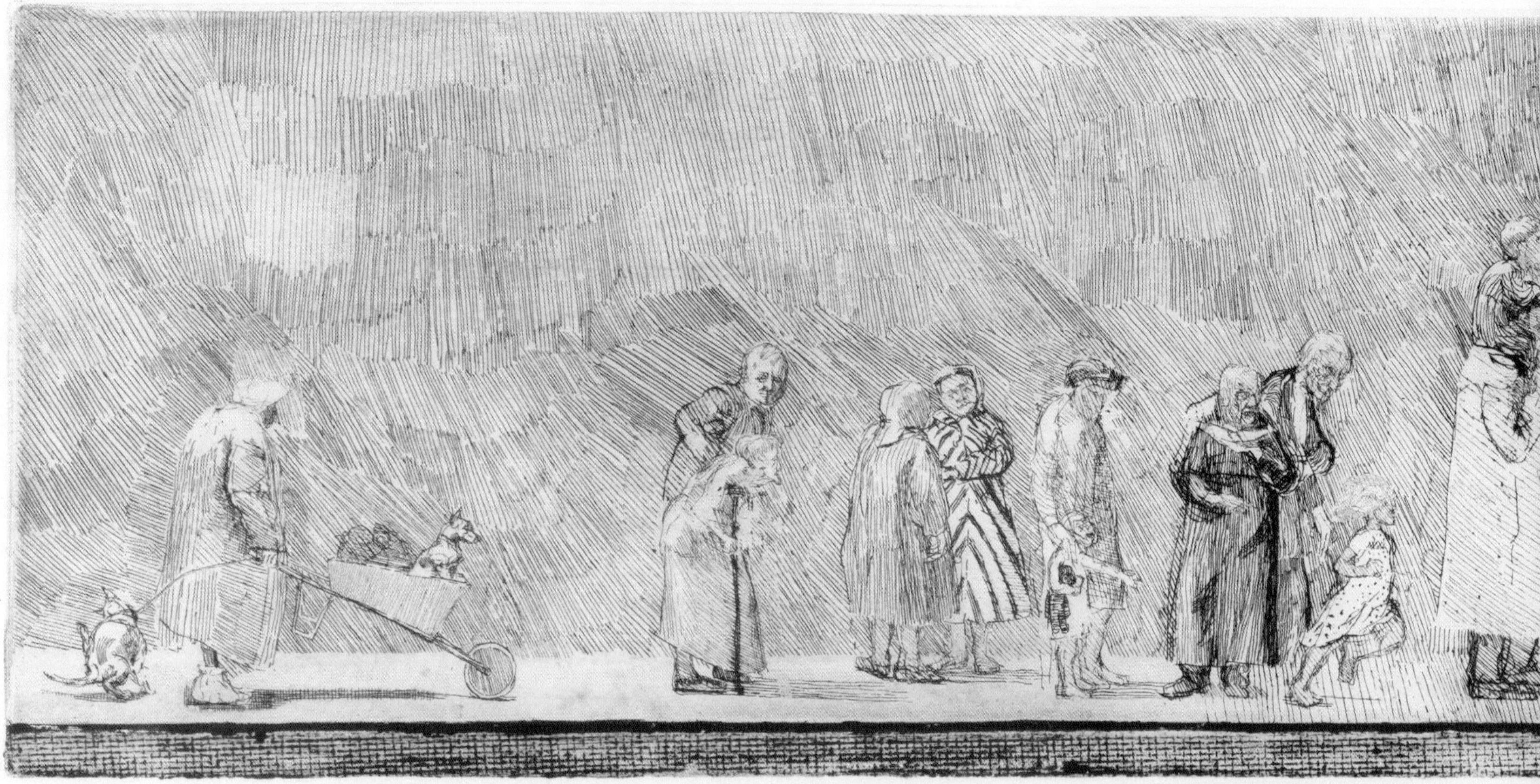

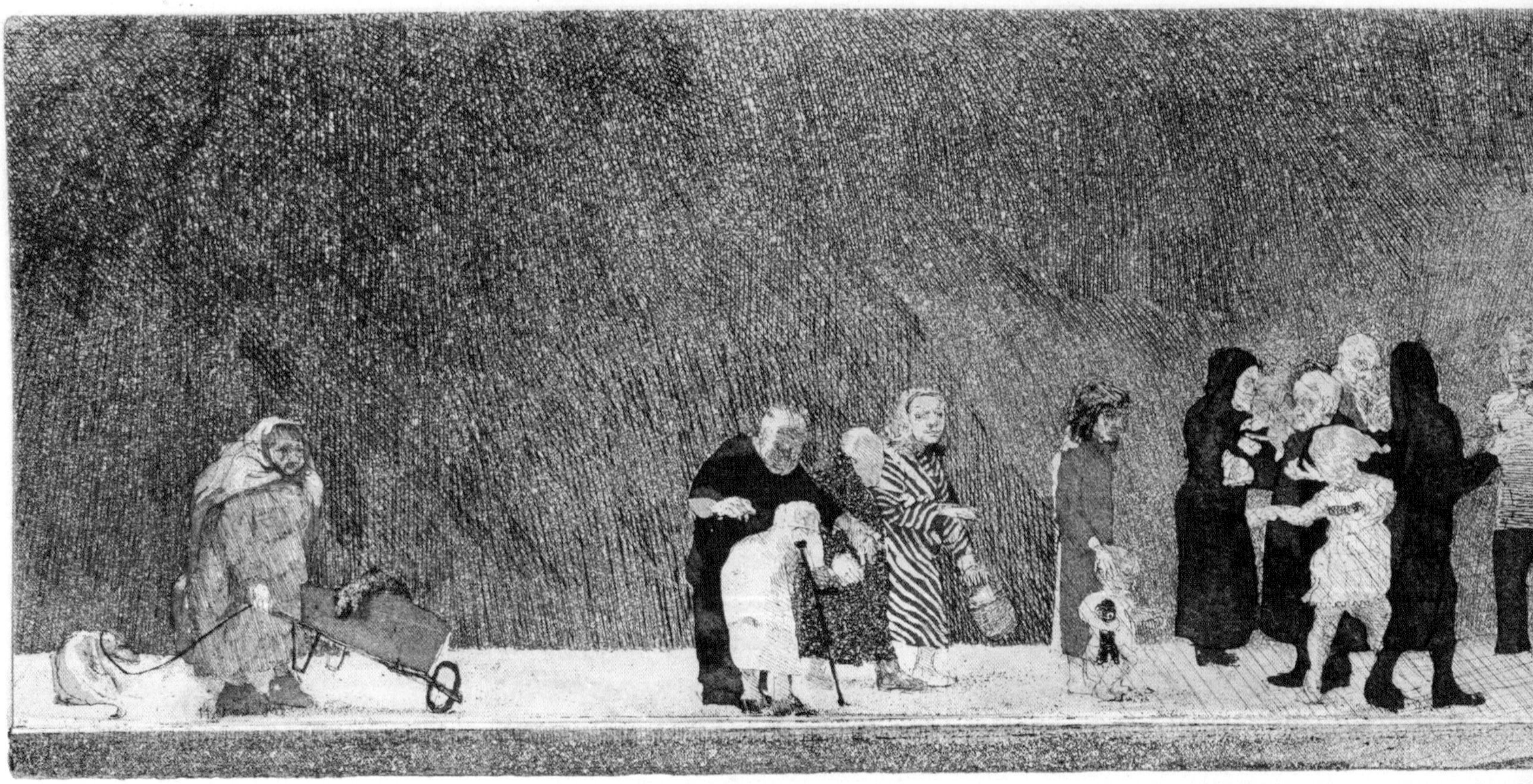

Top: 86. *The Gates of Heaven I*, early 1970s, etching, 12 x 49 cm

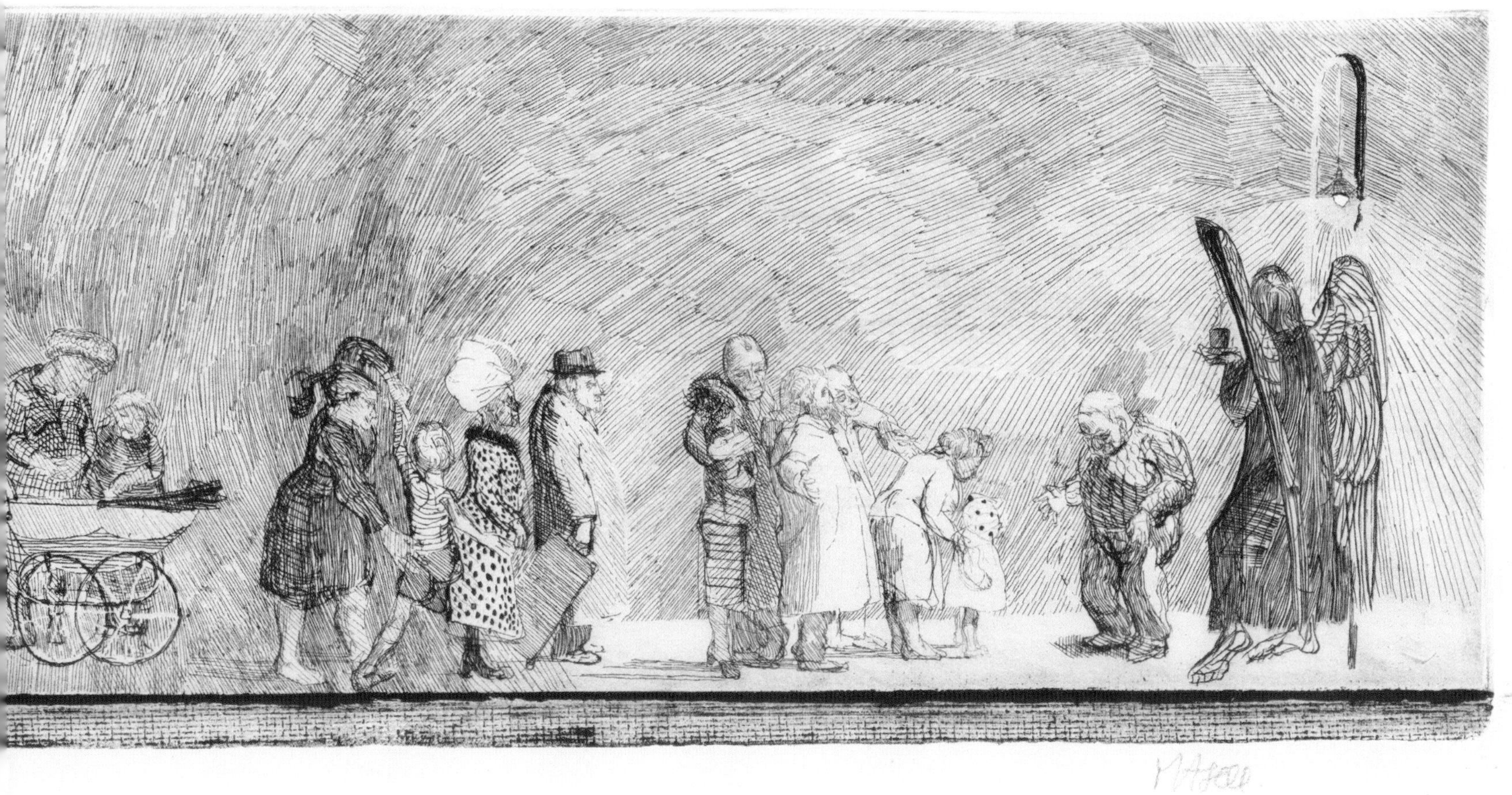

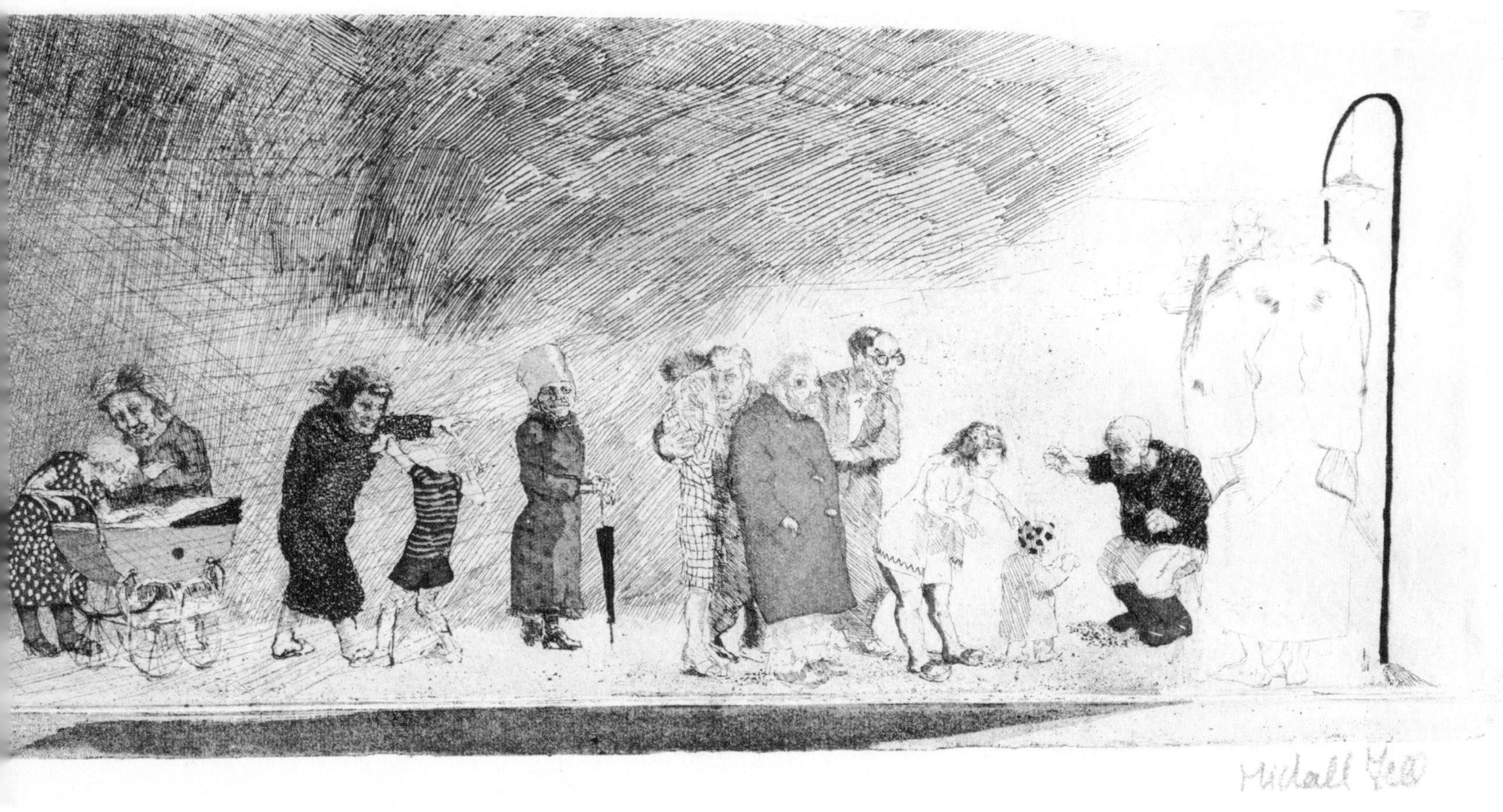

Above: 87. *The Gates of Heaven II*, early 1970s, etching and aquatint, 12 x 49 cm

Crucifixus

The climax of Fell's lifelong examination of his Catholic faith is the large canvas that is given a very late date – 2023 – in the catalogue of his works, with the title *Crucifixus* [88]. The word, meaning 'He was crucified', comes from the Creed, or formal declaration of faith, in the Latin Mass. Despite its late date this was, like all Fell's major pictures, the product of a long-drawn-out gestation. It might, indeed, take 'Credo' as its title, covering as it does a broad panorama of ideas related to Christianity and the faith that underlay Fell's thinking throughout his life.

It has in common with innumerable Christian images a representation of the Crucifixion itself, but in a far from common form. Christ appears not on the cross but hanging in space, apparently pinned to the night sky beneath Pontius Pilate's mocking label, in French – 'Roi des Juifs', 'King of the Jews'. He is naked, bereft even of a loin cloth, though the stark prickles of the crown of thorns are bursting into green leaf. In the depths of space behind him the planet Earth looks like a distant moon, and in front of him a young woman seated in the night sky on a low, probably straw-bottomed chair, under a red umbrella, holds up her baby son to the admiration of the miscellaneous crowds below: a highly unconventional, and moving, image of the Virgin and Child. Just as Pilate's notice appears in French, so the red umbrella situates the whole vision in the street market of Vic Fezensac: compare a similar umbrella in *Painting of the Priest* [6], which presents a ceremony in the church of St Pierre in that town.

Behind the Virgin and Child the dark sky is fragmented into oscillating irregular planes which we must read as the veil of the Temple, 'rent in twain', according to St Matthew, 'from the top to the bottom', when 'the earth did quake, and the rocks were rent; and the graves were opened'. The Chi Rho, or symbol of Christ (the first two letters of his name in Greek), hangs in the air between the Child and the Crucifix, and floating in space between sky and earth an enormous Star of David in yellow lines links the objects of veneration above with the teeming complexity of life below.

A man in red, who surely represents the artist himself, brings an offering of small trees to the Virgin, while before him the shepherds 'abiding in the fields' – evidently modern Gascon country people – are

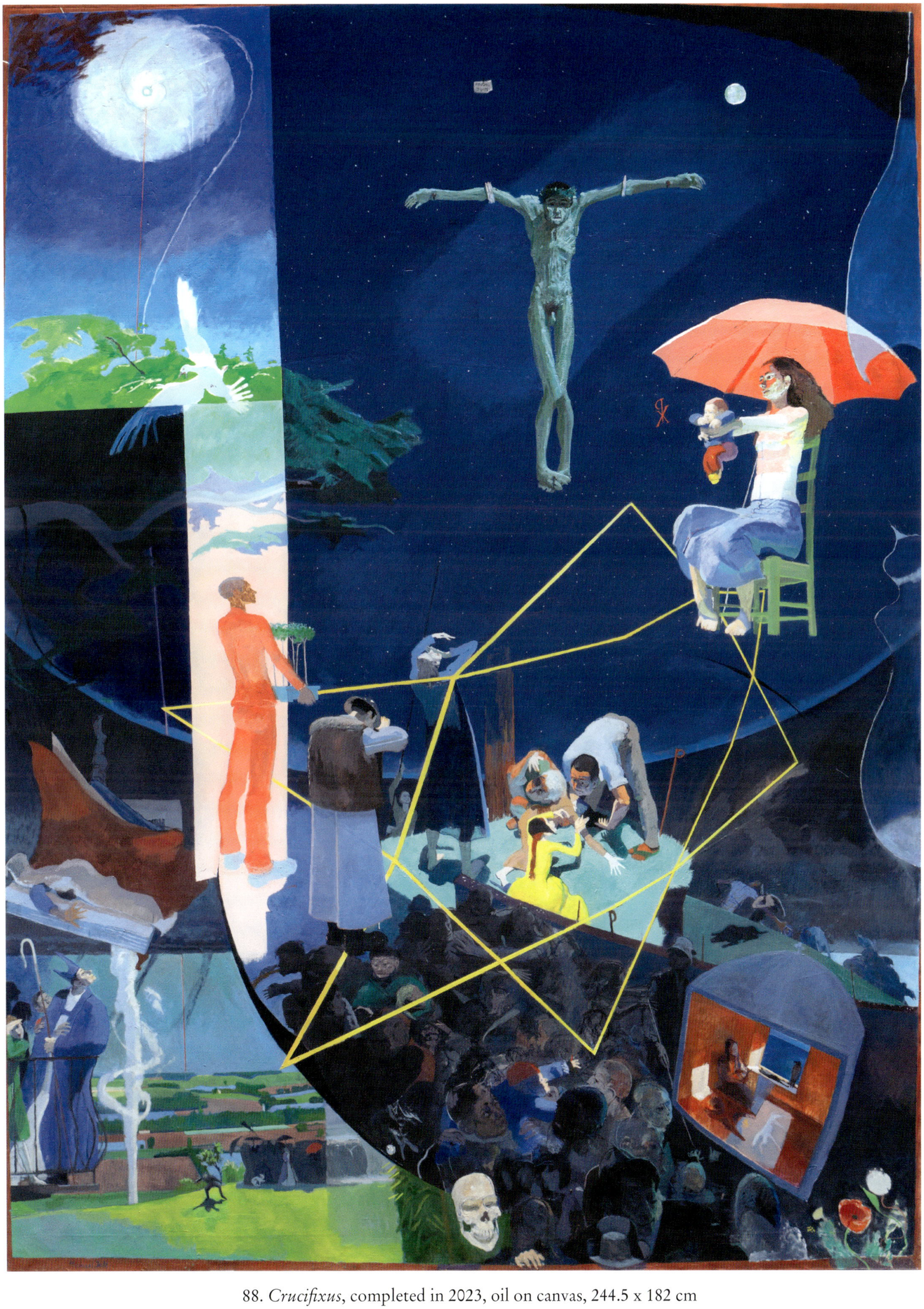

88. *Crucifixus*, completed in 2023, oil on canvas, 244.5 x 182 cm

dazzled by the light of a divine revelation shared with them by Mary Magdalen (in yellow): Mary was the devoted follower who was the first to see the resurrected Christ in the garden on Easter morning. An anguished figure, tossing sleepless in bed under a red blanket, has been interpreted as the guilt-ridden Judas Iscariot, and below, a bishop in a blue cope, on a balcony overlooking Fell's own Gascon landscape, stands next to a cloudy pillar, presumably referring to the phenomenon that accompanied the Israelites on their journey through the wilderness from exile in Egypt. Vertically above, a line links the dove symbolising the Holy Spirit and a Sun that we must understand as the presence of the all-powerful Godhead itself.

Occupying much of the lower right corner of the canvas is a crowd of figures partly obscured by darkness and dominated by a grinning death's head, which is placed exactly in the centre of the bottom edge of the picture. This lends the scene a macabre atmosphere that recalls work by the Belgian artist James Ensor (1860–1949). Some of the milling throng seem to be looking into an enclosed red room as though they were watching television. A window opens on to a view over an extensive calm blue sea, and on the sill sits a large black bird. Is this the raven of Edgar Allen Poe's poem, croaking for those who will listen 'Nevermore'? The picture doesn't gratify us with easy answers to any of its questions.

Painting

Painting

William Packer

Artists are creatures of the times through which they live and work, formed by the times even should they choose to react consciously against them, as some always will. All art is modern in its moment, or contemporary if you prefer, and shot through with its spirit, whether intended or not. Time leaves its mark, and the accuracy with which the experienced eye may, just by the look of it, set a work of art within a narrow span, is unremarkable. Over a long career one artist may follow a winding path with many sidetracks as the work grows and changes and develops, this way and that; another may follow a straight, un-diverted, single-minded course. Either is simply a function of temperament and circumstance. But whichever it may be, two things should be kept in mind. Any extended body of work, whether it vary markedly over the years in technique, subject interest or material, or remain within a narrow and consistent practice, will in all likelihood hang together all of a piece, the product of the same unifying hand and eye, brain and sensibility. It will also bear that more particular sense of its own identifiable moment, early, middle or late.

And Michael Fell was an artist of stimulating times, as perhaps they always are. Born early in 1939, he would, if fit, have still been eligible for National Service, but a place secured in higher education was ground enough for deferment if requested, which would seem to have been his case. The later 1950s thus saw him enrolled instead on the then standard two-year multi-disciplinary Intermediate Course at St Martin's School of Art, with a further two years in prospect for the more specialised National Diploma in Design (NDD) – presumably, for him, in Painting.

St Martin's at that time was, in its own eyes at least, the leading art school in London, if not the country: the Slade, the Royal College and the Royal Academy Schools were by then principally postgraduate institutions. And it would have been a lively place, as most art schools were, with its complement of older post-National Service students, along with many much younger, for one could be admitted at fifteen with no more qualification than the contents of one's portfolio. In consequence there would have been no formal hierarchy of age, only of practical experience and expertise. The tutors were artists too, and their knowledge and advice passed on quite as much by incidental conversation and example as by lecture or precept.

Nor was there over-much concern for certificates and diplomas: the work itself was the thing, and students came and went. The great museums and collections were on the doorstep, the commercial contemporary galleries where so much was going on, so much was new, just round the corner. Interests were shared informally, by word of mouth. As in all healthy institutions of education, the students went a very long way in educating themselves.

But the actual teaching regime, especially on that early course, was still set on the practical disciplines of craft, technique and close observation, with the life room and the model at its heart. I remember it well – life drawing of course, but also anatomy, perspective, architecture, life-modelling, casting and carving, lettering, a chosen craft (usually either printmaking or pottery), all subject to external examination before graduation to the specialisation of the NDD. One can see, all too well, how art school might have felt at once unsettling, unstructured and restrictive, and hardly be surprised by Michael's dropping out.

Perhaps it was simply a case of his not being ready, for the interest, indeed the ambition, clearly remained fully alive, and he continued to paint on his own account. After all, the late 1950s and early 1960s were years of significant shifts and movements in the visual arts, caught as they were in the cross-currents of Abstract Expressionism, Minimalism, early Conceptualism, Neo-Expressionism, Neo-Romanticism, and Pop Art – Pollock, Bacon, Vaughan, Sutherland, Rothko, Warhol, Hockney. It would all seep in. Italy was hardly a cultural desert, and the next several years Michael spent living in Rome and Florence would have been an education in itself. Was a visit ever made to a Venice Biennale? Was informal contact made with the British School at Rome? One imagines he would find its intriguing scholarly mix of archaeology, history, architecture and fine art especially sympathetic.

Whatever the reason, the experience in the interval had clearly confirmed Michael in his commitment to being an artist and a painter. He returned to London, and in 1965 enrolled on the painting and printmaking course at the City & Guilds Art School in Kennington, where Elizabeth Fitz Gerald was the Principal. It is significant that the City & Guilds, with its strong tradition not just in Fine Art but also across the broad range of the Fine and Applied Crafts, was then as now prominent among the handful of accredited art schools that remained quite independent of the State system of higher education. And 1965 was the moment at which, in the wake of the Summerson and Coldstream Reports to the Ministry of Education, those art schools within the system, in which St Martin's was of course so prominent, were about to embark on a radical programme of structural and curricular reform that would soon see the model banished from the life room, and freedom reign. The City & Guilds stayed as it was. The model remained, and so too, still in place for Michael now to follow, did that old more disciplined regime, with its emphasis on drawing, observation and technical probity, that he had walked away from only those few years before. He left in 1968, but would return as a tutor in the 1970s, and remain, eventually as Head of Foundation, until in the 1990s France at last called him away.

William Coldstream, distinguished painter himself and for many years Principal of the Slade, once remarked that 'the longer one remained a student, the longer one went on making student work'. A hard, yet in Michael's case a significant truth. For in the interval between his leaving St Martin's and enrolling at the City & Guilds he had continued to draw and paint, though the work was now affected by informal contact with friends and other artists, by what he sought out in galleries and churches or simply chanced to come across in the meantime, to say nothing of the general, bracing experience of being out and on his own in the world.

So by 1965, at twenty-six, with a body of work and the experience that came with it already behind him, he was rather out of the run to begin again as a student. But he was at least now clearer in his mind not only of the direction he should take but of what he needed to know and learn. And it is also clear that it was from this decisive point, through the particular course he undertook, that he would march equally in step with whatever his practice as a painter might prove to be. None of that earlier independent work is to hand, but what there is from this second and sustained period, though demonstrably still the work of a student, is by no means the work of a novice seeking a path to follow, but rather that of an already developed sensibility, and a mind that knew not only what it wanted but where to find it. And the lasting importance to Michael of that received instruction and foundation, late as it was, would find tacit acknowledgement in all he ever did.

And there is a sense in this work of the late 1960s, and its subsequent transition into renewed individuality and artistic independence in the 1970s, of a sympathetic identification, not with the predominant movements of the moment – though one might occasionally catch their flavour, and even their influence – but rather with the quieter figurative and narrative character of the earlier modern British School, its subjects drawn from close observation of the natural world, the human figure, and ordinary daily life. It is committedly figurative painting, impressionist in the broadest sense rather than expressionist, more tonal than colourful – though colour is always a central concern – and incidental and anecdotal, even picaresque, in its narrative, with nods to Degas, Forain, Sickert, Whistler and Wilson Steer.

It is the tradition instinct in the generation of artist-teachers who had held sway under that older pre-reformation art school dispensation, and which still clung on at City & Guilds and a few schools elsewhere, both outside the State system – at Heatherley's in Chelsea, the Byam Shaw in Holloway, and the RA Schools – and, for a while at least, one or two within the State system – Camberwell, Falmouth, Colchester. So one thinks not just of Roger de Grey but also of his late colleagues Ruskin Spear, Rodrigo Moynihan and Carel Weight at the Royal College; of Coldstream, Euan Uglow and Patrick George at the Slade; and James Fitton, Edward Bawden and Leonard Rosoman at the Academy. And there are too the artists Michael came to know as fellow teachers, or socially, especially after his move to Bungay in the 1980s – Richard Bawden, Peter Coker and Sargy Mann. Altogether it is a tradition that, far from dead, remains a powerful influence particularly on contemporary English painting, for all that today it passes for the most part critically and institutionally unremarked.

But Michael's work of those crucial, formative years at City & Guilds is of interest in more than just one respect. His willing submission to the demanding technical disciplines of printmaking, and to those of etching in particular, bears witness enough to his search for formal structure and control, yet the rapid growth in his confidence and technical assurance as a painter is no less remarkable. And with it too came a steady broadening in his scope of reference and interest that would only increase as time moved on.

The model posed in the life room was still a staple of student instruction. In *Nude* [94] there he is in his blue underpants, seen from behind, gently and somewhat oddly *contrapposto*, leaning upon a bicycle. Beyond, a fellow student at his easel across the studio sets the space. It is hardly more than an oil sketch, and there is still much to sort out between leg, back and bike, and perhaps the feet; but the freshness in the paint, the ease of handling, and the unforced accomplishment in the statement of the figures are striking – and are what count.

And then there is that other regular punctuation of art school life, the day out in the field – Smithfield and its meat market in this case [10] – sketchbook and *plein-air* kit in hand. But any market, busy street or local park would do, as in *Summer Football* [89]. Studies made on the spot might be worked up later back in the studio, either on their own merit and interest or as reference for larger narrative elaboration – of which student exercise Michael's costermonger's barrow in *A Vegetable Stall* [95] is an entirely typical example.

But rather more to the point is the degree to which he would continue to follow this particular strain or thread of interest – the imagined narrative composition confected from multiple references, both primary and secondary. He would pick it up and drop it, only to return to it again and again, not just in the immediately succeeding years but throughout his life. The large family parties and French café scenes left unfinished at his death, such as *Benoit's Christmas Party* [102], are not a world away from those of his first maturity as an artist. For even in those pictures of the early 1970s, in their complexity of composition, painterly sophistication and graphic wit, we find the same but younger artist growing so rapidly in confidence and authority. The lessons of close observation and careful note had been well learnt.

In *Looking into a Supermarket* [96] a gang of boisterous children play and squabble in the evening gloom outside, oblivious to the bright retail bustle within. Dark against bright, shadow into light is no mean challenge to a painter, and one Michael would regularly set himself. But no less so,

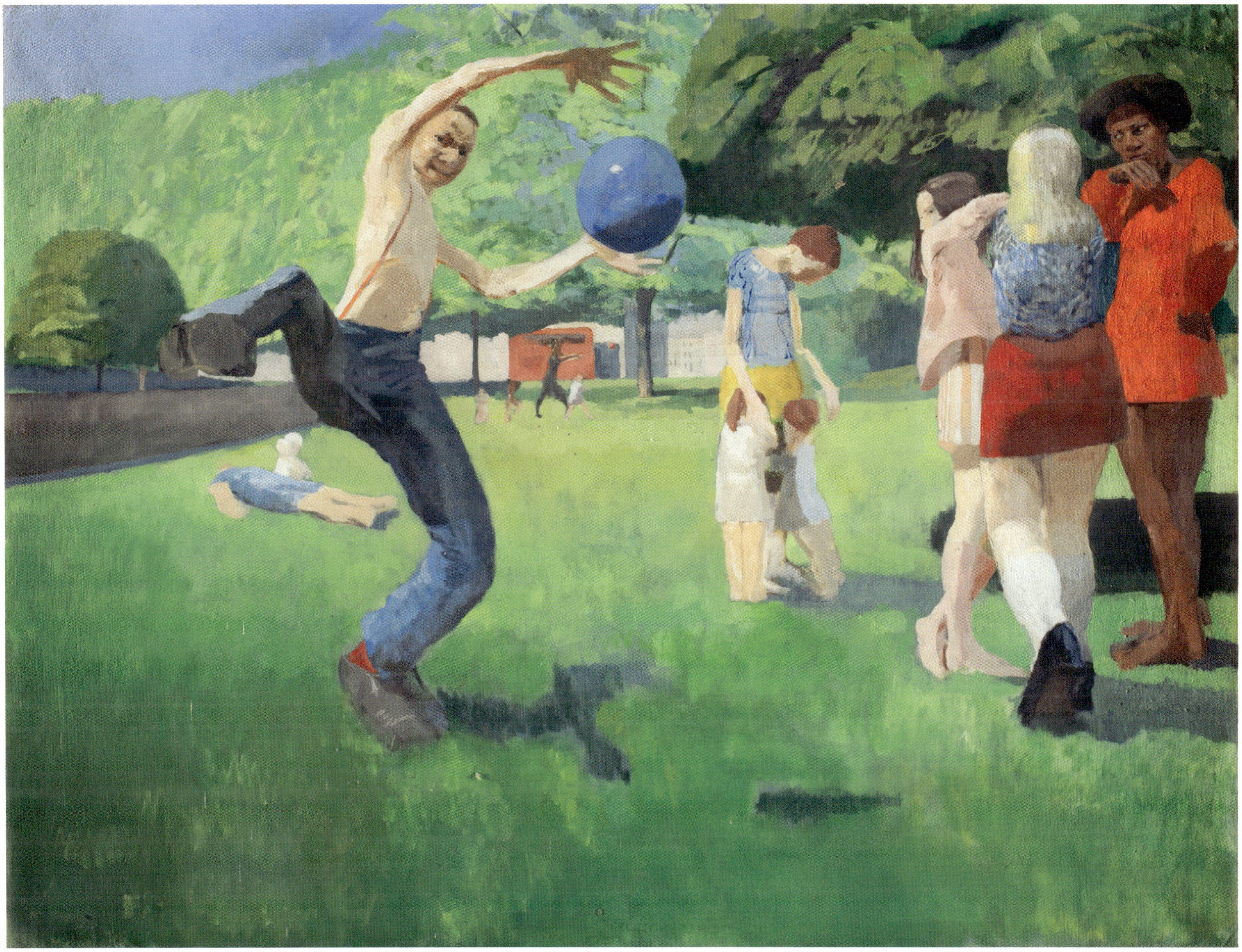

89. *Summer Football*, 1971, oil on canvas, 74 x 100 cm

with its shifting eye levels, is that tumble of figures in *Tube Train* [12] into a carriage on the Underground, an image quite remarkable in its pictorial organisation and resolution. Strong in the somewhat mannered drawing, beautiful in the paint and in the detail, it is also very funny, its humour resting quite as much in the way as the what of its expression.

And so Michael would continue, getting ever stronger and more adventurous in the liberties he would take not just in the games played with narrative and imagery but with the formalities of pictorial space and structure, tone and colour, light and dark. The dim interior, the spotlight and the shadow, indeed the shared and incidental public space, would be for him a lifelong staple and pictorial resort. But they would never be quite enough in themselves. There would be no sustained development of any particular radical approach or manner, but instead a shift of preoccupation for a while, and a crossing-over or sideways step to something more mundane, straightforward, ordinary, as circumstance allowed – a restorative return as it might be, though one no less serious in intention and ambition, to first principles. The move in the 1980s from Kennington to the large Music House at Bungay with his young family brought with it fresh pictorial material and opportunity: see *Robert at the Music House* [16]. And with Suffolk, just as with the permanent move to France some dozen years on, came a garden and a landscape to be painted for their own sake. There were wife and children to draw and paint. Yet the glimpse through the bannisters to the dark space beyond in *Painting at the Music House* [90] is hardly a world away from the mother with her child in *St John Southworth in Westminster Cathedral* [69] in the gloom of the Cathedral peering through a grille at the memorial figure on the tomb. And there was always the etching to keep experiment and pictorial adventure alive.

Indeed, by a strange inversion of normal expectation, it is with Michael as etcher that, far from working through the process stage by discrete stage, we find him at his more intuitively inventive. As painter, rich though his paint may be on the surface, and subtly inflected where need be in the handling and the detail, we often see him working directly to a carefully prescribed scheme. Oil paint of course is both the most flexible and the most forgiving of the pictorial media, print in general far

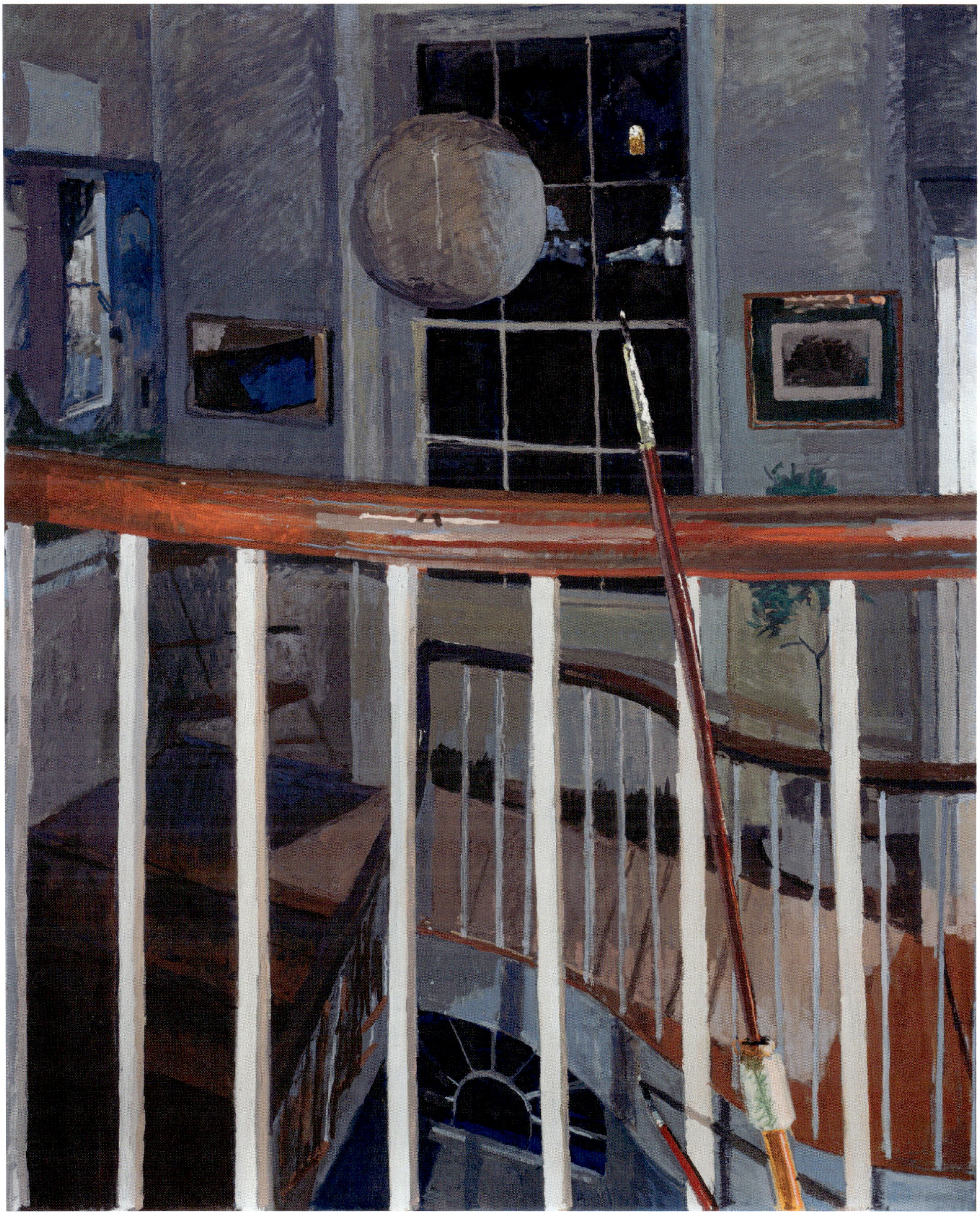

90. *Painting at the Music House*, late 1980s, oil on canvas, 89 x 74 cm

less so; but, that said, etching, with its scope for re-biting, scraping out, benign accident and experiment, is at the more generous end of the range. And of the various kinds of subject-matter that would draw Michael as a painter now this way, now that – the observed figure, the domestic circumstance, the landscape, townscape and still life – it was in the field of the imaginative figurative composition, drawn on reference taken from many sources, whether primary or secondary, and collage-like across a sometimes fractured or disrupted space, that the to-and-fro between print and paint proved most fruitful, radical and inventive.

He was never afraid of working on an ample scale, a relief perhaps from the narrower limits of the print, but even the somewhat smaller of these larger compositions carry a considerable visual punch. And whether the narrative they present occupies a coherent pictorial space or one more ambiguous and constricted, or even manifestly and deliberately inconsistent, they have much in common.

The narrative is inexplicit, unresolved, the mood, if not actively sinister, at the very least disconcerting. What, quite, is going on? In *Chess at Rozès* [91] is it check-mate and the game over? The thin lady's imperious flourish might well suggest so, her opponent's serene concentration quite otherwise. Who once was this ecclesiastic laid out on his tomb in scarlet vestment and black cap [69]? And in *Olivier Stalls* [3] quite where and what is going on, with its ghostly row of figures sitting rather as if in a waiting room? And are those lively musicians off to one side, playing away to the world beyond, a conscious art-historical nod to Sickert and his Pierrots on the Pier at Brighton? Michael didn't care to date his paintings, so any chronology is loosely general and circumstantial, but a painting of two distinct halves, of pilgrims to Lourdes from the 2000s, makes clear that Michael continued to produce such work, both in form and narrative, throughout his career [92].

But the narrative, or rather the mystery of it, is only a part of the matter, for all that it is the most likely part to command casual attention. And the putting together of it in its pictorial structure and organisation is a kind of narrative in itself. There is the broad centre of the piece that seems often to be left largely to look after itself. The nominal interest drifts to the sides and edges, and into the corners – but then all is interesting

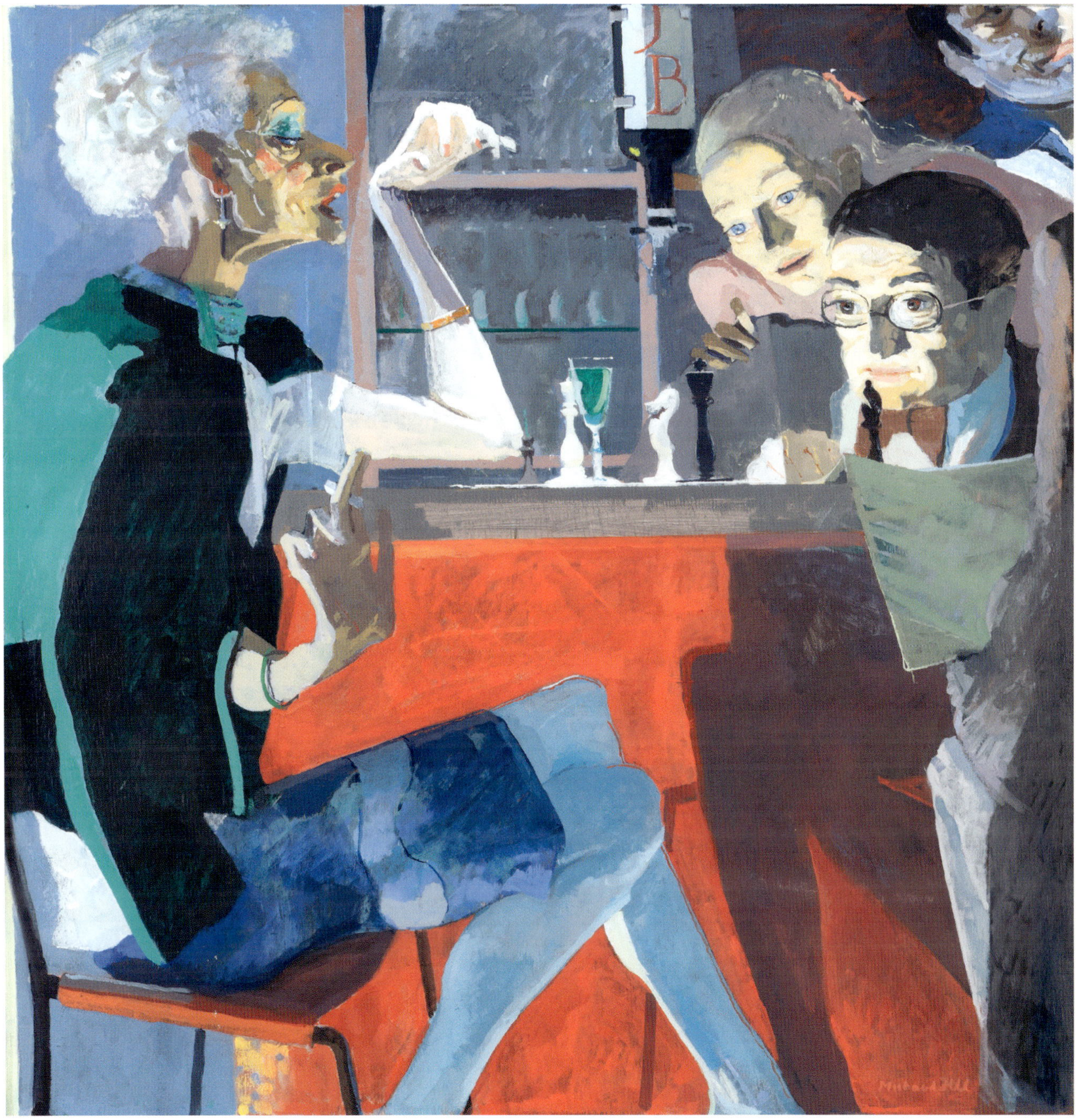

91. *Chess at Rozès*, late 2000s, oil on canvas, 60 x 60 cm

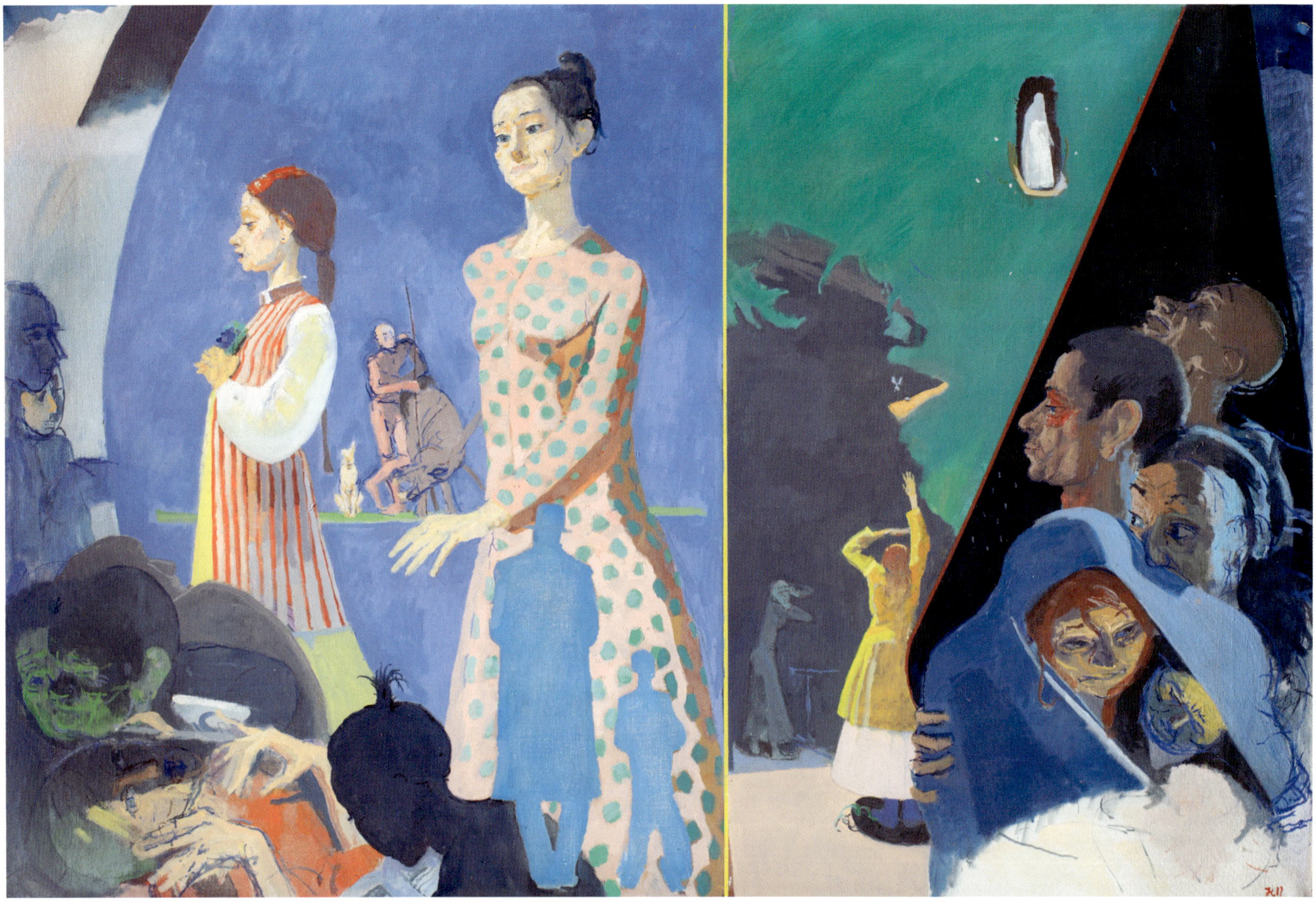

92. *Lourdes*, 2010s, oil on canvas, 79 x 119 cm

nevertheless, even the spaces and absences, the shadows and reflections. Figures turn away, move apart. Between the players at chess there is only the warm shadow cast by that elegantly thin lady's cool-blue crossed legs [91]. Beyond the picture, those musicians play to an audience out of sight. In *Lourdes* [92] the pilgrims approach an unseen shrine. Mother and child lean from the shadows of the church behind them and into the light, peering intently into the lowest, farthest, corner of the picture, transfixed by the cold pale face of the bright figure stretched out beneath them.

Olivier Stalls [3], at some 6 feet long and 4 feet tall, one of Michael's larger paintings, is quite as intriguing in what it is about, yet perhaps more complex than any in the formal problems it sets itself. Most of its upper part is occupied by an otherwise dark and empty wall, relieved only by a spot-lit notice indicating a row of seats in the stalls of the Olivier Theatre. But that wall, we then realise, is interrupted and the space in front of it formally articulated by what one takes to be two glass panels, one vertical down at the left-hand side of the painting, and another, somehow set behind it, running along the greater part of the lower edge. So we now read those shadowy figures not as a figment but as their reflection, sitting in a row behind us sheltering from the sun. In the bottom corner where the two panels cross are two heads tilted this way and that, one that of a young woman listening intently to the music, the other of her reflection in the glass behind her. And where screen and wall end not quite together towards the farther side, the musicians play away unobscured before another vertical panel intervenes, and the young woman's reflected face, now somewhat distorted, appears in the lower corner once again. A thin diagonal line, top left to lower right, arbitrarily establishes the picture plane and pulls all together.

The drawing, the handling of paint and surface, the control of colour, pitch and tone, light and shade, are again consistent in all these figurative compositions of whatever stage in Michael's career, founded on close observation later enhanced and manipulated back in the studio. And to speak of drawing in this context is to speak not of a distinct exercise, study or preparation but as drawing in and with the paint itself. With Michael it is wonderfully direct and to the point, vigorous and assured. But more than just a demonstration of technical accuracy and conviction, to say nothing of its skill, it is all the more remarkable for the graphic liberties he then takes in the disposition of the figures in his narratives. For there is quite naturally much of the illustrator in the relish he takes, sometimes wicked, sometimes amused, but always based on close observation and long experience, in his mannered emphasis or exaggeration of pose, gesture and expression – the disdainful sneer and pointed angularity of the lady at the chess board, the puffed cheek and bulging eye of the oboist, the elegant tilt and sway of the slim clarinettist – all so beautifully modelled in the paint.

This graphic command is no less evident in all his work, but it makes him no less of a painter for that. Rather, in this intuitive technical accommodation and reconciliation between painting, drawing and print, it is simply a natural demonstration of Michael's essential temperament and disposition as an artist. He makes great play with light almost as an image in itself in setting it sharply against deepest shadow. Colour, for all its apparent brightness, is in large part pitched low and light-absorbent; and though rich in the paint itself, he disposes colour often laid, either flat and unmodulated across broad areas of the painting, or its detail shrouded in shadow. Either way, colour is always contained, clean, clear and set in its place, every image carefully deliberated to point and serve the narrative. It may appear simple, but deceptively so, for here is painting of great subtlety: to pitch one colour effectively to sing against another, or set a tone precisely to set a sweet and gentle contrast, and all to serve the greater purpose of the painting, is no small thing.

While the narrative paintings make these points most clearly, in more nuanced and implicit form they apply no less to the landscapes and the domestic subjects and later compositions. And while the general palette might lighten, the tonal pitch lift, especially so after the permanent move to France, the technical approach would remain essentially the same. Though now somewhat looser in the statement and general handling, and the paint thinner on the surface, form and colour would be no less contained within the line, and the formal fascination with the play of light no less evident. Indeed nowhere is the demonstration more apparent than in Michael's enduring painterly delight in his pond at Barrère, which with its lilies and ornamental fish would become a particular preoccupation and subject to which he frequently returned, so much so as to produce in itself a distinct and significant body of work [54, 60, 61].

Monet made the lily pond and its watery depths so much a subject of his own that it is a brave artist who takes it on himself, inviting only impossible and readily mistaken or irrelevant comparisons. But the mysteries of transparency and reflection have long been of natural fascination to painters for the challenges they present of representing by inference and oblique suggestion rather than direct description that which isn't there, or can't quite be seen, let alone fixed. So why not? And now, for Michael, it would be the lily pads to set the surface plane and catch the sunlight, and the clear dim depths below to explore with characteristic acuity and tonal subtlety, rather than those deep shadows and reflected faces that had so engaged and intrigued him before. Here still was a close, almost domestic but now alfresco space.

And if another artist does come to mind, it is Matisse in his more graphic aspect rather than the intuitively painterly Monet – the flat, bright colour and simplified, sometimes schematic imagery, and all discretely ordered in the process of the work, state by state, layer by layer. And yet, in the close modulation of tone and colour – the fish, orange upon sky-blue and green where they are caught in the sunlight, red upon purple and the deepest blue down in the shadowy depth – so the delicate, subtle relation of method and effect is resolved.

The landscapes, which became so central a feature of his work, most especially after the final move to France, may seem at first sight to be rather different, indeed uncharacteristic in being apparently so much looser in the handling, thinner in the paint and sketchier in the drawing, as in *Valley of the Baïse – morning* [64]. Yet here again the appearance is deceptive. The contrast between light and shade remains no less marked, the colour still as clear, the drawing, that seems so free and light, no less direct and certain in the execution.

With Michael as with so many artists, whatever the preoccupation or particular interest of the moment – family and social life, the landscape, the pond in the garden, the lane through the trees, the observed and incidental narrative, the constructed composition – in a strange way that is not so strange at all, the work of a sustained career, first to last, comes together all of a piece.

But being the kind of artist one is is another matter, and rather more of temperament than principle. To specialise is a personal choice, with no more virtue to it than there is in the pursuit of variety for its own sake. The artist may hit by chance on material of endless fascination, or simple curiosity lead who knows where. The only true consideration either way is the quality of what is done. If it comes to the matter of critical or commercial success, however, there is a caveat to raise. The world on the other side of the easel is ever inclined to distrust the all-rounder. It likes to know where it stands, and what to expect – Jack of all trades: well, why can't Jack make up his mind? So to be various in one's work is to take a risk, and the question inevitably arises as to whether Michael would perhaps have been more widely acknowledged and valued as the artist he was had he followed a straighter and narrower path.

All we can say is perhaps, or perhaps not. Michael as an artist was what he was and his work is what it is, the product throughout of the same eye, hand and mind, and the same unifying sensibility, for all the digressions and asides, and especially, in his case, the burin, the acid and the etching press – though without them he would not have been the artist we know. And if here and there, in an early still-life painting of jars on a shelf, *Spice Rack* [97], or an incident-laden etching, or a lily pond, there may be perhaps a nod to Sickert, Gillray, Monet or Matisse, it was never any mere retreat into another's safe convention, but always an expression of wider interest and respect, made in his own way on his own terms. Influence is a tricky issue, much misunderstood. Good artists have always looked for and taken what they need from others. To do so betrays no surrender. Once on his own and with art school behind him, Michael the artist was ever his own man.

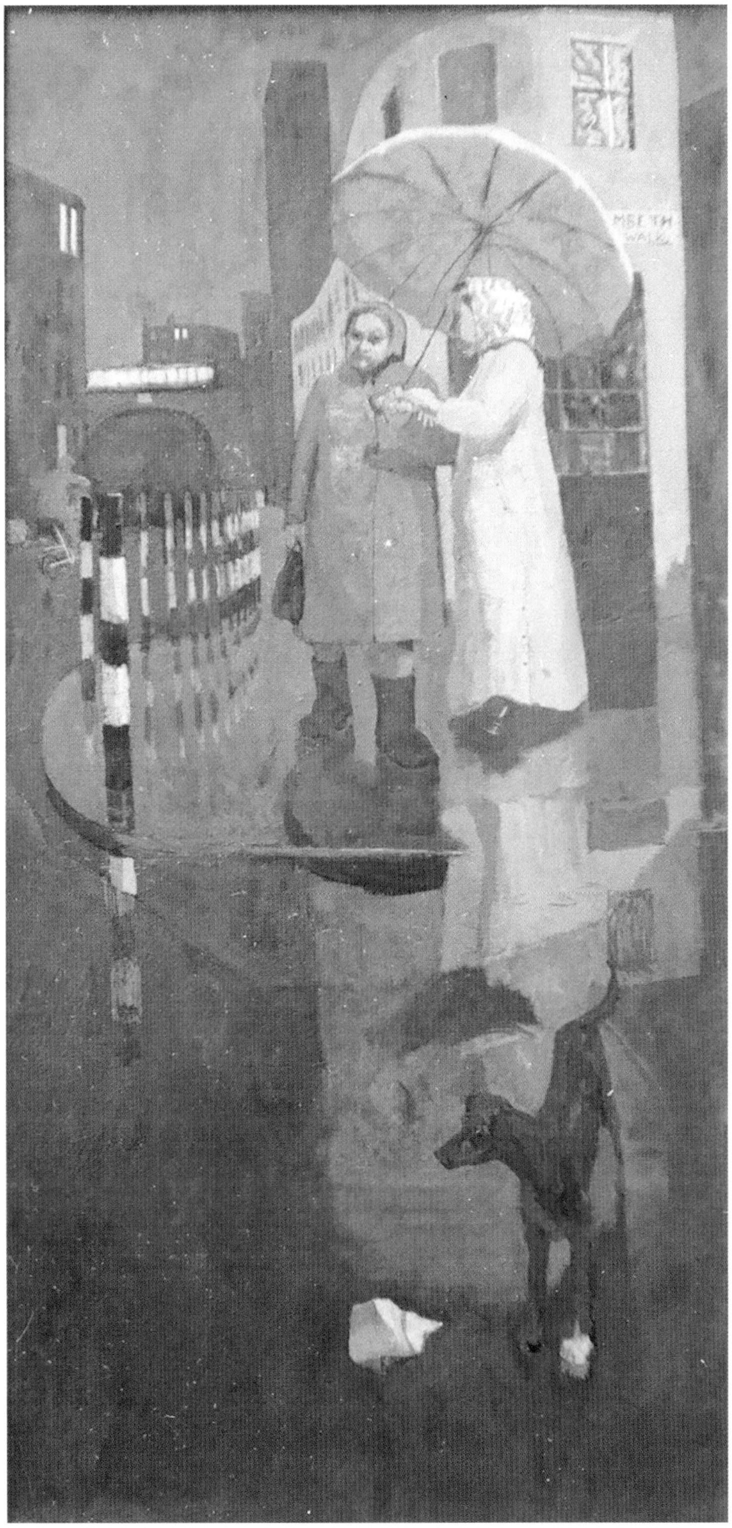

93. *Lambeth Walk, rain*, oil on canvas, date and dimensions unknown
Image obtained from the artist's papers

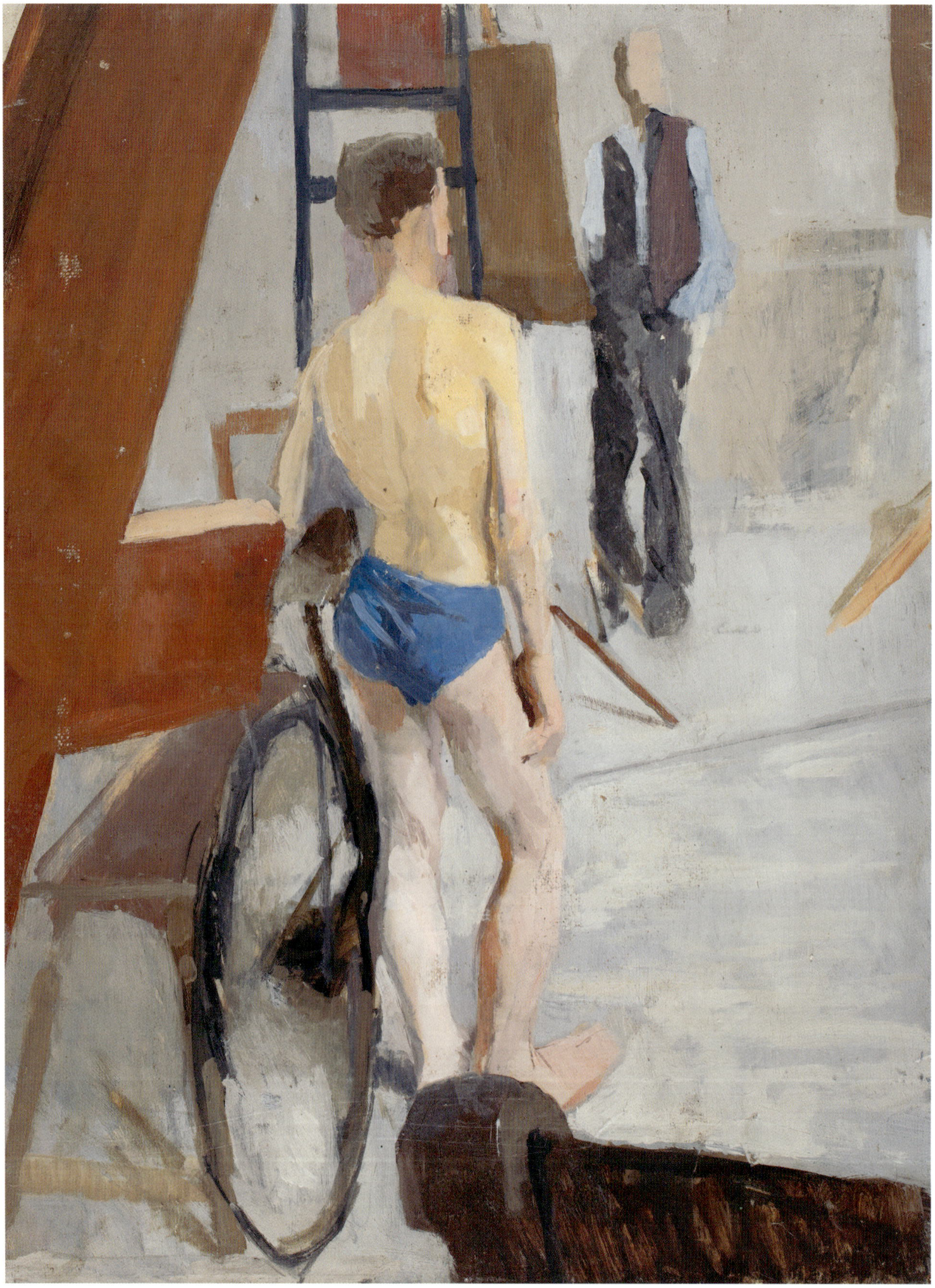

94. *Nude*, 1960s, oil on board, 61 x 46 cm

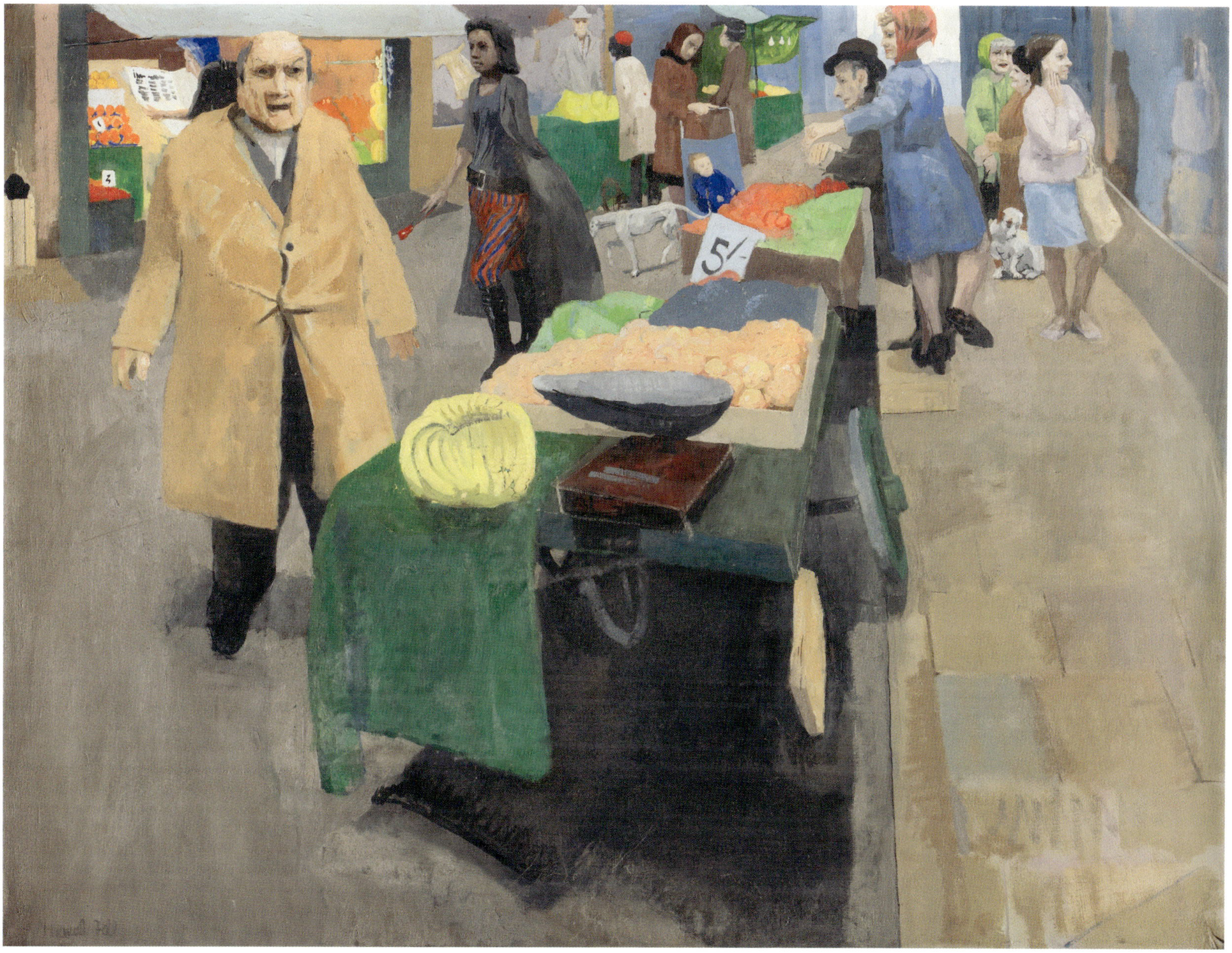

95. *A Vegetable Stall*, 1960s, oil on canvas, 75 x 100 cm

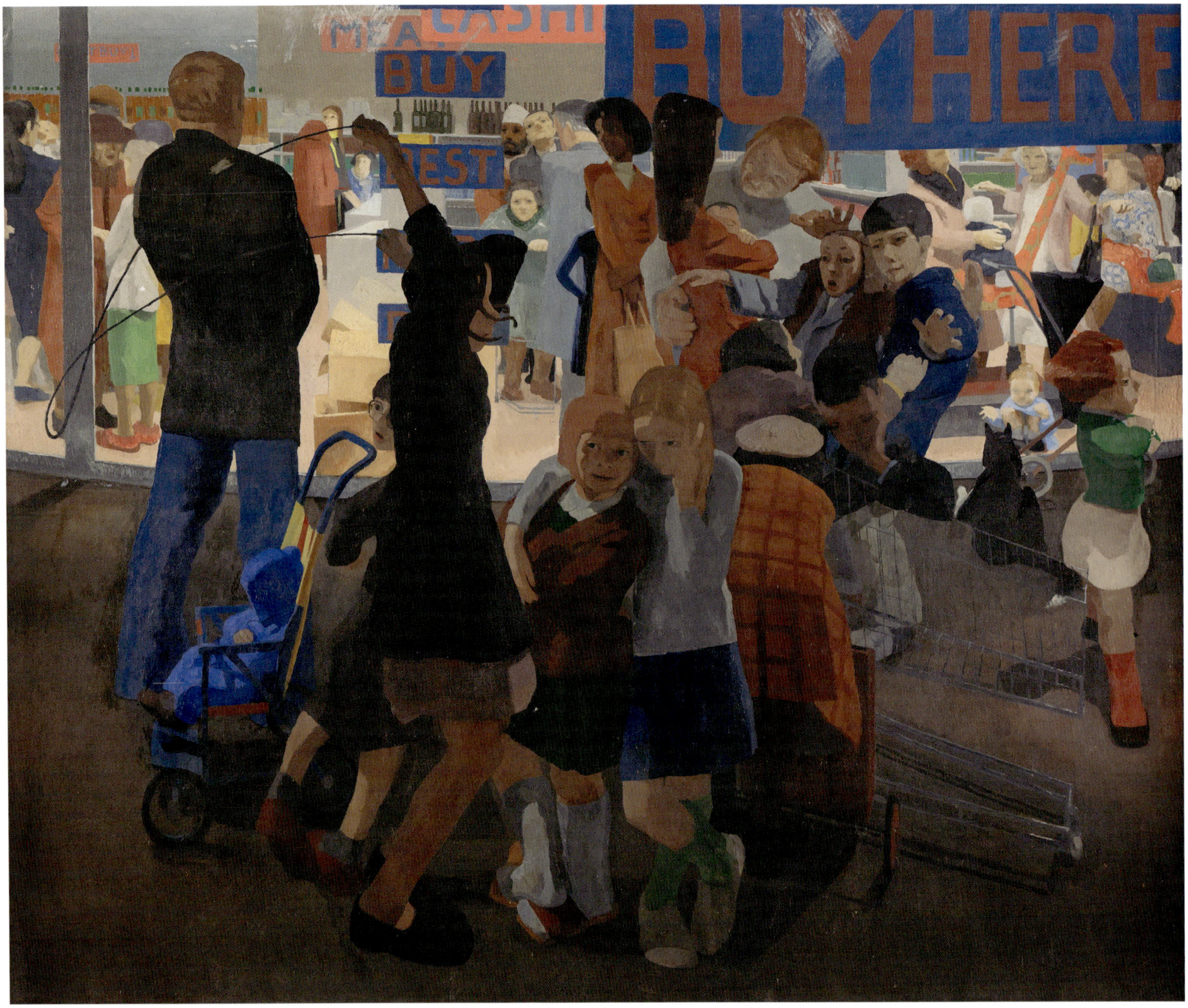

96. *Looking into a Supermarket from Outside*, 1970s, oil on canvas, 137.4 x 167 cm

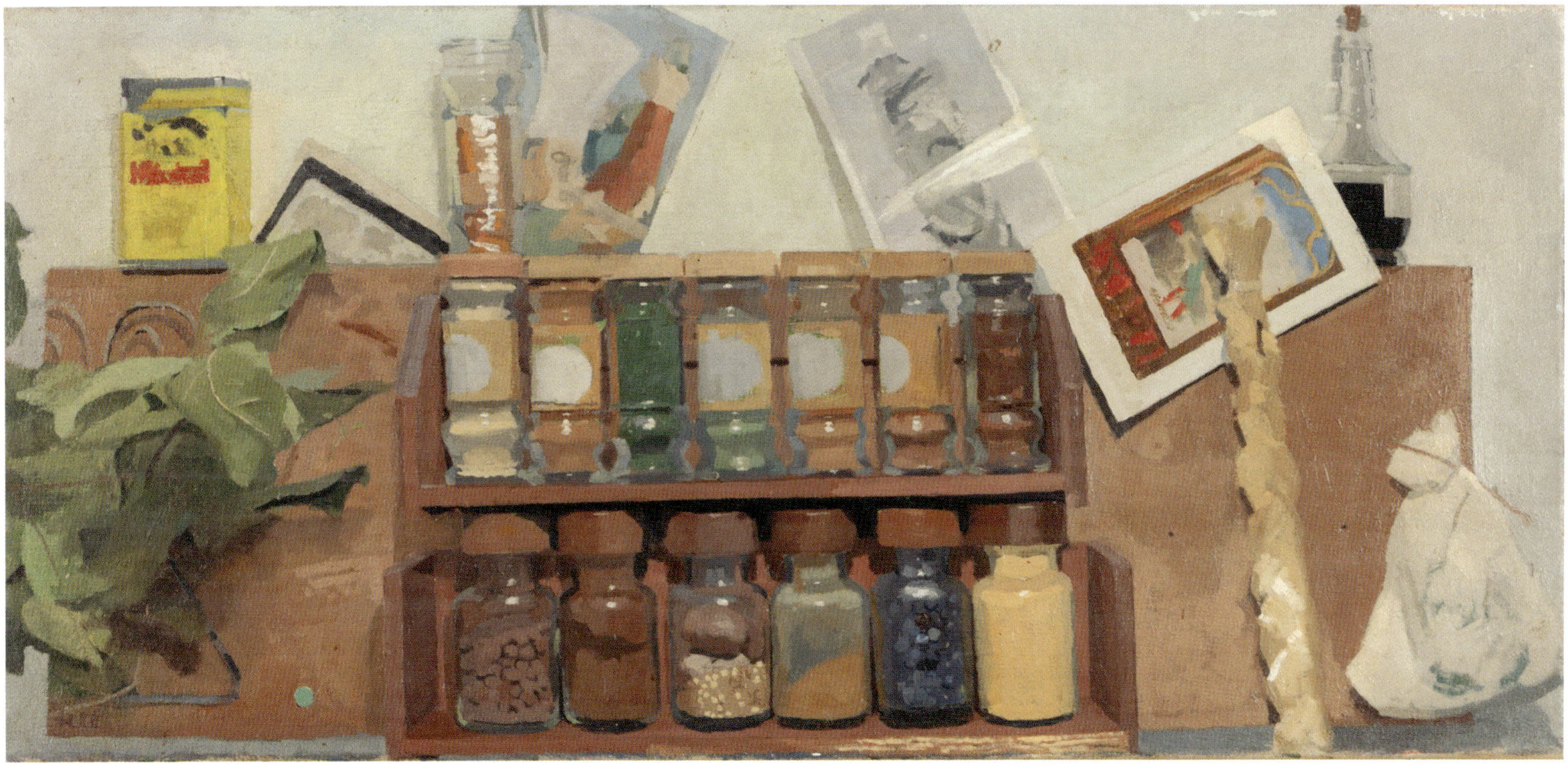

97. *Spice Rack*, 1970s, oil on board, 36 x 75 cm

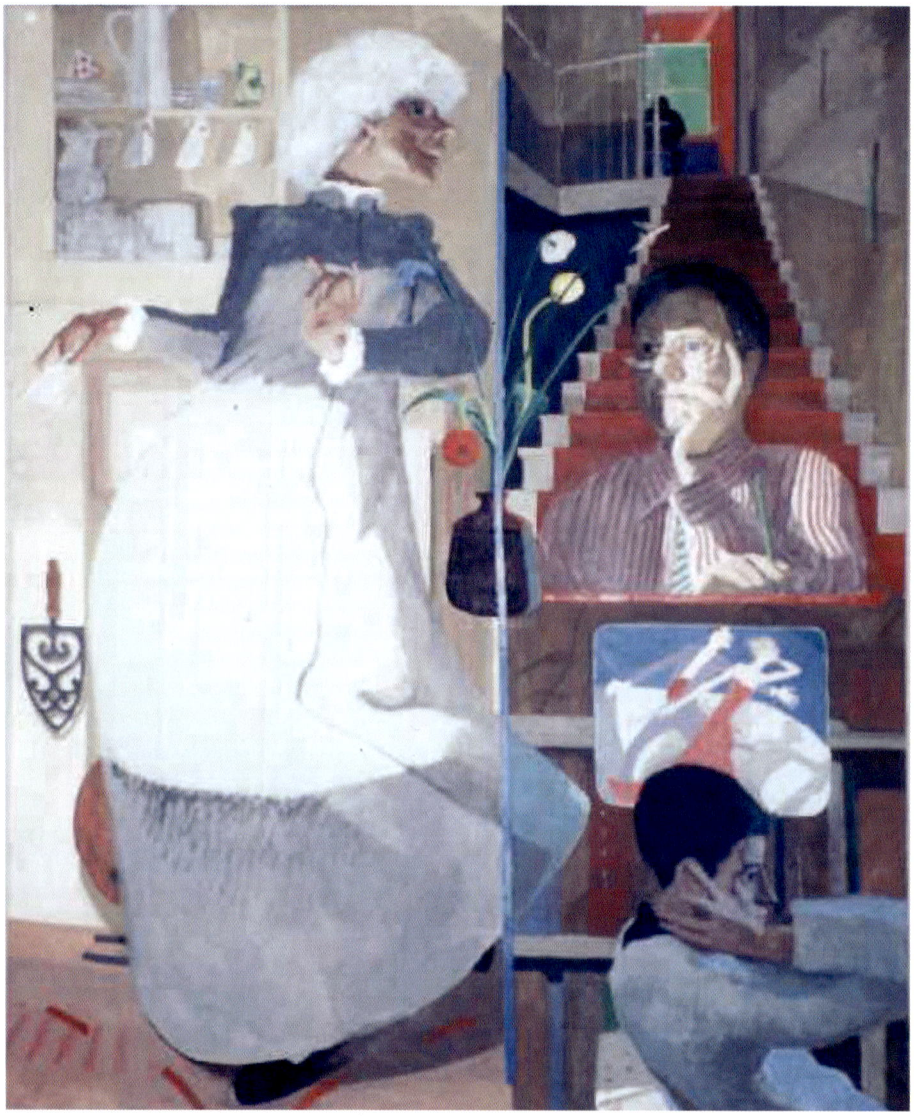

98. *The Ollington Family*, 1980s, oil on canvas, dimensions unknown
Image obtained from the artist's papers

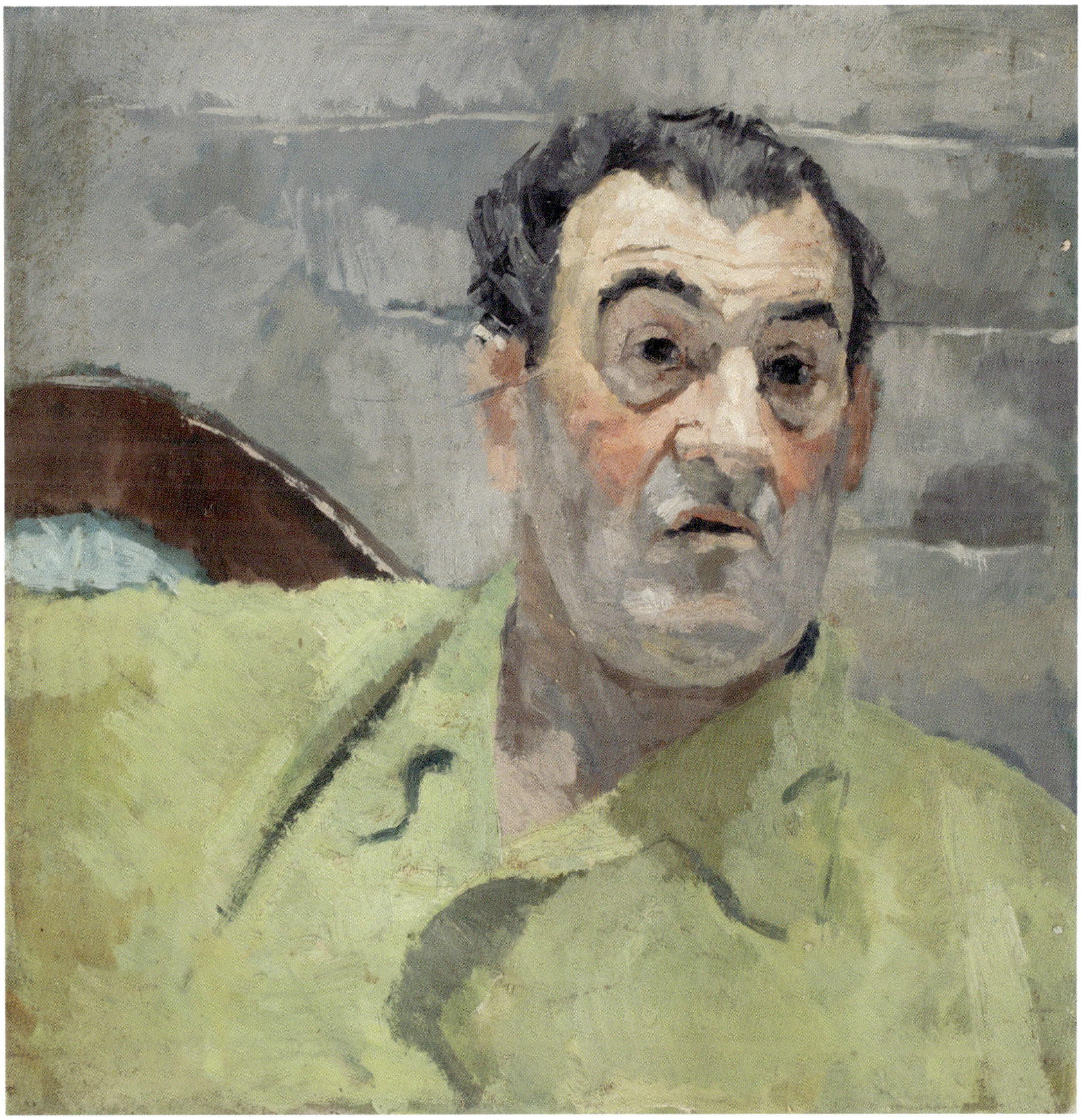

99. *Unknown man*, date unknown, oil on board, 46 x 46 cm

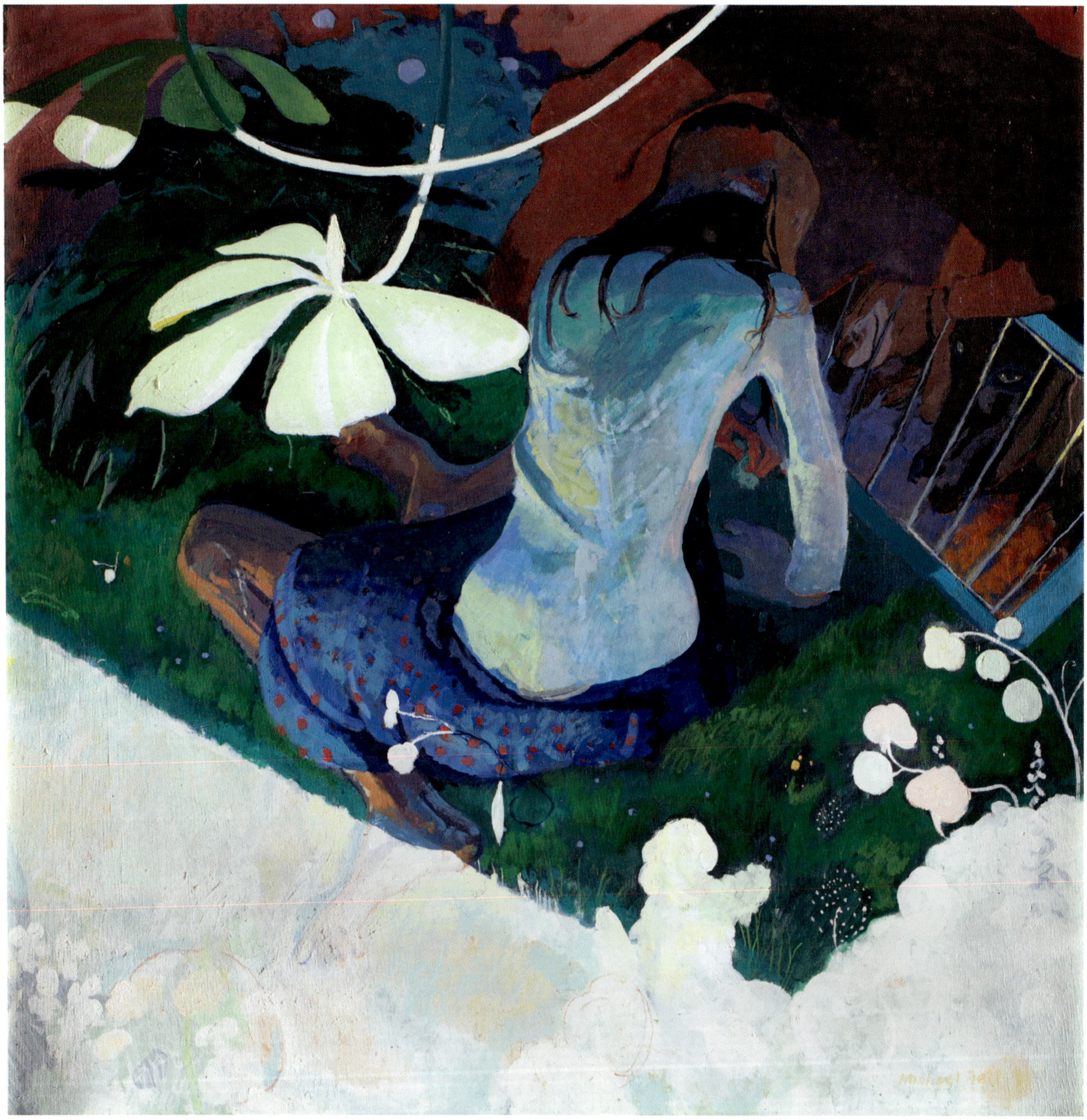

100. *A Girl*, 2000s, oil on canvas, 60 x 60 cm

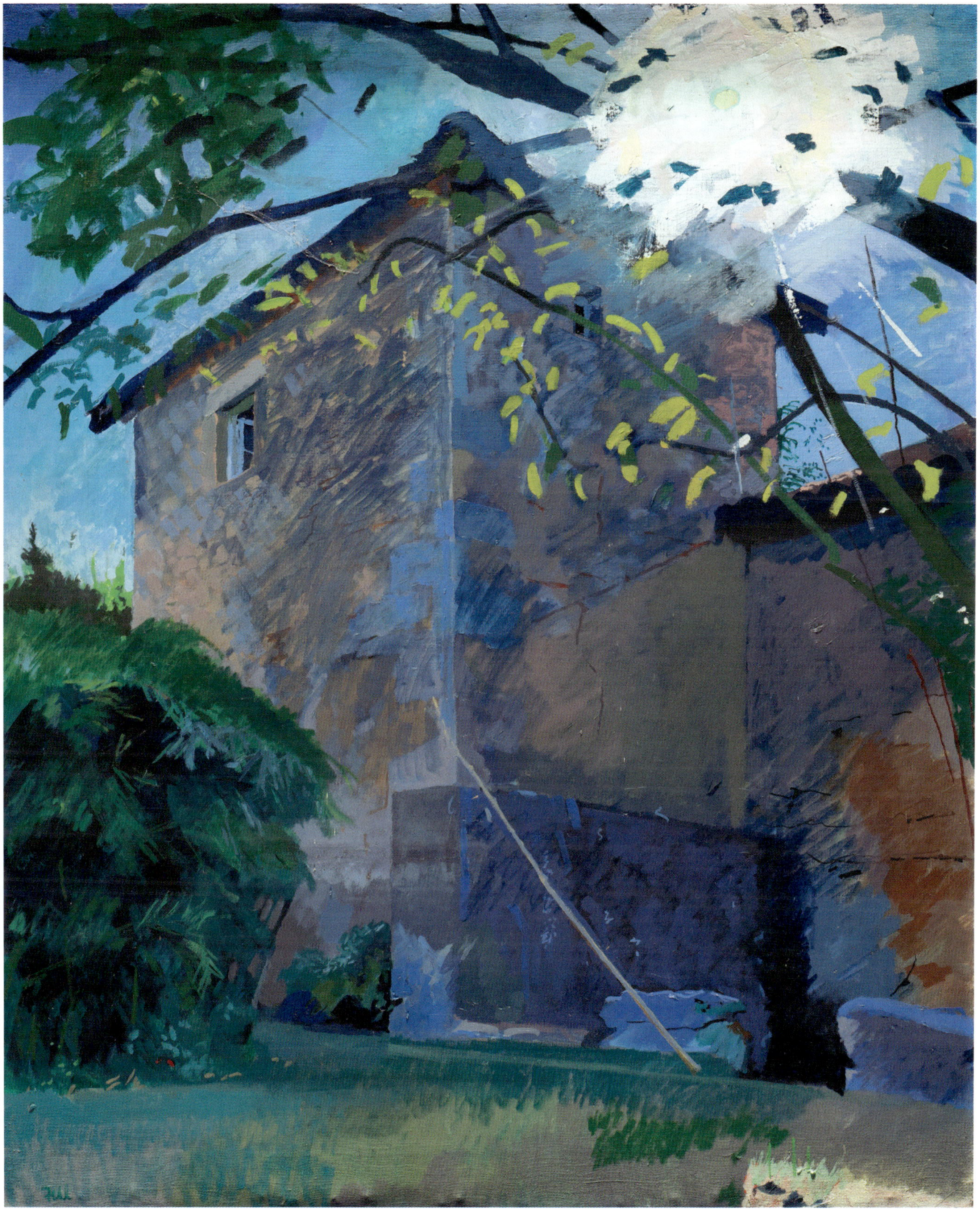

101. *The Tower*, 2010s, oil on canvas, 90 x 75 cm

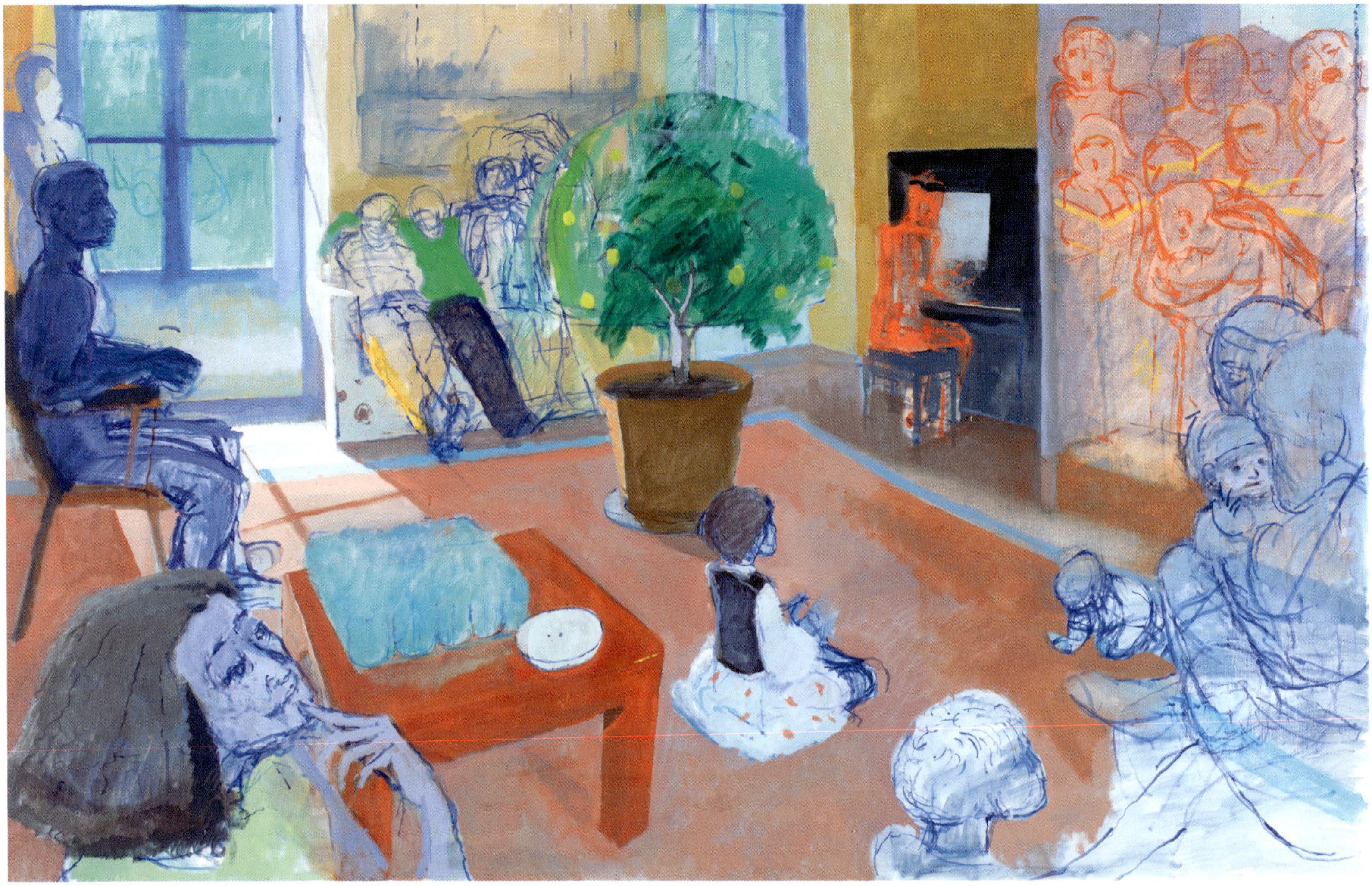

102. *Benoit's Christmas Party*, 2023, unfinished, oil on canvas, 73 x 116 cm

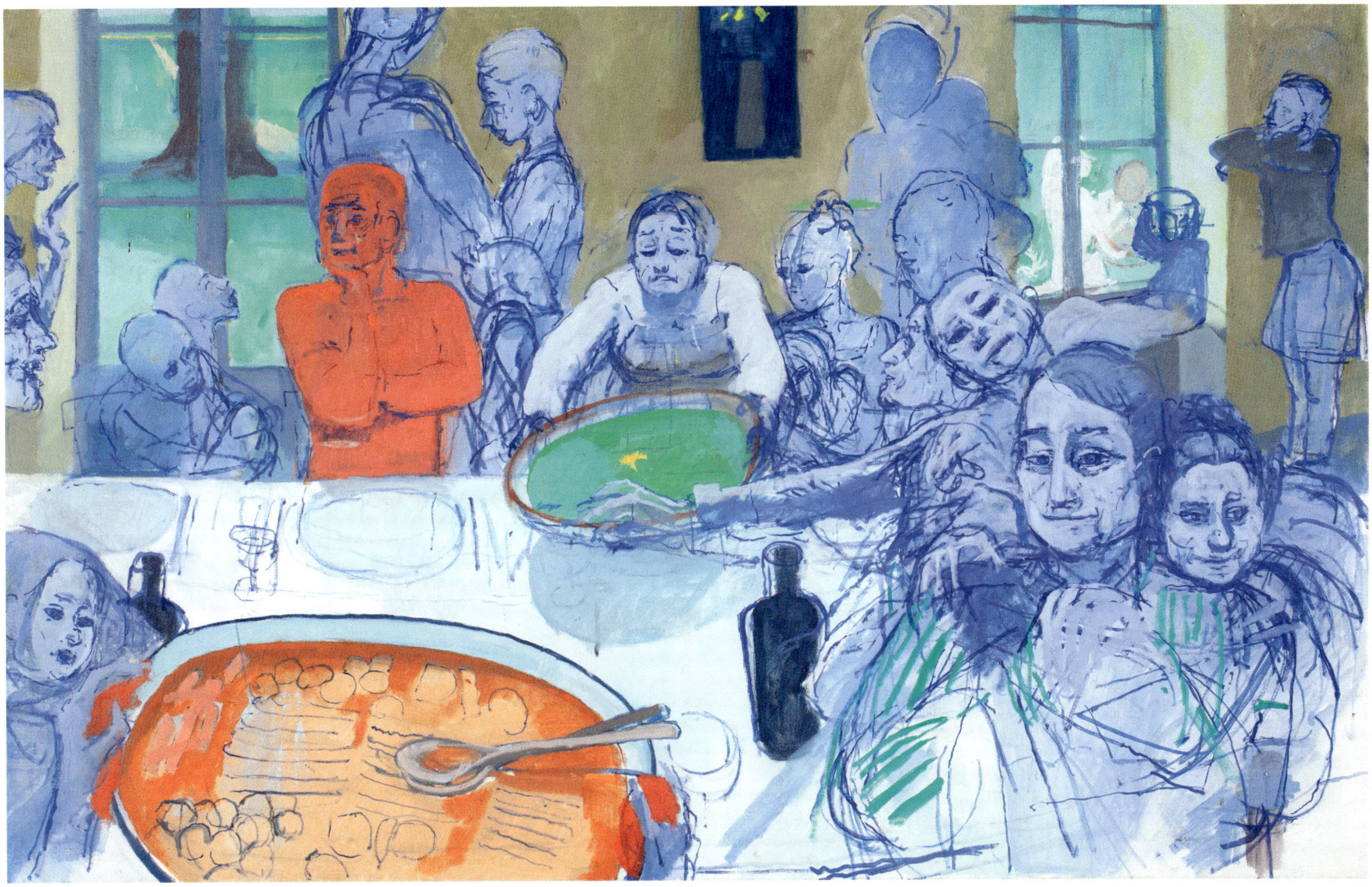

103. *Benoit's Easter Party*, 2023, unfinished, oil on canvas, 73 x 116 cm

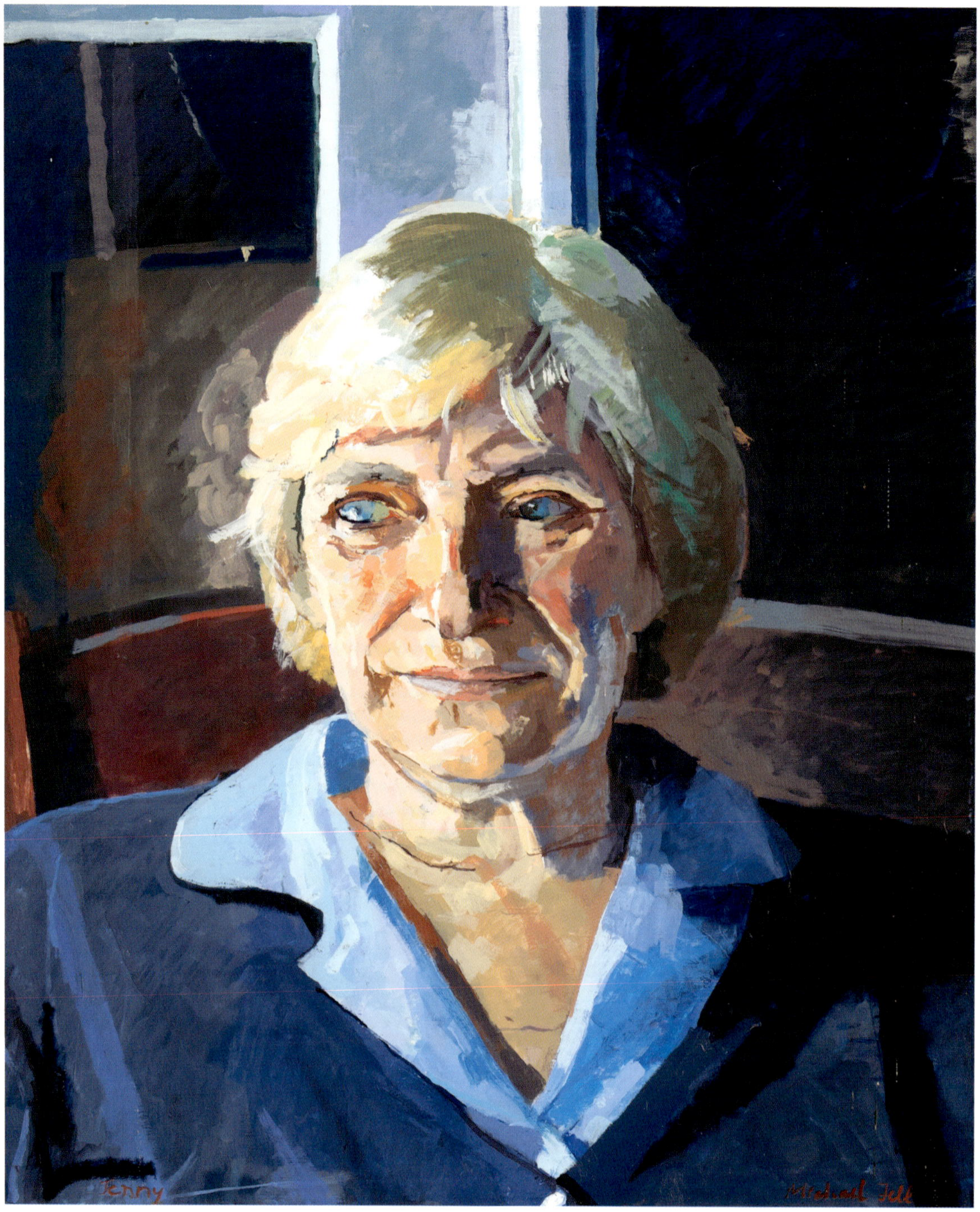

104. *Jenny Fitz Gerald*, 2011, oil on canvas, 47.8 x 40.1 cm

Acknowledgements

The editor and his colleagues are grieved to record the death in July 2024 of Adrian Bartlett, greatly respected artist and teacher, author of the Printmaking chapter of this book.

The editor and his colleagues would also like to thank Edda Abbagliati, Victoria Bartlett, Jacques Bosser, Alice Boyd, Jessica Boyd, Julia Boyd, Olivia Boyd, Jemima and Edith Boyd-Fell, Benoît Branthomme, Heather Brown, Daphne Casdagli, Richard Clavaud, Maria Cristina White Da Cruz, Frances Dakers, Slim and Annie Dinsdale, Susan Edward, Annette Emms, Michael Estorick, Phillip and Gillian Evans, Maureen Fell, Patricia Fell, Robert Fell, Maurice and Jenny Fitz Gerald, Jeremy Gadd, Professor George Gaskell, Tom Goodyer, Andrée Gorton, Sarah Grant, Tina Gray, Anne and Arnaud Guinard, Fr Peter Harris, Javan Herberg, Pascale Hertier, Russell Hurn, Trevor Hurrell, Diane and Tony James, Victoria Jenkinson, Tinkie and Mark Lake, Emily Lane, Peter Ledger, William Ledger, David Lee, John Lessore, Sanchia Lewis, Kristen Lippincott, Peter Mansell, Gilles de Margerie, Isabelle Martinez, Priscilla McDougall, Sylvie and Richard Mégevand, Marek and Angela Mierzejewski, Edna and Władysław Mirecka, Isobel Muir, Elaine Mummery, Robin Ollington, Reina Osumi, Ben Prestney, Bożena Przewlocka, John and Helen Radcliffe, Nicole Robertson, Daniel Rothschild, Emma Russell, Nicky and Maya Slater, and Dr Thomas Stammers.

Photographs:
Lucy Dawkins: front cover, 3, 6–17, 21, 22, 24–28, 47–53, 56–61, 64–69, 86, 88–92, 94–97, 99–104; Joe Humphrys: 4, 5, 18, 19, 23, 29–46, 54, 55, 62, 63, 70–85, 87; Dan Bernard: 20; Rob Henderson: 2; Marek Mierzejewski: frontispiece.

Works Illustrated

The artist did not always refer to works using the same title, and dates are estimates.

Page numbers follow the illustration numbers, in brackets.

1. (7) *The Nun's Family*, 1971, oil on canvas, dimensions unknown
2. (9) *A Lovely Summer's Day, if you can see it*, 1970s, oil on canvas, 110 x 90 cm
3. (10) *Olivier Stalls*, 1980s, oil on canvas, 80 x 150 cm
4. (12) *The Window*, 1980s, lithograph, 51 x 77 cm
5. (14) *The Gates of Hell*, 1974, etching and aquatint, 43 x 66 cm
6. (16) *Painting of the Priest (L'abbé Fabère)*, *c.* 2000s, oil on canvas, 181.7 x 182.1 cm
7. (22) *Self Portrait*, 1970s, oil on board, 60 x 43 cm
8. (23) *London Scene*, 1960s, oil on board, 43 x 61 cm
9. (24) *On the Grass in the Park*, 1960s, oil on canvas, 61.9 x 64 cm
10. (25) *Smithfield Butcher*, 1960s, oil on canvas, 91 x 85 cm
11. (26) *Printing Press at City & Guilds*, 1960s, oil on board, 61 x 46 cm
12. (29) *Tube Train*, 1972, oil on canvas, 152 x 76 cm
13. (32) *Maureen*, 1970s, oil on canvas, 45 x 60 cm
14. (33) *Mark is born*, 1979, oil on canvas, 63.1 x 75.8 cm
15. (36) *Bungay*, 1990s, oil on canvas, 172 x 177.4 cm
16. (37) *Robert at the Music House*, 1993, oil on canvas, 121 x 182.2 cm
17. (39) *Maurice Fitz Gerald*, 2011, oil on canvas, 47.8 x 40.1 cm
18. (42) *The Burning Babe 1*, 1970s, aquatint, 59.5 x 45 cm
19. (43) *The Burning Babe 2*, 1970s, aquatint, 66.5 x 50.8 cm
20. (44) *Cardigan Street*, 1979, oil on board, 71 x 63 cm
21. (45) *St Mary's at Bungay*, 1980s, oil on canvas, 32.5 x 37 cm
22. (46) *Virginie*, 1990s, oil on canvas, 121 x 91 cm
23. (47) *The Art School*, early 1990s, etching and aquatint, 59.5 x 48 cm
24. (48) *Isabelle reading*, 2007, watercolour, 41.9 x 27.1 cm
25. (49) *Isabelle*, 2011, charcoal, 75 x 59 cm
26. (50) *My Desk*, 2000s, oil on board, 89 x 89 cm
27. (51) *View from my Desk*, 2016, oil on board, 45 x 45 cm
28. (52) *Window at my Studio*, 2020–21, unfinished, oil on canvas, 60 x 92 cm
29. (57) *Riverscape*, *c.* 1976, aquatint, 38 x 54 cm
30. (59) *Italian Café, New York*, 1980s, etching and aquatint, 30.7 x 36.7 cm
31. (61) *Berthold Wolpe*, 1980s, etching and aquatint, 30.5 x 22 cm
32. (63) *Katie's Wedding*, 2007, etching and aquatint, 33.9 x 29.8 cm

33. (64) *Covent Garden – early morning*, 1968, etching, 14 x 11 cm
34. (65) *Covent Garden – market dustman*, 1968, etching, 14 x 11 cm
35. (66) *Covent Garden – late morning*, 1968, etching, 14 x 13.5 cm
36. (67) *St Anne's Vauxhall*, 1969, aquatint, 56.5 x 39.6 cm
37. (68) *Victoria Station*, 1968, etching and aquatint, 23.5 x 41 cm
38. (69) *Librarian*, 1970s, etching, 11.3 x 8 cm
39. (70) *My Friends*, 1980s, etching and aquatint, 15 x 20.5 cm
40. (71) *Theatre People*, 1980s, etching and aquatint, 28 x 40 cm
41. (72) *Travellers at the Elephant*, 1980s, etching and aquatint, 18.5 x 29.5 cm
42. (73) *Last Train Home*, 1990s, etching and aquatint, 11 x 17 cm
43. (74) *Canterbury Tales, The Prologue*, 1990, etching and aquatint, 60 x 77 cm
44. (75) *Telephones*, early 1990s, etching and aquatint, 60 x 77 cm
45. (76) *Cat*, *c.* 2000, etching, 6 x 6 cm
46. (77) *L'étudiante*, *c.* 2000, etching, 11.5 x 12.5 cm
47. (78) *Moto-Experience*, 2007, etching, 27 x 40 cm
48. (81) *The Family*, *c.* 2000, oil on canvas, 121 x 90 cm
49. (83) *Fête at Rozès*, 1996, oil on canvas, 182.1 x 182.5cm
50. (84) *Vineyards at Routgès*, *c.* 2000, oil on canvas, 75.8 x 90.9 cm
51. (87) *Rozès in February*, 2010, oil on board, 35.1 x 21.4 cm
52. (90) *Hillside at Barrère*, 1980s, oil on canvas, 118 x 93 cm
53. (91) *View from Barrère*, 1980s, oil on board, 40 x 50 cm
54. (92) *My Pond*, mid-1990s, oil on canvas, 172.1 x 101.4 cm
55. (93) *Winter in Gascony*, late 1990s, oil on board, 29 x 29 cm
56. (94) *Afternoon from Barrère*, *c.* 2000, oil on canvas, 122 x 76 cm
57. (95) *A View (Routgès)*, *c.* 2000, oil on canvas, 90.5 x 60 cm
58. (96) *Routgès*, *c.* 2000, oil on canvas, 75.5 x 75.5 cm
59. (97) *Drive at Routgès*, *c.* 2000, oil on canvas, 104 x 91 cm
60. (98) *Lily Pond*, 2000s, oil on board, 60 x 60 cm
61. (99) *My Fish Pond*, 2000s, oil on canvas, 75.3 x 121 cm
62. (100) *Field at Routgès*, *c.* 2000, oil on canvas, 104.5 x 180.8 cm
63. (101) *View at Routgès*, *c.* 2000, oil on canvas, 62.6 x 49.6 cm
64. (102) *Valley of the Baïse – morning*, *c.* 2000, oil on canvas, 74 x 151 cm
65. (103) *Charlie*, *c.* 2000, oil on canvas, 155 x 83 cm
66. (104) *View from a Window*, *c.* 2000, oil on canvas, 49.7 x 60 cm
67. (105) *Bright Light, early a.m.*, 2010, oil on board, 40.3 x 25.4 cm
68. (106) *Self Portrait*, 2023, oil on canvas, 75 x 90 cm
69. (109) *St John Southworth in Westminster Cathedral*, 1980s, oil on canvas, 122 x 91 cm

70. (113) *'Palm Sunday'* (from *A Simple Easter*), 1991, etching and aquatint, 10 x 7.5 cm
71. (113) *'Agony in the Garden'* (from *A Simple Easter*), 1991, etching and aquatint, 10 x 7.5 cm
72. (113) *'Lord, is it I'* (from *A Simple Easter*), 1991, etching and aquatint, 10 x 7.5 cm
73. (113) *'Pilate's troubles'* (from *A Simple Easter*), 1991, etching and aquatint, 10 x 7.5 cm
74. (114) *'The Sanahdrin'* [*sic*] (from *A Simple Easter*), 1991, etching and aquatint, 10 x 7.5 cm
75. (114) *'Way of the Cross'* (from *A Simple Easter*), 1991, etching and aquatint, 10 x 7.5 cm
76. (114) *'The disciples wait'* (from *A Simple Easter*), 1991, etching and aquatint, 10 x 7.5 cm
77. (114) *'Christ alone'* (from *A Simple Easter*), 1991, etching and aquatint, 10 x 7.5 cm
78. (116) *The Tomb* (from *A Simple Easter*), 1991, etching and aquatint, 10 x 7.5 cm
79. (116) *The Tomb* (from *A Simple Easter*), 1991, etching and aquatint, 10 x 7.5 cm
80. (116) *'The Tomb'* (from *A Simple Easter*), 1991, etching and aquatint, 10 x 7.5 cm
81. (116) *'Jesus Dies'* (from *A Simple Easter*), 1991, etching and aquatint, 10 x 7.5 cm
82. (118) *'God's despair'* (from *A Simple Easter*), 1991, etching and aquatint, 10 x 7.5 cm
83. (118) *'A Simple Easter'* (from *A Simple Easter*), 1991, etching and aquatint, 10 x 7.5 cm
84. (118) *'And He was parted from them'* (from *A Simple Easter*), 1991, etching and aquatint, 10 x 7.5 cm
85. (118) *St Peter's Faith*, 1991, etching and aquatint, 10 x 7 cm
86. (120–21) *The Gates of Heaven I*, early 1970s, etching, 12 x 49 cm
87. (120–21) *The Gates of Heaven II*, early 1970s, etching and aquatint, 12 x 49 cm
88. (123) *Crucifixus*, completed in 2023, oil on canvas, 244.5 x 182 cm
89. (131) *Summer Football*, 1971, oil on canvas, 74 x 100 cm
90. (133) *Painting at the Music House*, late 1980s, oil on canvas, 89 x 74 cm
91. (135) *Chess at Rozès*, late 2000s, oil on canvas, 60 x 60 cm
92. (136) *Lourdes*, 2010s, oil on canvas, 79 x 119 cm
93. (141) *Lambeth Walk*, rain, oil on canvas, date and dimensions unknown
94. (142) *Nude*, 1960s, oil on board, 61 x 46 cm
95. (143) *A Vegetable Stall*, 1960s, oil on canvas, 75 x 100 cm
96. (144) *Looking into a Supermarket from Outside*, 1970s, oil on canvas, 137.4 x 167 cm
97. (145) *Spice Rack*, 1970s, oil on board, 36 x 75 cm
98. (146) *The Ollington Family*, 1980s, oil on canvas, dimensions unknown
99. (147) *Unknown man*, date unknown, oil on board, 46 x 46 cm
100. (148) *A Girl*, 2000s, oil on canvas, 60 x 60 cm
101. (149) The Tower, 2010s, oil on canvas, 90 x 75 cm
102. (150) *Benoit's Christmas Party*, 2023, unfinished, oil on canvas, 73 x 116 cm
103. (151) *Benoit's Easter Party*, 2023, unfinished, oil on canvas, 73 x 116 cm
104. (152) *Jenny Fitz Gerald*, 2011, oil on canvas, 47.8 x 40.1 cm

Index